ARMS FOR THE ARABS

ARMS FOR THE ARABS:

THE SOVIET UNION
AND WAR IN THE MIDDLE EAST

JON D. GLASSMAN

THE JOHNS HOPKINS UNIVERSITY PRESS
BALTIMORE AND LONDON

The Johns Hopkins University Press, Baltimore, Maryland 21218
The Johns Hopkins University Press Ltd., London

Library of Congress Catalog Card Number 75-29254
ISBN 0-8018-1747-1

Library of Congress Cataloging in Publication data will be found on the last printed
page of this book.

CONTENTS

PREFACE

This book was written during a one-year leave from the Foreign Service. This respite from day-to-day tasks was made possible by receipt of an International Affairs Fellowship from the Council on Foreign Relations. The Council's fellowship provided me with time to reflect on my 1971–73 assignment in the Soviet Union and to expand my knowledge of Soviet foreign policy. Needless to say, I am extremely grateful to the Council and members of its staff for their truly superb and generous assistance.

During my fellowship year, I was fortunate to enjoy the hospitality of the Program on Science and International Affairs (PSIA) of Harvard University. My residency at PSIA provided me with not only invaluable logistic support but, more importantly, the companionship of intellectually stimulating colleagues. I am very thankful to the director of PSIA, Professor Paul Doty, for his kindness during my stay as well as for his sponsorship of my trip to Great Britain and Israel to conduct interviews.

In Israel, I wish to thank particularly the Office of the Presidency, the Ministry of Defense, and the Ministry of Foreign Affairs, as well as faculty members of Tel Aviv and Hebrew Universities, for their splendid help in arranging interviews for me. These interviews were truly invaluable.*

In addition to those who directly helped me with the book, I wish to express my gradidute to those teachers and friends who have had a major impact on my thinking on Soviet and international affairs, namely, Zbigniew Brzezinski, Marshall Shulman, William T. R. Fox, Alexander Dallin, Peter Berton, Martin Hickman, and Ross Berkes.

Finally, I want to acknowledge the support of my wife Debbie and daughter Mandy, who tolerated my neglect and often lifted me from despair.

---

* Interviews were conducted in January–February 1974 with the president of Israel, Dr. Ephraim Katzir, the director of the Eastern European section of the Foreign Ministry, Ambassador Avigdor Dagan, and military officers of the Planning Section of the General Staff and other organs of the Ministry of Defense, as well as academic specialists at Tel Aviv and Hebrew Universities. I have compared this interview data with published information on the subject as well as with the views of other analysts in order to verify its accuracy. Nothing I have seen or heard substantially contradicts the data presented in this book.

Although I owe a great debt to many people and institutions, any errors or shortcomings found in the book are strictly my own. The conclusions and analysis of the book do not, of course, necessarily represent the views of the Department of State or any other agency of the U.S. government.

Falls Church, Virginia
March 1975

ARMS FOR THE ARABS

CHAPTER ONE † DÉTENTE AND LOCAL CONFLICT

On 24 October 1973 in Washington, D.C., Soviet Ambassador Anatoliy Dobrynin delivered a letter addressed to U.S. President Richard Nixon from the General Secretary of the Communist Party of the Soviet Union, Leonid Brezhnev. Nixon and Brezhnev, whose summit meetings in Moscow and Washington had become symbols of international détente, would exchange messages that day which would highlight the fragility of cordial relations between the two political and ideological rivals. "I will say it straight," Brezhnev wrote, "[if the United States does not join with the Soviet Union to immediately compel Israeli observance of the recently negotiated ceasefire,] we should be faced with the necessity urgently to consider the question of taking appropriate steps unilaterally."[1]

Brezhnev's warning and the U.S. military alert that followed were the culminating actions of perhaps the most serious sequence of political-military events in recent years—the 1973 October War between Israel and its Arab neighbors. The United States and the Soviet Union stood, during the October crisis, if not at the brink of war, certainly far removed from the threshold of stable peace. A crisis that had begun with the rhetoric of the Moscow Summit ended with words reminiscent of the Cuban Missile Crisis. The tense denouement of the Middle Eastern events, some observers felt, owed much to Soviet behavior during the October War.

While some of the initial postwar judgments of Soviet conduct may have been overly severe, it is clear that certain Russian actions provided considerable basis for concern in the West. Prior to the Brezhnev warning, Western statesmen had already witnessed the absence of overt Soviet opposition to the massive Egyptian and Syrian surprise attacks on Israeli forces; the Soviet reluctance to restrain arms shipments to the combatants; a subsequent Soviet initiative to involve other parties in the conflict; the large-scale battlefield introduction of technically advanced Soviet weaponry, some of which had never before been employed in combat; the unprecedentedly rapid Soviet resupply of the Arab combatants during the course of hostilities; the introduction into the combat theater of Soviet weapons of regional strategic significance serviced by Soviet personnel; and the performance by Soviet and other Communist military cadres of various support and military advisory functions.

Given initial expectations, generated by détente, of Soviet restraint in the Middle Eastern war, American decisionmakers were understandably preoccupied with the scope of Russian commitment to the Arab military cause. Secretary of State Henry Kissinger, for example, felt it necessary in the closing days of the crisis to point out, albeit implicitly, that American tolerance of Soviet assertiveness was not boundless and that there were limits beyond which the United States could not go.[2]

The unprecedented degree of Soviet support for Arab military efforts raised questions as to the viability of détente. In the eyes of American officialdom, détente implied restraint. Indeed, the foreign-policy orientation of the American administration was premised on mutual forbearance and accommodation—negotiation—as a substitute for confrontation.

Soviet actions in the October 1973 Arab-Israeli war suggested that Moscow had not yet abandoned policies that could lead to a clash of Soviet and American interests. This fact caused many in the United States to question the value of détente. After all, should the United States exercise restraint vis-à-vis an antagonist that showed little or no reciprocity? Was détente not, in fact, a "cover" masking genuinely aggressive Soviet intentions?

Public skepticism in the post-October period was a natural response to earlier euphoric portrayals of the détente relationship. Administration spokesmen had been tireless in their praise of the emerging "structure of peace"—a supposed programmatic shift of Soviet-American relations from hostility to peaceful dialogue.

Soviet conduct before and during the October 1973 war suggested, however, that in contrast to Washington's monochromatic view, the Kremlin saw détente in a differentiated light. While Moscow wished to inaugurate a less tense relationship with the major Western regimes, these improved ties did not presage a lapse of Soviet support for anti-Western or belligerent "progressive" forces.* The Soviet leadership fully intended to promote simultaneously the seemingly contradictory policies of détente with the Western powers and opposition to Western-endorsed elements of the status quo.

---

*The term "progressive" is used by Soviet analysts and ideologists to identify states or movements, outside the West, that are predominantly anti-Western in their foreign-policy and military-supply orientation and that pursue or advocate anti-capitalist domestic transformation or national liberation. The principal states in the Arab-Israeli zone that were regarded as "progressive" in the 1956–73 period were Egypt, Syria and Iraq (after 1958). The term "progressive" is also applied to movements within the capitalist world that oppose the current socioeconomic order and seek to eliminate Western political, economic, and military domination of, or pressure against, other countries. Progressive movements inside and outside the capitalist world, therefore, share the common virtue in Soviet eyes of opposing Western attempts to manipulate or influence world events through use of political, economic, and military power.

The dilemma of balancing détente against support of the "progressive" movement, or peaceful coexistence against revolution, has been a longstanding concern of Soviet foreign policy. While emphases on one or the other policy pole have come and gone, the Soviet leadership has never completely abandoned concurrent pursuit of both goals. This dualistic policy has forced Moscow to measure and limit its actions carefully. Absence of restraint in one direction could discredit the alternate policy emphasis. Excessive support of the "progressive" movement could undermine détente, and vice versa.

This book examines the process of Soviet balancing and restraint in the Middle East during the last two decades. It seeks to define the limits that Moscow observed in supporting its "progressive" clients. It also explains how these limits eroded over time.

Specifically, the book examines the restraints to which the Soviet Union adhered in arming its Arab associates, particularly Egypt, for self-defense or conduct of war. These restraints (and their removal) affected Arab domestic politics and intra-Arab relations and played an important role in influencing the onset and course of three Middle Eastern wars—the 1956 Suez War, the 1967 Six-Day War, and the 1973 October War.

Soviet arms transfer and diplomatic restraints and cautions, limiting as they did the possibility of achievement of Arab ambitions by means of initiation and continuation of war, were meaningful indicators of Moscow's felt need to exercise caution or to promote closer relations with the capitalist world. The "progressive" Arabs' principal military antagonist, after all, was Israel, a state that enjoyed American and Western European political support of varying degree.[3]

Moreover, shortcomings in Russian military assistance were repeatedly criticized in the Arab world and eventually led to the 1972 expulsion of Soviet military personnel from Egypt and the (perhaps temporary) decline of Soviet-Egyptian relations after the October 1973 war. Considering the longstanding Soviet desire to cultivate the Arab "progressives," these costs were probably not incurred lightly.

The motives for Russian restraint—limitations which were observed during the entire eighteen-year period examined—were, of course, not always uniform. On some occasions, particularly when highly advanced equipment began to be supplied to the Middle East, restraint was probably motivated by the wish to preserve and protect the physical security and performance data of certain weapons. This probably explains in part the great Soviet reluctance to provide the MIG-25 *Foxbat* interceptor to Egypt despite repeated requests.

On other occasions weapons were withheld to signal displeasure over a client regime's conduct in domestic politics or in intra-Arab affairs. The cessation of Soviet arms supplies during President Nasser's campaign against domestic communism at the end of the 1950s, and after President Sadat's support of the Sudanese 1971 anti-Communist countercoup, were examples of this category of restraint.

Given the continuity and repetition of acts of limitation, however, a more persistent motive for abstinence was clearly present. This motive was probably Moscow's wish to avoid dangerous confrontations with the West. After all, Arab resort to, or involvement in, war would lead—and repeatedly did—to severe crises in Soviet relations with the major capitalist powers. Three times in twenty years the Soviets felt moved to threaten military intervention in Middle Eastern wars. On each occasion the United States responded, and the Soviets did not intervene. While these intervention threats and responses were more theatrical than real, nonetheless, they were actions that, through miscalculation or emotion, might have led to more serious Soviet-American confrontations, or even war. While Moscow was clearly willing to take chances if necessary, there is no reason to assume that the Kremlin welcomed heightened risks.

In the mid-1950s it behooved Moscow to avoid confrontations because the United States possessed the capacity to devastate the Soviet homeland—a capacity that the Soviet Union could not match. Later, the Soviet move to strategic, and increasingly conventional, military parity lessened but did not erase the threat represented by Western military power.

Concurrently, the growing sophistication of the Soviet economy increased the desirability of closer relations with the Western regimes. These closer ties, in the Politburo's eyes, would hopefully serve both to facilitate sale of Soviet industrial goods, raw materials, and energy resources and also to ease Soviet access to Western technology, consumer goods, and credit.

Warm relations with the capitalist nations also lessened Western public enthusiasm for increased defense budgets, a strengthened NATO alliance, and anti-Soviet domestic politicians.

Moscow's urge to maintain its identification with the "progressive" movement, however, often surpassed the Soviet interest in avoiding confrontation with the West—witness the intervention threats in the Middle East and the persistent erosion of the earlier-maintained Soviet arms restraints. What, in fact, were the benefits of association with the "progressives," an association which the Russians pursued so diligently?

Soviet inroads in the Middle East in the mid-1950s did, of course, deprive the West of the opportunity to turn the area into a firm link in the chain of military alliances that was being constructed around the Communist periphery. The military significance of this Soviet accomplishment, however, was considerably reduced by American deployment of intercontinental-range ballistic missiles, submarine-launched ballistic missiles, and heavy bombers in the late 1950s and early 1960s.

As far as economic benefits were concerned, the Soviet Union, being a net petroleum exporter during the period under study, stood to gain little from the area's principal resource. Moscow might, of course, have aspired to gain control of Western Europe's principal oil supplies, but Soviet Middle Eastern clients possessed little petroleum.

Soviet support for the "progressive" movement, in fact, was probably motivated by two fundamental considerations. Firstly, the Soviets wished to make the "progressive" states into models that would evoke the emulation, by means of either evolution or revolution, of the traditional, Western-oriented Arab states. Such a transformation of the Western-oriented regimes would remove, once and for all, the possibility of a return of the Western military presence to the area and would place Moscow's hands on the Western European energy jugular. Secondly, the Soviets recognized that the Middle East was an area where "progressive" forces were militarily threatened by a Western-oriented state, Israel. Military support provided by Moscow allowed these "progressive" forces to withstand their enemy. It also graphically demonstrated to restive elements in the Near East and far beyond that the Soviet Union was an exponent of "national liberation." The Soviets welcomed such an identification because of their deep-seated conviction that, over the long run, nationalist and socialist forces would increasingly prevail in most parts of the world. This belief often created the tactical necessity for balancing Soviet shifts toward closer ties with the capitalist West with moves seeming to favor the "progressive" movement.

These balancing moves, which in many cases involved the dropping of previously observed restraints, were often manifested through changes in the content of arms shipments to the Middle East. At such times of change, weapons previously withheld sometimes began to be supplied. In 1963, for example, first-line Soviet military equipment began to be dispatched to the Middle East. In 1970, ultra-modern air-defense equipment and thousands of Soviet air-defense personnel were committed for the first time outside the Communist camp. And, in 1973, surface-to-surface missiles of regionally strategic range (the *Scud*) were deployed outside of the Warsaw Pact nations for the first time.

The erosion of bounds of restraint in the arms-supply field is set out in some detail in this book. In discussing the maintenance and disintegration of restraint, however, a somewhat novel approach is utilized. Instead of simply enumerating the new types of weapons delivered at each juncture, as some earlier treatments have done, this study considers additional factors, namely: (a) the types of weapons possessed by the Soviet Union that were *not* delivered to the Arab "progressives," (b) the purpose and functions Soviet weapons could serve that had been provided or denied to clients (see Appendix 1 for an explanation of alternative weapons types and functions), and (c) the presence or absence of qualitative changes or shifts in the pattern of Russian weapons deliveries over time. Russian behavior, therefore, is treated, not simply as a continuing series of discrete acts, but rather as an amalgam of acts and inactions. This perspective takes into account possible Soviet caution as well as assertiveness and, hence, provides a more comprehensive view of Soviet behavior than sometimes appears in other Western studies.

In addition to weapons deliveries, a second important indicator of Soviet restraint or assertiveness are Moscow's diplomatic efforts to encourage or discourage the outbreak of war. Soviet attempts to convince Near Eastern clients either to avoid resort to hostilities or, alternatively, to display increased activism are detailed in the following chapters, as are the apparent motivations for these efforts. Particular attention is also directed at Moscow's moves during the course of the various wars either to seek quick ceasefires or to acquiesce to prolongation of hostilities. Besides Soviet diplomatic and political pressures, Russian utilization of wartime political-military instruments, such as intervention threats, weapons resupply, and dispatch of military personnel, are also surveyed. The overall focus of study is to determine changes and constants in Soviet views on the desirability of promoting favorable outcomes of local conflict (by means of initiation or prolongation of local combat or provision of additional Soviet support) as opposed to the urge to avoid or curtail such conflict because of the perceived danger or undesirability of escalation and expansion.

In sum, by codifying the evolution of Soviet diplomatic and arms-supply self-limitations, the dynamics of the process of balancing gain against risk in Soviet foreign and military policy become clearer. Hopefully, this increased clarity is useful in understanding the likely nature of Soviet policy in future local-conflict situations in the Middle East and other areas.

CHAPTER TWO † THE 1956 SUEZ WAR: THE SOVIET POLITICAL-MILITARY ROLE

At 5:00 P.M., 29 October 1956, Israeli paratroopers landed near the Mitla Pass in Egypt's Sinai Peninsula. The airborne assault was the first step of Operations Kadesh and Musketeer, the Israeli and Anglo-French invasions of Egypt.

The three-power incursion was motivated by a variety of factors, only some of which related to the Arab-Israeli conflict. The confrontation between Tel Aviv and its Arab neighbors, in fact, had remained relatively tranquil in the years after the 1948–49 Israeli war of independence. The few Arab-Israeli incidents of the early years generally involved small-scale terrorism and usually emanated from Jordan. Beginning in 1953–54, however, coinciding with the rise to power of the Egyptian Free Officers' Movement (ultimately headed by Gamal Abdel Nasser), cross-border violence rose in the area adjoining the Egyptian-occupied Gaza strip. These incidents culminated in 1955 with a large-scale Israeli raid on the city of Gaza and a subsequent increase of Egyptian government support for *fedayeen* guerrilla activity against Israel.

The rising tension on the Israeli-Egyptian border was paralleled by growing English and French irritation with Egypt's Nasser. By the time of the Suez crisis, the Egyptian leader and his colleagues had succeeded in nationalizing the English- and French-owned Suez Canal, had expelled British troops from Canal-Zone military bases, and provided support for the anti-French Algerian rebels.[1]

The leaders of England, France, and Israel, therefore, all had cause for animosity toward the Nasser regime. On 27 September 1955, an additional event took place that further galvanized their common concern: Egypt signed an arms-supply pact with Czechoslovakia.

The Czech-Egyptian arms agreement was, in fact, a Soviet-Egyptian accord effected through the Czechs.[2] The new arms pact, which provided Soviet weapons to the Egyptians in substantial proportions, marked the debut of the Soviet Union on the Middle Eastern political-military scene. Moscow's initial involvement would be repeated, and in the ensuing years the Soviet Union would become the principal arms supplier to the major Arab belligerents in the Near Eastern imbroglio.

Soviet military involvement outside the Communist bloc, however, even in the form of military aid and sales, was a novel element in the international politics of the 1950s. Many in the West thought that the Soviets were seeking to disrupt the fragile East-West equilibrium that had prevailed since the 1951 stalemate in Korea. The Soviets had, after all, leaped over the Baghdad Pact, the Middle Eastern link of the West's cordon sanitaire around the Communist bloc.

Not only the global balance but also the regional Middle Eastern balance was shaken. The American-British-French Tripartite Declaration of 1950, which bound its parties to maintain an Arab-Israeli arms balance, was effectively breached by the addition of Russia as a major arms supplier. The possibility of a Middle Eastern arms race, or even war, was apparent. Harold Macmillan later wrote: "If we armed Israel in return, we should lose all hold upon the Arabs, if we refused, Israel might be tempted into a preventive war."[3]

The Soviets were probably little disturbed about the possibility of breaking down the Western-dominated political status quo. Indeed, such a course probably recommended itself. The Soviet leadership was discarding the ideological shackles of Stalinism. Unlike their late leader, the new Presidium majority, led by Nikita Khrushchev and Nikolai Bulganin, saw great advantage in cooperating with "nonaligned" nationalist leaders, such as India's Nehru and Egypt's Nasser. Western power could be broken down incrementally with the aid of the West's renegades, the new Soviet line held, not just by cataclysmic war and Communist revolution.

At the same time, however, the Soviet leadership was making cautious, conciliatory gestures toward the main capitalist powers. After many years of little progress, the Austrian State Treaty was signed in 1955, and Soviet occupation troops were withdrawn from that country. Later in 1955, as a consequence of the Four Power Geneva summit conference, there was a temporary interlude in the cold war, assertedly infused with the "spirit of Geneva." The Soviet leadership in contacts with the West, in a refreshing change from the Stalin period, appeared guardedly civil.

The arms deal with Egypt, while consistent with Moscow's interest in supporting Nasser and the progressives, seemed, because of its large size, to contradict Soviet desires temporarily to placate the West. Indeed, in retrospect, the basic motivations for the arms deal appear clear, though the reasons for its magnitude do not. Presumably, it would have been possible to satisfy Nasser's desire for arms, but in reduced quantities. Arms shipments that would upset the Arab-Israeli military equilibrium, as Harold Macmillan noted, could create the prerequisites for a

Middle Eastern war and a possible Soviet-American confrontation. Considering the strategically inferior position of the Soviet Union in this period, a Soviet-American military clash might well have proven fatal to the Soviet Union. With this in mind, why would the Soviet leadership have consciously sought to disrupt the military balance in the Middle East? The American government, also asking itself this question, initially sought to dissuade the Kremlin from shipping arms to Egypt because such deliveries would make war more likely. However, the Russians, in reply, minimized the unsettling consequences of the weapons shipments.[4] The sanguine Soviet response to American concerns may have been motivated not only by opportunism but also by a conviction that the Soviet Union was only balancing Israeli arms acquisitions and an increasing Western threat to Egypt.

What could have prompted Moscow to believe that its large arms shipments would contribute to military balance rather than to chaos in the Near East? The answer may lie in Egypt's 1955 approach to the Soviet Union.

Nasser's associate Mohamed Heikal reports that in 1955 the Egyptian leader felt threatened by the budding Western-dominated Baghdad Pact, which, in the eyes of Nasser, was meant to serve as an instrument to isolate revolutionary Egypt from the other Arab states. Moreover, Israel had recently inaugurated a policy of military reprisal raids in retaliation for Arab terrorist attacks. Heikal states: "He [Nasser] had to get arms from somewhere. He had to equip his army to face the threat posed by [Israeli leader] Ben Gurion. . . . At the same time our Intelligence Service began to get information about the Israeli arms purchases from France that had started in 1954."[5]

Nasser echoed this concern with the reported Israeli arms build-up. Shortly after signature of the "Czech" arms pact, he told a *New York Times* correspondent that Israel allegedly had received a commitment from France for the delivery of advanced AMX tanks and Mystere jet fighters *prior to* the Egyptian arms deal. Nasser added: "I am thinking of Israel's Army not as it is today but what it will be tomorrow. . . . Now we will be meeting Mysteres with MIG's. This is better than meeting Mysteres with nothing."[6]

It is natural that the Egyptians would use the argument of impending large French deliveries to Israel to convince the Soviets of Egypt's acute need for large quantities of arms. Certainly, Egyptian concern was not entirely specious. On 31 July 1954 Israel had concluded a secret agreement with France for the supply of arms, including first-generation Ouragan jet fighters.[7] Subsequently, in August 1955, reports appeared in the Western press that France had agreed to sell highly advanced Mystere IV jets to Israel.[8] The real extent of French shipments to Israel remained cloaked in secrecy, however. The clandestine nature of the deliveries to Israel was such that shipments were received, not in ports, but rather out at sea, from camouflaged ships that could not be seen from the air.[9] Because of this acute secrecy and the limited aerial-surveillance capability of the day, it was easy and prudent for Israel's enemies to err on the side of caution.

The extent of Egyptian concern, coupled with the absence of precise information on the content of secret French deliveries to Israel, may have caused the Soviets to overrespond in their efforts to curry Egypt's favor. The large Soviet arms deliveries may have been intended only to offset what the Egyptians described as a large growth in Israeli military capabilities and an increase in the Western military threat against Egypt. That the weapons deliveries in fact initially outstripped Israeli capabilities may have been either unexpected or a consequence of the effort to balance the threat of other Western powers. While this conclusion can be tentative at best, it is interesting to note that the Soviets maintain, at least retrospectively, that Israel and France were conspiring to attack Egypt more than one year before the actual invasion and that Israeli armed forces were then, one year before the attack, undergoing a "rapid growth."[10] Indeed, the United States did nothing to contravene this Soviet view when Secretary Dulles rejected Israeli requests for arms after the "Czech" deal on the grounds that American weapons deliveries would further spur a Middle Eastern arms race.[11]

What were the dimensions and composition of Soviet deliveries to Egypt before the 1956 war?

The value of Soviet arms shipped to Egypt under the first Egyptian-Czech agreement has been variously estimated as between $90 million and $200 million. The arms were purchased under a twelve-year barter arrangement involving the exchange of weapons for Egyptian cotton and rice. The barter mechanism allowed Egypt to obtain a quantity and quality of weapons whose value far exceeded Cairo's foreign-exchange holdings.[12]

Contradictory reports on the content of Soviet arms shipments to Egypt abound. The difference in estimates may be partially due to the fact that, not one, but two arms pacts were apparently concluded between Egypt and the Soviet Union before the Suez conflict. Nasser in 1966 disclosed that a second major arms agreement, equal in value to the first, was signed before the 1956 war in response to reports of new French arms shipments to Israel. The new pact provided Egypt with the more advanced MIG-17 jet fighter to replace the earlier delivered MIG-15 as the prime Egyptian air-defense interceptor. The total value of the two arms pacts reached $336 million, Nasser reportedly said.[13]

Before the 1955–56 Soviet and French arms deliveries to the Middle

East, a relative arms balance prevailed between Israel and its principal antagonist, Egypt. Egypt had eighty jet aircraft and Israel had fifty. Both parties had approximately two hundred tanks.[14] As a result of Soviet deliveries, Egyptian stocks of tanks were increased by over 50 percent, and the jet aircraft inventory was more than doubled. While the exact chronology of the Israeli-French weapons-supply situation is still murky, it appears that initial Soviet deliveries to Egypt placed Israel in a position of considerable arms inferiority. The heavy influx of French arms, however, in the months immediately preceding the Anglo-French-Israeli invasion significantly reduced this deficiency.

Moshe Dayan asserts that the Soviet arms shipment added the following items to the Egyptian inventory: 530 armored vehicles—230 tanks, 200 armored personnel carriers, and 100 self-propelled guns; approximately 500 artillery pieces of various kinds; almost 200 fighter aircraft (MIG-15), Ilyushin bombers (IL-28), and transport planes (IL-14); and a number of naval vessels, including destroyers, motor torpedo boats, and submarines.[15] Another author, quoting an alleged "American official estimate," states, on the other hand, that Egypt received 80–100 MIG fighters (MIG-15), 30–45 light jet bombers (IL-28), 100 Stalin (IS-III) and T-34 tanks, several hundred armored personnel carriers, as well as artillery, tanks, bazookas, small arms, and ammunition.[16] Former British Ambassador to Egypt Sir Humphrey Trevelyan, relying on British estimates, asserts that Nasser received 300 medium and heavy tanks, more than 100 self-propelled guns, 2 destroyers, 4 minesweepers, and 26 motor torpedo boats.[17] British professor John Erickson places Soviet deliveries to Egypt as 80 MIG-15 fighters, 45 IL-28 strike bombers, 115 Stalin and T-34 tanks, several hundred self-propelled guns, armored personnel carriers, and supporting equipment.[18]

Taken together, these conflicting figures indicate that before the 1956 war, the Soviets probably delivered to Egypt *at least* one hundred medium T-34 and heavy IS-III Stalin tanks of World War II vintage, eighty MIG-15 Korean War–era fighters, thirty IL-28 jet bombers, plus large quantities of self-propelled guns, armored personnel carriers, artillery equipment, several naval vessels, small arms, and ammunition. Actual quantities of weapons delivered may have been significantly higher, of course. Nonetheless, even these low-estimate figures, showing 50 percent and 100 percent increases in the number of Egyptian tanks and jet aircraft, were enough to alarm Egypt's opponents. Qualitatively, Moshe Dayan points out that the MIG-15's and IL-28's were "two stages ahead" of Israel's Meteors and Ouragans, and the Soviet T-34 tanks were "infinitely better" than Israeli Sherman Mark 3's.[19]

Before the beginning of the 1956 war, however, France openly, as well as covertly, supplied Israel with considerable amounts of military equipment. Israel, for instance, obtained from France advanced Mystere IV jet fighters, which were considered superior to the MIG-15's supplied to Egypt.

Dayan states that at the beginning of the war, Israel possessed thirty-seven Mysteres, fourteen to sixteen of which were operational.[20] Another source maintains, however, that Israel had received seventy-five Mystere IV's.[21] With regard to armor, the most up-to-date equipment received by Israel were French AMX light tanks equipped with Nord SS-10 antitank missiles. At the beginning of the war, Israel possessed one armored battalion and two armored squadrons of these very fast, but lightly armored, tanks.[22] (The Nord missiles, incidentally, would be the first weapons of their kind ever used in modern warfare.)

The general Western view of the Soviet arms supply to Egypt in the pre-1956 period is that the Russian deliveries destabilized the Middle Eastern arms balance and contributed to pressures for a preventive war against Egypt, certainly on the part of Israel. As discussed previously, there may be grounds for believing that Russian shipments were meant to balance the supposedly increased Western threat to Egypt and to anticipate French deliveries to Israel and were not intended necessarily to exceed Israel's military capacities. To judge this hypothesis more critically, it is useful to survey the most important categories of arms delivered by the Soviets—tanks and aircraft—in order to determine the degree to which Russian deliveries were restrained. To the extent that weapons available to the Soviet armed forces were excluded from delivery, it is likely that the Russians sought to balance, rather than outstrip, the Israelis and their Western associates.

With regard to fighter aircraft, Moscow's delivery of eighty-odd MIG-15's provided Egypt with a versatile, dual-purpose interceptor/ground-support aircraft that had been the standard combat aircraft of the Communist forces during the Korean War, terminated only two years previously. It is conceivable that Soviet or Egyptian anticipation of delivery of a substantial sum of Mystere jets to Israel spurred the Soviet Union to double Egypt's jet aircraft inventory.[23] Indeed, there is some correspondence between the suggested figure of eighty MIG-15's shipped to Egypt and various Western claims that sixty to seventy-five Mysteres were delivered to Israel before the 1956 war. Moscow's failure initially to supply Egypt with the more advanced and available MIG-17 (supplied under the second Soviet-Egyptian agreement) also lends credence to the hypothesis that Soviet intentions were to balance rather than overwhelm anticipated Israeli and Western air capabilities.

A similar argument could be made with regard to the T-34 medium tanks and the IS-III heavy tanks. The introduction of large numbers of these tanks, as well as considerable sums of self-propelled guns and armored personnel carriers, gave Egypt a substantial quantitative advantage over Israel in mobile firepower and means of rapid infantry transport. However, again, Nasser had purportedly anticipated that the Israelis would receive substantial quantities of AMX tanks (along with the Mysteres) from the French. Presumably, he may have convinced the Russians of the possibility of large deliveries.

The Russian provision of medium and heavy tanks to compensate for delivery of light tanks on the surface might seem to be far from an act of balance. Nonetheless, it must be recalled that until 1955, the Soviet forces deployed no postwar light tanks.[24] The simple availability of the T-34 and IS-III tanks may have dictated their delivery to the Egyptians.

The IS-III Stalin heavy tank sent to Egypt had originally been deployed by the Soviet forces in January 1945; by 1955 it had been superseded by two more advanced heavy tanks, the IS-IV and the T-10. The T-34 medium tank had also appeared in the Soviet forces in many models in World War II and had since been replaced by the T-44 and T-54 medium tanks.[25] The latter were the tanks that accompanied the Russian forces that put down the Hungarian revolt in 1956, at the same time as the Suez War. Thus, as in the case of the MIG-15 aircraft, the Russians had not initially given the Egyptians their best available tanks.

The Russian commitment to the Egyptians of thirty-odd IL-28 medium bombers with a range of fifteen hundred miles would seem superficially to place in doubt Soviet intentions as a balancer. Other than a pair of World War II B-17's, the Israelis had no strategic bombing capacity, nor were aircraft for this role on order.[26] While British air bases on Cyprus were within range of the new bombers, their penetration possibilities were small given the limited range of Egypt's MIG-15 escorts and the vulnerability of the aircraft over the entire route to British and French carrier-based aircraft. Hence, provision of the IL-28 primarily made sense in relation to proximate targets such as Israel.

In a peacetime defense situation, a first strike by the IL-28's against Israel presumably could have been thwarted, especially after the arrival of the Mystere IV's. However, to the extent that Israeli fighter aircraft were required for wartime offensive or defensive tactical ground support and air cover, there would be an increasing probability of penetration of Israeli airspace by the IL-28's. Peter Calvocoressi has pointed out that "when Egypt began to get Russian arms, Israel assumed that Egypt would reply to any Israeli offensive by bombing Tel Aviv and other places in Israel. To meet this threat . . . it was essential for Israel to have active French support in the shape of air cover. . . ."[27]

Thus, because of the difficulty for Israel of offensive activities when it was subjected to the threat of strategic bombing, it is possible to conceive of the IL-28's as largely intended only to provide a deterrent against Israeli offensive action. Indeed, the nonemployment and withdrawal of the IL-28's from Egypt during the course of the Suez hostilities (when deterrence had failed) lends greater credence to this hypothesis. On the other hand, had the IL-28's not been withdrawn and had Israel operated offensively or defensively in isolation, without British or French air support, the presence of the IL-28's would have forced Israel to maintain a greater number of fighter aircraft committed to strategic air defense and would have given the Egyptians a far greater possibility of obtaining tactical air superiority and hence the capacity to operate offensively.

In summary, then, Soviet arms deliveries to Egypt in 1955–56 can be seen as a means of fortifying the Egyptian regime that had opposed the Western-dominated political and military status quo in the Middle East. Whether these deliveries were intended to give Egypt military superiority over its principal local competitor, Israel, is uncertain. While it is undoubtedly true that the Soviet arms deliveries did, in practice, give Cairo an important, initial weapons advantage over Israel, it is possible that the Russians intended, not to disrupt the regional arms balance, but, rather, to counter perceived increases in Israeli armed strength and a growing Western threat to Egypt. The rising power of Israel's armed forces, bolstered by French supplies, was apparently an element of deep Egyptian concern. The Soviets may well have taken Egyptian claims of a rapidly mounting Israeli and Western challenge at face value. Soviet intentions may have been defensive and cautious rather than destabilizing and aggressive. Furthermore, it was probably perfectly clear to the Soviets that the novel nature of Soviet military sales and their substantial quantity would cause a shocked reaction from the West. The fact that the arms deal was executed under the "cover" of Czechoslovakia reveals the fundamental Soviet temerity and the desire to avoid directly challenging the West during this period.

II Soviet caution vis-à-vis the Western powers was graphically illustrated during the Anglo-French-Israeli invasion.* This caution was undoubtedly heightened by the concurrent combat operations being conducted by the Soviet army in Hungary. Consequently, not even a verbal threat on behalf of the Egyptians was uttered until November 5,

---

* The key dates in the chronology of the Anglo-French-Israeli invasion are as follows: 29–30 October, the Israeli invasion of Sinai; 30 October, Anglo-French ultimatum to Egypt and Israel to stop fighting; 30–31 October, British and French begin bombing Egypt; November 5, Anglo-French "police action" begins with assault on Port Said; November 7, U.N. ceasefire is accepted by British and French.

seven days after the Israeli invasion of Egypt and six days after the commencement of the intensive Anglo-French aerial bombardment of Egyptian targets. (The actual Anglo-French airborne and amphibious landings in the Canal Zone did take place, however, on November 5. Also, on November 4, the Soviet army launched its decisive, final attack on the Hungarian rebels.) The initial Soviet government statement on October 31, the day after the Israeli invasion, called only for U.N. actions to restrain the British, French, and Israelis.[28]

Moscow's passivity (which may also have been partially due to President Eisenhower's attempts to restrain the invading parties) was not taken lightly by Nasser's supporters. Syrian President Shukri al Kuwatly, who visited Moscow at the time of the Suez invasion, allegedly made an impassioned plea to the Soviet leaders for direct intervention. According to Mohamed Heikal, Soviet Defense Minister Marshal Zhukov at this point spread a map in front of Kuwatly and said, "Mr. President, here is the map, look at it, how can we intervene?" Kuwatly replied, "Marshal Zhukov . . . , do you want me, a poor civilian, to tell you, the star of World War II, how to intervene? You must intervene." The Soviet leaders then purportedly tried to calm Kuwatly, referring to the impossibility of military intervention and the necessity to use political means and to take action through the United Nations. Kuwatly, according to Heikal, was "near to tears with rage and frustration."[29]

The veracity of Heikal's account cannot be determined, but it is clear that the Russians, certainly in the preliminary stages of the war, showed no sign of any inclination toward intervention. Khrushchev, five years later, boasted that the Soviets had not remained passive, in spite of the Hungarian revolt: "The representatives of the imperialist states whispered to us—well, you have your difficulties in Hungary and we have difficulties in Egypt, therefore do not interfere in our affairs. But we gave these whisperers a worthy answer. . . . We intervened and wrecked their aggression."[30] The Soviet intervention, however, was much less bold than Khrushchev's words might indicate.

On 5 November, one week after the beginning of Middle Eastern hostilities, Nikolai Bulganin, chairman of the Soviet Council of Ministers, addressed messages to the leaders of France, Britain, and Israel.[31] Bulganin's notes raised the specter of a Soviet strategic rocket strike on the French and British homelands. Israel was exempted from this specific threat presumably because it was only considered a "tool" in the hands of Britain and France. (The Soviet note to Israel did say, however, that Israeli actions put "a question mark against the very existence of Israel as a state.") The Soviet communication to British Prime Minister Sir Anthony Eden rhetorically asked, "In what situation would Britain find herself if she were attacked by stronger states, possessing all types of modern destructive weapons? And such countries could, at the present time, refrain from sending naval or air forces to the shores of Britain and use other means—for instance, rocket weapons. Were rocket weapons used against Britain and France, you would, most probably, call this a barbarous action. But how does the inhuman attack launched by the armed forces of Britain and France against a practically defenseless Egypt differ from this?"[32]

The implicit threat to employ rockets was hardly a credible one. The Soviets in 1956 possessed only one long-distance rocket in large quantity—the T-1 (M-101), a single-stage, liquid-fueled rocket of the German V-2 type, capable of delivering an eight-hundred-pound nuclear warhead some 450 miles. Longer-range IRBM's had been tested but had not yet been deployed on any scale.[33] Lack of Soviet mention of the U.S.S.R. bomber force reflected that branch's capabilities in this period.

Initial British reaction to the Soviet rocket threat was calm. In Sir Anthony Eden's words, "We considered that the threats in Marshal Bulganin's note need not be taken literally."[34] Harold Macmillan states that the British leadership never took Bulganin's threats "too seriously" because "a nuclear attack on Britain must have led to a general nuclear war in which the Americans could not have failed to take part. At that time the balance of armament in this field was overwhelming against Russia."[35] President Eisenhower shared Macmillan's conviction that an attack on Britain and France would lead to a major war involving the United States.[36] A specific public reply to the Russian threat was made through nondiplomatic channels, presumably with the authorization of President Eisenhower. U.S. General Alfred M. Gruenther, outgoing Supreme Allied Commander, Europe, told reporters on 13 November 1956 that the Soviet Union would be "destroyed" if it attacked the West. Specifically concerning the Soviet threat to attack Britain with rockets, Gruenther said, "Whether or not such rockets exist, they will not destroy the capacity of NATO to retaliate. No nation is going to press that button if it means national suicide—that is just what it would mean."[37]

Thus, the reality of the Soviet threat to employ strategic rockets against Britain and France was largely dismissed in the West. There was (a) doubt that the Soviets possessed the capacity to engage in a strategic rocket attack; (b) confidence that the West possessed overwhelming strategic superiority over the Soviet Union; and (c) no uncertainty, even in a time of serious intra-Alliance disunity, that the United States was ready to strike and capable of annihilating the Soviet Union if that nation were to attack the West.[38]

Another Soviet threat caused greater concern. On November 5, in addition to the notes to Britain, France, and Israel, Chairman Bulganin sent a letter to President Eisenhower proposing that the United States and the Soviet Union act together militarily to halt the fighting in Egypt.[39] Concurrently, Soviet Foreign Minister Shepilov submitted an appeal to the president of the U.N. Security Council. The appeal contained a draft Security Council resolution which stated in part: "The Security Council . . . considers it necessary that all the United Nations member-states, and primarily the United States and the USSR, as permanent members of the Security Council which have powerful air and naval forces, render armed and other assistance to the victim of aggression, the Egyptian Republic, by dispatching naval and air forces, military units, volunteers, instructors, materiel, and other aid . . ." if Israel, England, and France do not cease military operations within twelve hours and withdraw their forces from Egypt within three days.[40] In the aforementioned notes to France and England, but not to Israel, the Soviet Union made reference to its proposals to the United States and the United Nations and added, "We are fully determined to crush the aggressors by the use of force and to restore peace in the East."[41]

The United States categorically rejected Bulganin's proposal and warned that no Soviet or any other military forces should enter the Middle East without a U.N. mandate. If new forces were introduced, the American statement continued, "it would be the duty of all United Nations members, including the United States, to oppose any such effort."[42] In addition, a gradual increase in readiness of U.S. forces was ordered. President Eisenhower stated, however, that "in order to avoid creating a stir," he did not want a general alert declared all at once.[43]

The "stir" that Eisenhower apparently feared was the creation of a pretext for Soviet intervention in the Middle East. Eisenhower's concern was that the Soviets, "seeing their failure in the satellites [Hungary and Poland], might be ready to undertake any wild adventure. . . . [They] are as scared and furious as Hitler was in his last days. There's nothing more dangerous than a dictatorship in that frame of mind."[44] In spite of his advisors' belief that any Soviet military intervention in the Middle East would be "extremely difficult," Eisenhower counseled British Prime Minister Sir Anthony Eden to accept the U.N. ceasefire resolutions "so as to deny Russia any opportunity to create trouble."[45]

Though the French and English initially considered Soviet threats as little more than bluffs, American diplomatic pressure to achieve a ceasefire, prompted in some measure by concern over Soviet intentions, coupled with a great drain on English gold and foreign-exchange reserves brought about by much selling of sterling, particularly in New York, convinced the British and French leaderships that they could no longer pursue their military enterprise.[46] Consequently, on November 7, a ceasefire took hold in the Suez combat zone in accordance with a decision of the United Nations.

A recent Soviet book has stated that "only after they were convinced in London and Paris that the Soviet Union was ready to quickly and unilaterally act against the aggression in Egypt was the decision for a ceasefire taken."[47] Until the November 7 ceasefire, however, the Soviets had only implied the possibility of unilateral Soviet action. Soviet initiatives regarding the introduction of forces into the Middle East had all been formally stated in terms of joint action with the United States and other members of the United Nations. No reservations were made regarding the possibility of unilateral Soviet action in the Middle East should cooperation not be forthcoming from the United States and other U.N. members.

After the English, French, and Israelis accepted the U.N. ceasefire and it was clear that they had submitted to the pressures of Washington and Moscow, Soviet diplomacy became more strident. For the first time, unilateral intervention to compel British, French, and Israeli forces to withdraw from the occupied areas was specifically threatened. This threat was issued on 10 November 1956, three days after all hostilities had ceased in the Middle East. The Soviet threat, conveyed in a TASS declaration, stated that "numerous statements" had been received from "Soviet citizens, among whom there are great numbers of pilots, tank men, artillery men and officers who took part in the Great Fatherland War [World War II] and are now in reserve, asking to be allowed to go to Egypt as volunteers so as to fight together with the Egyptian people for the expulsion of aggressors from Egyptian land." If the English, French, and Israelis did not withdraw from Egypt, the TASS declaration continued, "the appropriate authorities of the USSR will not hinder the departure of Soviet citizen volunteers who wish to take part in the struggle of the Egyptian people for their independence."[48]

The somewhat tardy threat to dispatch volunteers to Egypt may have been the result of a restoration of Soviet military confidence in the wake of the crushing of the Hungarian revolt. Indeed, it may be more than a coincidence that the TASS declaration of November 10 appeared on the same day that the last elements of resistance were extinguished in Hungary.[49] It is more likely, however, that the threat was an attempt to reestablish Soviet standing with the Egyptians, which had been tarnished due to Soviet passivity during the days of combat. Nasser reportedly stated, for example, that during the hostilities Russia offered Egypt arms and technicians, but no volunteers. Since Egypt had plenty of arms, particularly aircraft, but a shortage of pilots, the Soviet offer was unhelpful.[50] In addition, the Soviet lack of support, even on the verbal level, during the days of devastating French and English bombing and Israeli ground advances could not have passed unnoticed in Cairo.

The postwar Soviet intervention ploy was not the only example of a Russian attempt to recoup lost prestige in Egypt. Immediately after the Suez War, another Egyptian-Soviet arms deal was concluded that provided Cairo with weapons to replenish its wartime losses.[51] The Soviets also kept up a diplomatic offensive directed toward securing the withdrawal of France, England, and Israel from the Egyptian territories occupied during the war. When the withdrawals were well on their way to completion, the Soviets on 8 December 1956 issued a TASS declaration that stated that Britain, France, and Israel had been "compelled" to withdraw their forces. These withdrawals, according to the TASS statement, "naturally eliminate the question of departure of Soviet volunteers for Egypt."[52] The Russians thus tried to claim credit for securing the withdrawal of the invaders from Egyptian soil by their threat to dispatch volunteers. As we have seen, the Russian threat to send volunteers had some impact, mainly because it fortified already existing American opposition to the Anglo-French-Israeli invasion. The main factors, however, that caused England and France to accept the cease-fire and to subsequently withdraw their troops from Egypt were American diplomatic pressure and a rapidly deteriorating British financial situation. The Soviet intervention threat, mainly because of its low credibility, was a secondary factor.

III If direct Soviet involvement was not a decisive factor in the 1956 war, what impact did Soviet weapons have on the course of hostilities? One of the immediate consequences of the Israeli invasion and the Anglo-French bombardment of Egypt was the decision, presumably taken or concurred to in Moscow, to withdraw both the IL-28 bombers and Soviet technicians and advisers from Egypt. The IL-28's had been used in from two to six missions against Israel or Israeli-held territories on the second and third nights of the war (October 30 and 31) with little effect.[53] With the commencement of the Anglo-French bombardment of Egypt on October 31, Nasser reportedly ordered the Egyptian air force to cease operations because of the attackers' overwhelming air superiority.[54] Most Egyptian aircraft that had thus far survived were withdrawn to the south of Egypt.[55] The IL-28's were moved back from Cairo West Airport to Luxor on the southern Nile. Unlike most of the other Egyptian aircraft, however, the IL-28's were ultimately evacuated from Egypt to Syria via Saudi Arabia. This decision was presumably motivated by the desire of the Soviets or of Egypt to avoid their destruction or capture.[56] In fact, according to one French general, French F-84's flying from Israel and British bombers from Cyprus caught eighteen of the thirty IL-28's on the ground at

Luxor and destroyed them. Only twelve reportedly escaped from Egypt.[57]

The approximately three hundred eighty Soviet and Czech advisers in Egypt also were quickly withdrawn to Khartoum in Sudan. Presumably, this pullback was a Soviet decision. The removal of the Russians and Czechs gave a sense of relief to the invading allies because the latter had feared that the advisers might become "volunteers" to pilot the insufficiently manned MIG-15's and IL-28's in Egypt.[58]

At the time of the Israeli invasion, only two squadrons (totalling thirty aircraft) of Soviet-supplied MIG-15's were considered operational.[59] Two hundred additional Egyptian pilots for the new aircraft were undergoing training in Poland and other areas in Eastern Europe and the Soviet Union at the time of the invasion but were still not available for service.[60] The MIG-15's, in their two days of operation over the Sinai (before Nasser's withdrawal orders) functioned as escorts for Egyptian Vampire and Meteor aircraft engaged in attack on Israeli forces. They also provided air cover and ground support for the Egyptian First Armored Brigade Team in Sinai. Dayan states that the entire Egyptian air force flew only forty sorties (less than one per plane) on the first day of the campaign and ninety sorties on the second day. The MIG-15's engaged the Israeli aircraft in fourteen brief air battles, during which at least four Egyptian MIG's, three Vampires, and one Meteor were downed by the Israelis. No Israeli aircraft were lost in air combat, though at least ten (only one jet) were shot down by antiaircraft gunfire while engaged in close ground support. Egyptian air ground-support attacks resulted in an estimated ten Israelis killed, twenty wounded, as well as the loss of several weapons and vehicles.[61]

The Egyptian MIG-15's apparently made only a few interception attempts against the incoming French and English bomber aircraft. Five or six British and French aircraft were lost as a result of Egyptian action,[62] principally antiaircraft fire. By the morning of November 2, three days after the inauguration of the Anglo-French aerial bombardment, those parts of the Egyptian air force that had not been evacuated to the south were, for all practical purposes, destroyed.[63]

With regard to ground combat in Sinai, the Soviet-supplied equipment apparently functioned well but was used with little tactical ingenuity. The Egyptians relied on static defensive positions, which were easily circumvented by Israeli forces. As Moshe Dayan pointed out, "The Egyptians made a fatal assumption in thinking that their fortified defense positions . . . would prevent our penetration into Sinai . . . without requiring their armored and air forces to join in blocking our breakthrough, and without their men having to go out and fight us beyond the perimeter of their posts."[64]

elements. The Soviets responded to Nasser's anti-Communist harangues by launching vitriolic attacks against the Egyptian leader.[4]

By the early 1960s, however, Soviet-Egyptian animosity abated, and there was a gradual reconciliation between the two countries. In August 1960, the Soviets agreed to continue financial support for the second stage of the construction of the Aswan High Dam[5] and, from 1961, Soviet-Egyptian arms deals of ever-increasing magnitude were concluded biannually. From the early 1960s to the beginning of the 1967 Six-Day War, Soviet-Egyptian relations, as well as Moscow's relations with the other non-Western-oriented Arab countries, continued on a reasonably even keel.

II The post-Suez arms pacts negotiated between the Soviet Union and Egypt had their origin in the 1957 agreement to replace Egypt's wartime equipment losses.[6] In addition to replenishment of destroyed equipment, the first postwar agreement, valued at $150 million, added 200 MIG-17 fighter-bombers to the Egyptian inventory to replace the MIG-15's delivered earlier. Naval vessels, including submarines, were also delivered, and Soviet and Czech instructors were sent to Egypt to man military-equipment training stations.

In 1959, in the midst of the Soviet-Egyptian "cold war," Moscow demonstrated its pragmatism by agreeing to deliver to Egypt a reduced, though still substantial, $120-million military-equipment package which included some one hundred twenty MIG-19 all-weather interceptors. The provision of the MIG-19's provided a step forward in Egypt's strategic air-defense and tactical air-cover capacity but still did not provide Egypt with a distinctly offensive weapon. Under the 1959 agreement, some construction of military infrastructure was also undertaken, including the establishment of a submarine base at Abukir, near Alexandria, and five new airfields in the Sinai Peninsula and along the Egyptian Red Sea coast.

By 1961 Egyptian-Soviet relations had improved, and Moscow increased the value of its new military equipment package to an estimated $170 million. Conventional warfare materiel was supplied to equip six Egyptian infantry and armored divisions, and the Egyptian armed forces were completely restructured on the Soviet organizational model. To facilitate reorganization, some thirteen hundred Soviet and Eastern European advisers (nine hundred Soviet) were reportedly dispatched to Egypt.

The next agreement, whose value has been estimated at anywhere from $220 million to $500 million, was concluded in June 1963. This agreement was clearly the most significant of the pre-Six-Day War pe-

For all practical purposes, Nasser's decisions on October 30 and 31 to concentrate Egyptian armored and ground forces along the Suez Canal to obstruct the impending English-French invasion,[65] plus the destruction of the Egyptian Air Force, sealed the fate of Egyptian units remaining in Sinai.

The Anglo-French landing in Port Said on November 5 and shore operations in the following days were resisted by the Egyptians. However, because of its short duration (three days) and circumscribed geographical scope, combat consisted primarily of small arms clashes that did not involve use of large amounts of Egyptian heavy equipment.[66] By the time of the landings, the British and French had, of course, won complete mastery of the skies, and any concentrated Egyptian effort would have been most difficult. The U.N. ceasefire on 7 November, therefore, came as a godsend to the beleaguered Egyptians.

IV In summary, then, a Soviet involvement in the events preceding and during the Suez War can be seen as cautious—and largely futile. Soviet military supplies to Egypt, which presumably were meant to deter Israeli and Western offensive actions, in fact acted to spur the invasion. The dangers created for Israeli and Western military action by Egyptian air superiority led only to massive Anglo-French bombings that destroyed the Egyptian air force and, with it, any chance for successful Egyptian defensive action.

During the course of the war, Soviet influence on the course of Middle Eastern events was hampered by the lack of physical means to threaten the British and French homelands credibly and to project forces rapidly into the Middle East. At the same time, military activities in Hungary effectively tied Soviet hands. Soviet reluctance to more vigorously challenge the West in such circumstances was understandable.

Nonetheless, the Russians, through a skillful use of threats and blandishments in the final days of the crisis, were able to influence the key actor in the Western camp—the United States. American pressure and lack of support for Britain and France, heightened particularly after the Russian intervention threat of 5 November, was the key element in aborting British, French, and Israeli military action against Egypt. While achievement of this goal might have been regarded as in the American interest regardless of Soviet action, U.S. pressure on its allies as the result of a Soviet threat set an unfortunate precedent. Henceforth the Soviets would view the possibilities of exploiting conflicts in the Western camp as an area of great promise.

CHAPTER THREE † THE SOVIET UNION AND THE SIX-DAY WAR

On the morning of 5 June 1967, as Israeli pilots systematically destroyed Arab air forces in the first stages of the Six-Day War, U.S. Secretary of Defense Robert McNamara informed President Lyndon Johnson that the Soviet Union had just activated the hot line connecting Moscow to Washington. For the first time in its four-year history the Moscow-Washington communications link, designed to prevent nuclear war by miscalculation, was being used by the Russian leadership to pass a message urgently to an American president.

Soviet alacrity in responding to the 1967 outbreak of hostilities sharply contrasted with the hesitancy that had been displayed during the Suez events eleven years before. The seriousness of Soviet concern reflected the expanded political and military involvement of the Soviet Union in the Middle East after the 1956 Egyptian debacle—a heightened role manifested in grossly expanded weapons deliveries.

Though the zone of confrontation between Egypt and Israel largely remained peaceful between 1956 and 1967, partially due to the presence of a U.N. Emergency Force in Sinai, the arms competition between Egypt and Israel moved to unprecedented heights. The motor for this expansion of weapons inventories was not only the conflict between Cairo and Tel Aviv but also the emerging aspiration of Egypt to play a leading role in Arab affairs.

Cairo's heightened ambition coincided with a burst of political change in the Near East. In the years between the Suez War and the Six-Day War, two Middle Eastern monarchies (Iraq and Yemen) fell, pro-Western regimes in Jordan and Lebanon were nearly toppled, and Syria joined Egypt in a short-lived federation. In addition, a civil war broke out in Yemen, to which Egypt dispatched troops and weapons. The influence of Egypt's President Nasser was felt in all these events.

Because of Egypt's growing role in the anti-Zionist cause and in intra-Arab affairs, Moscow viewed Nasser as a highly promising associate. Consequently, the Kremlin hierarchy, ignoring Nasser's periodic campaigns against domestic communism, generously supplied the Egyptian leader with arms to buttress Cairo's growing activism. Tel Aviv, in turn, sought to match these Egyptian acquisitions.

On Israel's northern border with Syria the situation was far less tranquil than in Sinai. Between 1956 and 1967 the Syrian-Israeli frontier was the scene of numerous clashes, most of which stemmed from Syrian shelling of Israeli farmers and fishermen followed by retaliation on the part of Tel Aviv. Tension further mounted in connection with an abortive Syrian plan to divert water from the Israeli Jordan River irrigation project. The confrontation on the northern border was exacerbated, particularly from 1965 to 1967, by a build-up of Arab *fedayeen* guerrilla activity emanating from Jordan. The tension in the Syrian-Israeli zone drew Damascus into ever-increasing dependence on the Soviet Union.

To understand the evolution of events that transformed the Soviets into major backers of the "progressive" Arabs, it is necessary to look back at the period after the 1956 invasion. Immediately in the wake of the 1956 Suez War, the Soviet Union had agreed to replenish wartime Egyptian military equipment losses and to supply Syria with large sums of military supplies.[1] Henceforth, as a result of a succession of Soviet-Syrian and Soviet-Egyptian arms deals, Israel would face two Soviet military-aid recipients along its borders. The 1958 revolution in Iraq and the realignment of Baghdad's policy from a pro-Western to a pro-Soviet orientation would place a third object of Soviet military support within striking distance of Israel.

Moscow's increased ties in the Middle East would quickly prompt its new Arab clients to seek direct Soviet military involvement in Near Eastern political disputes. In 1958, for example, after the Iraqi coup against the Western-oriented Nuri as-Said government and the American intervention in Lebanon, Egyptian leader Gamal Abdel Nasser hastened to Moscow to seek a Soviet military action or threat that would protect the Iraqi revolution from possible Western interference. Khrushchev on this occasion told a miffed Nasser that the Soviet leadership could not contemplate any more active intervention than announcement of a maneuver of twenty-four Soviet army divisions the Bulgarian-Turkish border.[2] Khrushchev later explained that S restraint was motivated by the fear that unlimited support of N would prompt the "impulsive" Nasser to undertake some type of lateral military action, a course the Soviet Union opposed.[3]

If Soviet hesitancy to support Nasser directly in the Iraqi epis partially due to concern about the Egyptian leader's stability a logical trustworthiness, these doubts were unquestionably heigh the domestic anti-Communist campaign which Nasser con 1959–60. Nasser's ire during this interlude was aroused by pected actions of the Iraqi revolutionaries in persecuting serites, a move which Nasser thought was instigated by Iraqi riod. Its wide scope may partially have been stimulated by a Soviet desire to support, though not participate in, Nasser's military intervention on behalf of the "progressive" revolutionary government in the Yemen, a military effort which the Egyptian leader would carry on from 1962 until 1967.[7]

In addition to the Yemen events, other Middle Eastern developments, particularly the 17 April 1963 tripartite pact concluded between Egypt, Syria, and Iraq, may also have encouraged the Soviets. This agreement had as one of its declared goals the creation of a military partnership that would "be able to free the Palestine Arab homeland from the Zionist danger."[8] Though short-lived, the tripartite pact may have convinced the Soviet leadership that a united anti-Western Middle Eastern bloc could be cemented by encouraging joint Arab military efforts aimed against Israel.

The 1963 arms agreement introduced a qualitative improvement into the Egyptian ground forces by providing two Egyptian armored divisions with T-54B medium tanks to replace the older T-34 medium and IS-III heavy tanks that were transferred to Egyptian infantry divisions. As of 1963, T-54 and later model T-55 tanks were the standard first-line battle tanks of the Soviet armed forces. The 1963 pact marked the first time in the eight-year history of the Egyptian-Soviet military relationship that the most contemporary equipment deployed in the Soviet armed forces had been sent to Egypt.

With regard to aircraft, the 1963 agreement provided two new additions, both of which represented qualitative advances. MIG-21 supersonic interceptors were introduced for the first time in the Middle East (the first deliveries were in 1962), and by late 1964, fifty of these first-line Soviet aircraft were located in Egypt. According to Egyptian accounts, the MIG-21's were acquired to balance Israel's acquisition of advanced aircraft from France.[9] Western accounts, however, dispute this Egyptian observation.

The second key aircraft addition was embodied in the Soviet commitment to provide TU-16 medium bombers, capable of carrying a twenty-thousand-pound bombload to Egypt. Of the aerial weapons yet placed in Arab hands, these bombers provided the heaviest payload and were perhaps the most significant delivery of the 1963 arms pact. In addition, the 1963 agreement provided further shipments of IL-28 light bombers, more MIG-17 and MIG-19 fighters, plus twenty-four large AN-12 transport planes, twenty-four IL-16 medium-range paratroop carriers, and forty-plus MI-2 helicopters. The provision of the transport aircraft was motivated, in all probability, by the Egyptian need to supply its expeditionary forces in Yemen. SAM-2 ground-to-air missiles also were reported in Egypt in April 1963. By fall 1964, about ten batteries of ground-to-air missiles, which may have been either SAM-1's or SAM-2's, were located in Egypt. The 1963 agreement also provided for delivery of thirty-six guided-missile gunboats of the *Komar* (2 missiles) and *Osa* (four missiles) classes, two *Tallin*-class destroyers, and two W-class submarines.

A final Soviet-Egyptian arms agreement before the Six-Day War was concluded in Moscow in August 1965. Though the agreement, whose value has been estimated at some $310 million, substantially increased the Egyptian air, ground, and naval inventories, no new weapons types were provided.

By the commencement of hostilities in June 1967, the Arab clients of the Soviet Union reportedly possessed the following weapons *inter alia* (major Soviet weapons delivered are indicated in subheadings):

Egypt
1,200 tanks and assault guns:[10]
   350 T-34 medium tanks
   500 T-54/55 medium tanks
    60 IS-III heavy tanks
    50 PT-76 light tanks
   150 SU-100 self-propelled guns
1,500-plus artillery pieces:[11]
   540 field guns
   130 medium guns
   200 120-mm mortars
   695 antitank guns
   A few *Snapper* (Soviet designation *Shmel*) antitank missile units
   Katyusha-type tactical rocket launchers
   A few other tactical surface-to-surface rockets
500 combat aircraft:[12]
    30 TU-16 medium bombers
   40–43 IL-28 light bombers
  120–163 MIG-21 C/D interceptors
   40–80 MIG-19 all-weather fighters or fighter-bombers
   15–55 SU-7 fighter-bombers
  100–150 MIG-15 and MIG-17 fighter-bombers
   150 SAM-2 *Guideline* surface-to-air missile installations[13]

Syria
500 tanks and assault guns:[14]
   400 T-34 and T-54 tanks (of which 200 were believed operational)
    50 SU-100 self-propelled guns
   Artillery pieces up to 155 mm[15]

Some 80–120 first-line combat aircraft:[16]
    4–6 IL-28 light bombers
   30–40 MIG-21 interceptors
   20 MIG-19 interceptors
  30–60 MIG-17 fighter-bombers
   10 SAM-2 *Guideline* surface-to-air missile installations[17]

Iraq
Some 600 tanks (400 of which were believed operational):[18]
   Approximately 450 T-34 and T-54 medium tanks
Approximately 200 combat aircraft:[19]
   Some TU-16 medium bombers
   10 IL-28 light bombers
   60 MIG-21 interceptors
   30 MIG-17 and MIG-19 fighters

Soviet military equipment delivered to Arab clients in the years preceding the Six-Day War was distributed in the following dimensions. Before the Suez War and in its aftermath, World War II-era tanks (T-34's) were supplied to Egypt, Syria, and Iraq in large numbers. These tanks were all surplus to Soviet requirements since they had been replaced in the Soviet army inventory by T-44 and T-54 tanks in the early and mid-1950s.[20] After the 1963 Soviet-Egyptian arms agreement, T-54 tanks equivalent to those in operation in Soviet and Eastern European forces began to be provided to the Arab clients. It is perhaps more than coincidental that the T-62 medium tank, a follow-on model to the T-54/55 series, had entered serial production in the Soviet Union in 1961 and would soon begin replacing some of the T-54/55 tanks in first-line service in the Soviet forces.[21] Soviet anticipation of the ensuing surplus may have prompted or eased the decision to qualitatively upgrade the Arab tank inventories.

To balance the Soviet shipment of T-54's to Egypt and Syria, Israel in 1963 requested that the United States supply M-48 Patton tanks (at that time the principal American battle tank) to the Israeli armed forces. Since the United States before this time had not supplied weapons to Israel, (with the exception of the Hawk antiaircraft missile system discussed below), the Israeli request caused some consternation. Ultimately, however, the United States agreed to the Israeli proposition and authorized West Germany, which since the early 1960s had been quietly supplying Israel with limited quantities of arms under the Israeli-West German reparations agreement, to ship American-produced M-48 tanks to Israel. A West German-Israeli agreement to this effect was signed in October 1964. Egypt, however, discovered the German-Israeli tank pact and, by threatening Arab punitive action against West Germany, caused the latter to break all arms agreements with Israel. The United States subsequently, in 1965, however, agreed to make up for the West German default and began shipping M-48 tanks to Israel (as well as to Jordan).[22]

The American M-48 shipment, prompted by large Soviet tank deliveries to the Arabs, established the precedent for U.S. participation as a major arms supplier to Israel. Before this time, Israel's principal arms suppliers had been France, Britain, and West Germany. As Secretary of State Dean Rusk observed in relation to the M-48 tank shipments to Israel, ". . . we have been interested in some sort of reasonable balance in the armed forces in that area. . . . Western Europe has been the primary arms supplier to Israel. We ourselves have tried not to be active in the Near East in the arms field, although we have taken some steps in that regard because for some years we have been trying to find some way in which to put some ceilings on this neighborhood arms race in the Near East."[23]

Decisionmakers in Washington thus hoped that the M-48 tank deliveries would induce the Soviets to limit their shipments to the Middle East. Presumably, the American view was based on the probably reasonable premise that the Soviet Union was striving to provide its clients with certain military advantages over the Israelis. Should these advantages, as a consequence of American weapons deliveries to Israel, elude the Arabs, the Soviet Union would be persuaded to limit arms supplies to the Middle East. The American scheme, however, was frustrated by the sheer magnitude of Soviet shipments to the Arabs.

The total number of tanks and self-propelled guns that the Russians supplied the Arab states bordering on Israel (approximately seventeen hundred, plus an additional four hundred fifty Soviet-supplied tanks in nearby Iraq) significantly exceeded the estimated eleven hundred tanks and self-propelled guns possessed and acquired by Israel.[24] Though by the beginning of the Six-Day War Israel had received some two hundred of the M-48 tanks (the most modern tank obtained by Israel),[25] plus a large number of late-model British Centurion tanks, the number of these contemporary armored vehicles supplied to Israel was much less than the number of T-54's alone that had been dispatched by the Soviet Union to the Arab countries, not to mention the many older Soviet tanks that had been shipped previously.

While it is unclear whether the extensive Soviet shipment of tanks was an opportunistic attempt to achieve political gain or was prompted by a perceived renewal of the Israeli-Western and "reactionary" Arab threat to the "progressive" Arab states, it is readily apparent that on any absolute scale, Soviet shipments constituted a manifold increase over the level of tanks introduced by the Soviet Union into the Middle East before 1956. The growing scale of tank supply alone was indicative of the increasing Soviet commitment to the "progressive" Arab cause.

Nevertheless, the extensive Soviet tank deliveries in isolation may not have constituted, in the Russian view, a factor that provided superiority to the Arabs. Considering the heavy loss ratio inflicted by Israeli aircraft and armor on Egyptian armored forces during the 1956 campaign, it is likely that Russians realized that both an extensive Arab air and ground superiority over Israeli forces would be required before the Arabs could defend themselves against the Israelis, much less defeat them.

Moshe Dayan has noted, for instance, that in the series of Israeli contacts with the Egyptian First Armored Brigade team in Sinai in 1956 the Israelis lost one tank and one half-track (with one person killed and ten wounded), while the Egyptians lost thirty T-34 tanks (of which eight were destroyed by Israeli armor and twenty-two by the Israeli air force); five SU-100 self-propelled guns; and about forty armored personnel carriers (mostly hit by air attack).[26] While complete figures for Egyptian and Israeli losses for the 1956 war are not available, Dayan's description of Israeli-Egyptian comparative performance is probably reasonably representative. Taking into account this historical background, the Russians probably assumed that a significant Arab reserve of tanks was required even if Israeli air superiority were neutralized.

To the extent that Soviet tanks supplied to the Middle East were obsolescent and surplus (such as the T-34), their provision in large numbers to the Arab states represented little economic and defense cost to the Soviets. However, when deliveries shifted to the currently deployed T-54/55's, the costs involved must have appeared more pronounced. While newer T-62 tanks were becoming available to replace some of the T-54/55's in front-line Soviet service, shipment of the T-54's to Egypt deprived the Soviet and Warsaw Pact forces in Europe of equipment that could have played a useful war-fighting reserve role, as well as a training role. These shipments, moreover, took place against a background of rising Soviet-United States tension generated by the growing American intervention in Vietnam.

Thus, the almost one thousand T-54/55 tanks introduced into the Middle East from 1963 to 1967 represented a meaningful cost for the Soviets and a significant commitment to the Arab military effort.[27]

Qualitatively, the T-54 tanks were faster and had a longer cruising range than the British Centurions and American M-48's acquired by the Israelis. Nonetheless, the T-54's firing accuracy, rate of fire, and armor thickness were faulted by some observers in comparison with Western tanks.[28] (The Israelis had been able to reduce some of the comparative disadvantages of their Western-supplied tanks by refitting them and installing new guns.)[29]

The ultimate significance of the added Arab tanks would only be determined, of course, by the ability of the Arabs to use their tanks, aircraft, and other antitank and antiaircraft weapons together to neutralize and destroy Israeli armor and aircraft, the means which the Israelis had used to inflict substantial losses on Egyptian armor in 1956. This fact gave great significance to the type and quality of aircraft with which the Soviets supplied the Arabs. (It should be recalled that in 1956 the Egyptian air force had been eliminated from combat on the second day of the war as a consequence of French and English bombings.)

The Soviets, in the period after the Suez War, continually upgraded the Arab fighter-aircraft inventory. By 1963, first-line Soviet interceptor aircraft had been committed to the Arab clients (the MIG-21 whose prototypes had first appeared publicly only in 1956).[30] These interceptor aircraft were called upon, in the first instance, to provide a strategic air defense for Egypt against the counterforce threat posed by the growing Israeli air force. (Before the Six-Day War, the Israeli air force, because of the limited payload capacity of its principal fighter aircraft, the Mirage III and Super Mystere, and the relatively few light bombers possessed, represented only a very limited threat, at least with conventional weapons, to Egyptian population centers.) Because of the decisive effect of French and English bombing of the Egyptian air force during the Suez War, the Soviets and Egyptians were presumably quite sensitive to the possibility of an Israeli counterforce strike. Soviet and Arab concern with this counterforce threat was further revealed by the decision to begin deploying SAM-2 antiaircraft missile systems, in addition to the MIG-21 interceptor defense, in Egypt and Syria. By the start of the Six-Day War, some twenty-seven SAM-2 sites were installed in Egypt in the Nile Delta, the Nile Valley, and the Sinai.[31]

The second and most important task of the Soviet interceptors supplied to the Arab countries would be to deny Israel control of the air space over any future Arab-Israeli battlefield. The high losses that the Israeli air force had inflicted on Egyptian ground forces during the 1956 Suez contest made air superiority, or at least an aerial stalemate, a *sine qua non* of Arab military action. The one hundred and fifty to two hundred MIG-21's that the Soviets shipped to Egypt and Syria (plus the sixty MIG-21's delivered to Iraq) substantially exceeded the seventy-two Mirage III and twenty Super Mystere first-line interceptors received by Israel.[32] In spite of individual cases of poor Arab pilot performance (on 7 April 1967, for example, the Israelis shot down four to six Syrian MIG's with no confirmed Israeli losses[33]), the incidence of Arab-Israeli aerial combat in the previous years had been infrequent enough to give the Arab leaders the impression that the numerical ratio of first-line interceptor aircraft favoring the Arabs reflected their actual combat potential for achieving air superiority. Nasser told British scholar and diplomat Anthony Nutting thirty-six hours before the beginning of the Six-Day War that the Egyptian intelligence service had assured him that his Soviet-supplied aircraft were "more than a match for anything possessed by Israel."[34] Soviet provision of a disproportionally large number of interceptor aircraft permitted the Arabs to contemplate more sanguinely a possible confrontation with Israel.

The Israelis counted on reducing the Arab numerical advantage in interceptors in the coming years by (a) obtaining fifty French Mirage V interceptors to combat Arab aircraft and (b) acquiring additional strictly ground-attack planes (American A-4 Skyhawks) to free Israeli dual-purpose aircraft such as the Mirage III for interceptor duty as well as to increase the number of aircraft that the Arab interceptors would eventually have to destroy to protect the Arab ground forces. Neither the Mirage V's nor the Skyhawks were delivered, however, before the Six-Day War.[35] The disproportion of aircraft in favor of the Arab side in 1967, with its potential for Arab tactical air superiority, therefore created strong incentives for an Israeli first strike on the eve of the Six-Day War. It should be pointed out, however, that Israeli plans for such a first strike apparently antedated the large growth in Arab aircraft inventories.[36]

Arab confidence before the Six-Day War may have been heightened by the belief that the increased Egyptian strategic threat represented by the presence of TU-16 medium bombers and IL-28 light bombers would tie down a great portion of Israel's interceptor inventory in strategic air defense and prevention of deep interdiction. The Egyptians and their Soviet mentors undoubtedly recalled that, in 1956, French air force units had provided air defense for Israeli territory, thereby freeing the entire Israeli air force for tactical air cover, interdiction, and ground-support tasks. This French help was no longer available. The Arabs might thus expect decisive air superiority over the battlefield.

In the interim, however, Israel, in 1962, presumably to counter partially the strategic threat posed by the TU-16 bombers, had acquired Hawk antiaircraft missiles from the United States.[37] By the beginning of the Six-Day War, some fifty Hawk installations were put into position, reportedly about half to protect the Israeli nuclear plant at Dimona and half just south of Tel Aviv.[38]

The Hawk missiles offset, to a limited extent, the need for additional commitment of Israeli interceptors to strategic air defense. The Soviets, however, demonstrating that their provision of a limited strategic threat to the Egyptians was meant to be preserved, next supplied the Egyptians with air-to-surface missiles, reportedly of the *Kennel* variety. (These missiles were first displayed in Egypt in 1965–66.)[39] Two of these subsonic missiles could be carried under the wings of a TU-16 medium bomber. The missiles had a range of some fifty miles and carried a one-thousand- to two-thousand-pound warhead.[40] The range of the *Kennel* missiles would permit the TU-16 launching aircraft to attack Israeli targets and yet remain outside the twenty-two-mile slant range of Israeli Hawk antiaircraft missiles (and also give the launching aircraft additional time and space to evade interceptor aircraft pursuit). Once launched, the *Kennel* missiles, though vulnerable to interceptor aircraft and Hawk antiaircraft missiles, would multiply the number of attacking objects with which Israeli air defense would have to cope and, hence, tie down significant numbers of Israeli interceptors in a strategic defense role.

As a trade-off, however, for engaging in a stand-off attack (as well as for carrying the heavyweight stand-off missiles), the Egyptians would initially have to forgo use of the high payload (twenty-thousand-pound), overhead bombing capability of the TU-16's. Thus, if all thirty Egyptian TU-16's had been used in a stand-off strike with *Kennel* missiles against Israel, and even if 100 percent penetrability were achieved, only sixty one-ton conventional warheads would have hit Israel—a painful but inconsiderable sum.

Although Soviet supply of *Kennel* missiles to Egypt preserved a limited strategic threat for the Egyptians, it did not provide Nasser with a decisive offensive or deep interdiction capability, or a means to degrade Israeli strategic air defense seriously. Soviet provision of many more TU-16's or IL-28 light bombers (plus training of additional Egyptian air crews) would have served more significantly to force Israel to divert more interceptors to strategic air defense as well as to increase the potential severity of strategic strikes inflicted on Israel, itself a greater incentive to the Israelis to maintain more interceptors in an air-defense role.[41] (If, as a result of increasing the number of attacking bomber aircraft, the Egyptians had been capable of penetrating only twelve TU-16 bombers directly over Israeli targets, they would have delivered bombs of at least twice as much explosive force as thirty TU-16 bombers launching *Kennel* missiles in a stand-off attack.)

Though Soviet restraint in not increasing the Egyptian bomber inventory may have been motivated on this occasion more by economic considerations than by political-military considerations (for example, the *Kennel* missiles were presumably considerably cheaper than additional bombers and extensive air-crew training), there are grounds for believing that at this stage, before the Six-Day War, the Soviets were concerned with not giving the Egyptians an extensive strategic bombardment capability. In 1959, for instance, during the Soviet-Egyptian quarrel, Khrushchev reportedly had denied Nasser's requests for medium-range bombers and missiles. Khrushchev justified his decision by stating that ". . . we had in mind that in a state of excitement . . . , you might have undertaken some undesirable action leading to war." The Soviet leader added: "If the need to use these rockets should arise . . . it would evidently be best to launch them from our territory. Therefore you have no need for such rockets, but you can count on us rendering you assistance with these rockets from our territory if the aggressors unleash war against you."[42] The Soviet leaders apparently feared that Egyptian possession of a formidable strategic bombardment capacity might tempt the Arabs into offensive action against the Israelis.[43] It should be noted that, in spite of the many years of reasonably satisfactory Soviet-Egyptian relations before the Six-Day War, the Soviet Union apparently never remedied the guidance-system difficulties that plagued the medium-range missiles (*al-Zafir*, *al-Kahir*, and *al-Ared*) designed in Egypt by German technicians in the early 1960s,[44] nor did the Soviets supply available tactical and medium-range missiles of the *Frog* and *Scud* series to the Arabs.

In addition to their potential strategic bombing role against Israel (and possibly against the Yemeni royalists), TU-16 bombers with *Kennel* missiles may have been provided to Egypt to deter action by the U.S. Sixth Fleet in any future Middle Eastern crisis. The *Kennel*-type missiles, presumably because of their high cost per unit of explosive force, were believed by Western sources to be designed primarily for high-value targets, such as ships.[45] (Considering the small size and concentrated nature of the Israeli economic and logistical infrastructure and population, use of these weapons against Israeli strategic targets would, of course, also make economic good sense). The commitment of the TU-16 medium bombers to the Arab states coincided with the beginning of permanent Soviet naval deployments in the Mediterranean (mid-1964),[46] and one can hypothesize that both decisions presaged a Soviet intention to deprive the United States and the West of their former military free hand in the region.

The Israelis originally sought to counter Egyptian acquisition of long-distance bombing capability by obtaining similar, heavier payload weapons. As a consequence, in March 1958 it was announced that Israel would acquire one squadron of French twin-jet Vautour light bombers, similar to the Soviet IL-28.[47] Eventually, some fifty of these aircraft would be obtained. The trend toward acquisition of bombers, however, would be halted by Israel in favor of purchase of multimission aircraft capable of employment for strategic air defense and tactical air superiority, as well as for interdiction missions, limited strategic bombing, and ground support.[48] This Israeli decision was eased by the growing payload capacity of available multipurpose interceptor/fighter-bombers.[49] The Mirage III supersonic interceptor/fighter-bomber ordered by Israel from France in 1962 was the first fruit of this decision to acquire multimission aircraft. While one source states that the Mirage III was ordered to counter the reported acquisition of MIG-21's by Egypt,[50] it should be recalled, as mentioned earlier, that the Egyptians asserted that their acquisitions of MIG-21's were meant to balance Israeli purchases of high-performance aircraft.

The Soviet Union had been less generous in supplying the Arabs with aircraft for ground-support and battlefield-interdiction roles than they had been with other categories of aircraft. This may have been due to the feeling that specialized ground-attack aircraft, as distinguished from interceptors, were suitable only in an offensive role. A Soviet book on the Six-Day War, for example, describes the American A-4 Skyhawk ground-support aircraft as "a purely offensive weapon."[51]

The Arabs, before the Six-Day War, had received only obsolescent MIG-15's, MIG-17's, certain models of the MIG-19, and relatively few modern SU-7 ground-strike aircraft to use in a ground-support role. The most contemporary and specialized Soviet ground-attack aircraft delivered, the Sukhoi SU-7, had only been in service in the Soviet air force since 1960.[52] Therefore, relatively few SU-7 aircraft may have been available to the Soviets for supply to the Arabs. Nonetheless, MIG-21 interceptors, which made their appearance in the Soviet air force at about the same time, were delivered to Egypt and Syria in quantities several times greater than the number of SU-7 ground-attack aircraft delivered (an estimated one hundred forty to two hundred MIG-21's delivered as against fifteen to fifty-five SU-7's). This disproportion invites speculation that the Soviets may have been consciously structuring the Egyptian and Syrian air forces on a defensively oriented model. This hypothesis is strengthened by the great numerical advantage in interceptors that the Soviets provided the Arabs over the Israelis.

Before the Six-Day War, because of the dearth of Arab-Israeli air engagements, there was little demonstrated evidence that Arab air combat losses would be relatively much greater than Israeli losses. Moreover, as mentioned previously, the Arab leaders apparently felt confident in their air superiority. Nonetheless, the Soviets provided Egypt and Syria collectively with an approximately two-to-one first-line interceptor advantage over the Israelis. One wonders whether, if the Soviets had intended to give the Arabs an offensive capability, they would not have somewhat reduced the quantitative advantage in interceptors in order (at the same cost) to provide additional modern ground-attack aircraft to the Arabs. The Soviets, of course, also had the option of simply providing additional contemporary ground-support aircraft to the Arabs. (The Arab air forces, of course, did have significant numbers of aging MIG-15's and MIG-17's that could be used in a ground-support role.)

It should be pointed out, by way of reservation, that Soviet military writings, particularly in the early 1960s, emphasized the use of artillery and tactical surface-to-surface missiles in preference to ground-attack aircraft for the purpose of accomplishing tactical fire support and, to a certain extent, battlefield interdiction. These tactical conceptions were derived from the doctrinal conclusion, echoed in Khrushchev's 1960 statement, that the day of the manned aircraft had passed, in favor of the rocket.[53] Heavy Soviet deliveries of artillery to the Arabs may have been intended, in the Russian conception, to accomplish the fire-support role.

At the same time, however, it is necessary to recall that before the Six-Day War, the Soviets had not provided the Arabs with tactical surface-to-surface missiles of the *Frog* variety (maximum range 25–50 km.), which initially made their appearance in the Soviet armed forces in the late 1950s.[54] Such weapons would have been useful in a battlefield interdiction or deep fire-support role. Nasser in fact requested these missiles from Khrushchev in 1958–59.[55] The Soviet denial of the missiles to the Arabs may have been tied to the fact that, with the pre-1967 boundaries, *Frog* missiles deployed in the Gaza Strip could have been used strategically to bombard population centers on Israel's coastal strip south of Tel Aviv. In addition, of course, it is possible that conventional warheads for the *Frogs* were simply not available in the early 1960s. At any rate, neither modern, specialized ground-attack aircraft nor tactical rockets were delivered to the Arabs in significant numbers. These deficiencies reduced the flexibility and mobility of Arab fire-support and battlefield-interdiction capabilities. Because of this, Arab forces could be expected to have greater difficulty penetrating Israeli lines, and Israeli forces would be relatively more free to deliver reinforcements to threatened points.

Another tactical deficiency was the failure to provide the Arabs with significant numbers of modern antitank weapons. Though a few *Snapper* wire-guided antitank weapons were supplied, no great quantities were dispatched; nor were newer antitank rockets such as the *Sagger* (which made its first public appearance in 1965) sent.[56]

To summarize, Soviet weapons deliveries before the Six-Day War demonstrated a pattern of constant quantitative and qualitative improvement of Arab clients' weapons inventories. These deliveries appeared to be motivated by the Soviet appreciation of the "progressive" role that Arab military strength played in (a) facilitating sociopolitical change in the conservative Arab states (as typified by the Egyptian military intervention on behalf of the Yemen rebels), (b) cementing the unity of the "progressive" Arab states by making confrontation with Israel (and its Western supporters) a realizable possibility and thus a constant common preoccupation, and (c) increasing the Soviet role and influence within individual Arab states and in Middle Eastern politics in general.

Presumably because of Soviet satisfaction with the political effects of this military aid, from 1963 onward certain weapons currently deployed in the Soviet armed forces, and not simply surplus items, began to flow to the Arab states. The quantity of most categories of Soviet equipment delivered to Egypt alone significantly outstripped the quantity of similar weapons supplied by the West to Israel. These quantitative advantages gave Arab leaders a sense of confidence and played an important role in the Egyptian decision to move troops into Sinai in May 1967, the event which served as the prelude for the Six-Day War.[57]

While each new Soviet weapons system given to the Arabs was balanced qualitatively by a new Western weapons system provided to Israel (MIG-21 fighter—Mirage III fighter, T-54 tank—M-48 tank, TU-16 bomber—Hawk missile), the quantitative dimensions of Soviet aid were such that the Arab military supply position vis-à-vis the Israelis was steadily improving. Soviet tanks and aircraft in the Middle East that numbered in the tens before Suez were present in the hundreds by 1967. The Soviet leadership was undoubtedly aware that any war that resulted with this great quantity of weapons would be significantly larger and more explosive than any previous Middle Eastern conflict. Particularly after the involvement of the United States as a partial military supplier to Israel in the early 1960s, the possibility of any Arab-Israeli conflict escalating to include American participation became more likely. With these factors in mind, the Soviet leadership may have taken a decision to provide the Arabs with sufficient weapons for defending themselves and engaging in limited offensive action but not to allow contemplation of a successful first strike or total victory.

Though it appeared that the Arabs had been given sufficient tanks and interceptor aircraft to neutralize the offensive threat of Israeli armor and aviation, they had been denied significant numbers of contemporary ground-attack aircraft and tactical rockets, which would have improved their fire-support and, hence, their offensive capabilities. The Soviets had provided the Arabs with a strategic threat that would tie down a portion of the Israeli interceptor force in air-defense duties, but they had structured the long-distance forces in such a way that Arab strategic strikes would probably not have been decisive or even significant.[58] Because of the limited nature of the Arab strategic threat, more Israeli aircraft would be available to contest Arab air forces over the tactical battlefield.

In sum, the Soviets had given the Arabs the capability to engage in political braggadocio and threat but not some of the means at the Soviet Union's disposal that would have better ensured Arab military victory. The Soviets apparently wished to give the Arabs the illusion, rather than the reality, of overwhelming military superiority. Because of the gaps in Arab capabilities and the possibilities of U.S. intervention, one would have expected the Soviets to approach the 1966–67 build-up of tension in the Middle East with considerable concern. Actual Soviet performance is outlined below.

III On 14 May 1967, Egyptian leader Gamal Abdel Nasser ordered Egyptian troops to enter the Sinai Peninsula, an event which would serve as a key precipitating cause of the Six-Day War. Nasser justified his decision on the basis of reports he had received indicating that an Israeli military build-up had taken place on the borders of Syria, Egypt's ally as the result of a defense pact signed on 3 November 1966.[59] The link between Egypt and Syria, and the favorable Soviet attitude toward it, would be crucial in generating the events that preceded the Six-Day War.

The conclusion of the 1966 Syrian-Egyptian defense pact had coincided with the reestablishment of diplomatic relations and friendly ties between Egypt and Syria, links which had been broken since the 1961 split of the short-lived (1958–61) Syrian-Egyptian United Arab Republic. The Egyptian-Syrian reconciliation was regarded by the Soviet Union as an important positive manifestation of growing "anti-imperialist" unity in the Middle East. (Soviet Chairman Kosygin had called only a few months before, on 17 May 1966, in Cairo for a "united front" of the four "progressive" Arab states—Egypt, Syria, Iraq, and Algeria.)

In the months before and after the Egyptian-Syrian agreement, tension had risen on the Syrian-Israeli frontier as the result of infiltrations into Israel by Palestinian Arab terrorists. In answer to Israeli appeals to the Soviet Union for assistance in stopping the terrorist incursions, Moscow asserted that "it is possible that incidents of the kind were organized in a special way by certain [Western] services or by an agency of those services for the purpose of provocation."[60] The Soviet Union thus did not feel moved to condemn or even to admit the existence of Arab terrorism against Israel. The ludicrous Soviet accusation against Western intelligence services did, however, reveal an important element of the Soviet outlook. The Russians apparently believed that the Western powers, using Israel as their tool, were seeking to undermine the "progressive" Syrian regime and to disrupt the blossoming of Egyptian-Syrian "anti-imperialist" ties. These alleged Western moves were regarded as threatening because the encouragement of an "anti-imperialist" (that is, anti-Western) orientation among the states of the Middle East had been a prime goal of Soviet policy since the 1955 Egyptian arms deal.

On 13 November 1966, perhaps partially as a signal to the new Egyptian and Syrian alliance partners, the Israelis engaged in a major antiterrorist retaliatory raid on the Jordanian village of Es Samu. In the months that followed, terrorist incidents increased, particularly on the Syrian-Israeli border, and a number of artillery and small-arms duels took place between Syrian and Israeli forces.[61]

On 7 April 1967, after a sharp artillery exchange, Israeli Mirages and Syrian MIG-21's clashed near the Sea of Galilee. According to the Israelis, six MIG's were shot down with no Israeli losses. The Syrians claimed that five Israeli planes were destroyed and acknowledged a loss of four Syrian aircraft.[62]

The April 7 battle was one of the largest armed clashes in the Middle East since the Suez War. The humiliating losses inflicted by Israel on the Syrian air force, which had been equipped with the latest Soviet interceptors, would be greeted with great anger in Moscow as virtually a direct affront to the Soviet Union. In addition, the Soviet leaders would quickly seize upon statements of Israeli political and military leaders that seemed to reflect a desire to upset the "progressive" Syrian government. These Israeli actions and intentions, in the view of Soviet decisionmakers, would require a firm response from the Soviet Union.

The Soviet official reaction to the April 7 air battle, reflecting its importance, came after a two-week delay. On 21 April 1967 the Israeli ambassador to the Soviet Union was summoned to the Soviet ministry of foreign affairs. Soviet Deputy Foreign Minister Malik delivered an oral statement to the ambassador in which the April 7 incident was qualified as a "dangerous playing with fire on the part of Israel in an area near the borders of the Soviet Union. . . ." Israel was equated with the United States ("The forces responsible for the situation in Vietnam are also responsible for provocations in the Middle East . . .") and was warned that continued verbal and physical threats against Syria would "result in serious consequences."[63] Given the two-week delay in Soviet response to the April 7 incident, the April 21 oral statement in all probability represented a considered Soviet policy stand of some importance. Moscow apparently wished to signal to Israel that it would not tolerate threats of violence to Syria's regime. Deep Soviet concern with Israel's threats was meant to be highlighted by the assertion that Israel was serving the interests of the Soviet Union's prime enemy, the United States, and by the geographic hyperbole placing the Israeli threat near the Soviet border.

On 25 April 1967, for no apparent reason, the Israeli ambassador was again summoned to the Soviet foreign ministry and this time was presented with a written statement by Deputy Foreign Minister Semyonov. The contents of this statement would set the stage for the chain of events that followed. The Russian note asserted: "The Soviet Government is in possession of information about Israeli troop concentrations on the Israeli-Arab borders at the present time. These concentrations are assuming a dangerous character, coinciding as they do with the hostile campaign in Israel against Syria."[64]

Whether the Russians initially believed that Israeli forces were actually concentrating on the Syrian border is still not clear. Nonetheless, in the days that followed it became evident that the Russians would attempt to use the Israeli troop-concentration report to convince Israel to cease further military actions against "progressive" Syria and simultaneously to strengthen the ties between Syria and Egypt and the other Arab states. As Polish commentators later pointed out, from the Communist perspective, "an overthrow of the left-wing Baathist government in Syria, as threatened by Israel, would mean infinitely more than a mere prestige setback. It would, in fact, mean a blow against the front of progressive Arab states. . . ."[65] In order to fortify the Syrian government and to protect Egyptian-Syrian unity, the Soviets probably concluded that they would have to spur the Egyptians into greater action against Israel.

The need for urging the Egyptians onward probably became particularly evident to the Soviets as the result of certain events that allegedly took place in the weeks after the April 7 Syrian-Israeli air battle. According to a Soviet account, "imperialist and reactionary Arab circles began to circulate a story, especially in Syria, to the effect that Egypt was participating in the common Arab confrontation with Israel only with words. In fact, it was sitting snugly behind the U.N. forces . . ." in Sinai. According to the Soviet account, the "Voice of Israel" in its Arabic broadcasts was declaring that if Israel struck at Syria, Egypt would not intervene. In the words of the Soviet observers, "it is completely evident that the imperialists by these means wished to stir up anti-Egyptian sentiments."[66]

In order to firm the ranks of Arab solidarity, Moscow on April 27 published an account of its first (21 April) protests to Israel on the issue of armed provocations against Syria.[67] (The published account, however, omitted the April 25 claim of Israeli troop concentrations.) Most importantly, on April 29, Soviet Chairman Kosygin told Anwar Sadat, who was visiting Moscow as head of an Egyptian parliamentary delegation, that the Soviet Union had information that the Israelis had massed two brigades on the Syrian border.[68] According to Nasser, who may well have been exaggerating, the Soviets told Sadat that an "invasion of Syria was about to take place."[69]

In the first two weeks of May 1967, two more major Arab terrorist incidents took place in Israel, and the Soviet press began publishing accounts of the purported Israeli troop concentrations on the Syrian border. According to U.S. President Lyndon Johnson, information available to the American authorities indicated that the purpose of the Soviet reports of troop concentrations was "to pressure Egypt into military support of Syria."[70] U.N. Secretary General U Thant also informed the U.N. Security Council on 19 May that reports from U.N. observers "have confirmed the absence of troop concentrations and significant troop movements on both sides of the (Syrian-Israeli) line.[71]

The Israeli foreign ministry, on May 12 and 19, and the Israeli prime minister, on May 29, invited Soviet Ambassador Chuvakhin to visit the Syrian border area to see for himself whether troops were concentrated there. On each occasion the Soviet ambassador refused.[72]

In spite of all the evidence to the contrary, the Soviets at the beginning of May continued to hold that the Israelis were about to attack the Syrians. As Premier Kosygin stated to the United Nations on 19 June 1967, "in those days, the Soviet Government, and I believe others too, began receiving information to the effect that the Israeli Government had timed for the end of May a swift stroke at Syria in order to crush it and then carry the fighting over into the territory of the United Arab Republic [Egypt]."[73]

The Soviets, whether or not they really expected the Israelis to attack Syria, were clearly set on convincing the Egyptians that they should take a firm stand against the Israelis. By making a demonstrative move (such as a return of Egyptian troops to the Sinai), the Egyptians would confront the Israelis with their strong Soviet-supplied army and force the Israelis to think twice before undertaking any further adventures against "progressive" Syria.

On 14 May, purportedly on the basis of information received from Egyptian intelligence, the Syrians, *and the Soviet Union,* Nasser alerted his armed forces and ordered them into the Sinai Peninsula to forestall the supposed Israeli attack on Syria.[74] On 16 May, the Egyptians requested that the United Nations remove its truce-observer troops from Egypt's Sinai border with Israel. Subsequently this request was amended to include the U.N. troops at Sharm el-Sheikh. On 18 May, U.N. Secretary General U Thant agreed to remove the entire U.N. Emergency Force (UNEF) from Sinai.

Though the Soviets formally supported the Egyptian right to remove UNEF,[75] there was reason to believe that the Russians were beginning to feel uneasy about the extent of Egyptian moves. According to a knowledgeable observer of U.N. affairs, "it became authoritatively known that . . . the UAR (Egypt) did not consult with the Soviet Union about the withdrawal of UNEF. Moscow was taken by surprise by Cairo's demand for withdrawal and Soviet diplomats assiduously inquired from all who might have some special knowledge of Arab intentions why Nasser had taken this step and how far he was prepared to go."[76]

Cairo's move in seeking UNEF's expulsion would put the Egyptian forces in direct proximity to Israeli forces. The situation became even more dangerous when Tel Aviv's forces were brought to full mobilization, in the period between May 18 and May 21.[77] The force demonstration that Moscow had desired now might risk transformation into war. At this point the knowledge of the various deficiencies that had been built into the Egyptian armed forces and the danger of escalation of any Arab-Israeli war undoubtedly began to penetrate Moscow's consciousness. Not only did the Soviet leadership have to restrain Israel, but it now became a question of urgency to caution the Egyptians. The urgency became particularly great after the May 22 Egyptian decision to close the Straits of Tiran to Israeli shipping, a move which shortly would be defined by the Israelis as an "act of aggression."

President Johnson dispatched a letter to Soviet Chairman Kosygin on May 22 (before the closure of the Straits of Tiran) which, though pitched in pacific terms, probably made clear the possibility of dangerous developments arising out of the Middle Eastern situation. Johnson's letter stated: "Your and our ties to nations of the area could bring us into difficulties which I am confident neither of us seeks. It would appear a time for each of us to use our influence to the full in the cause of moderation. . . ."[78] Kosygin, perhaps partially in response to the veiled threat contained in the Johnson letter, made the first major Soviet move to restrain the Egyptians. Between May 25 and May 28 he reportedly told visiting Egyptian Minister of War Shams el Din Badran: "We are going to back you. But you have gained your point. You have won a political victory. So it is time now to compromise, to work politically."[79] Kosygin's purported message of restraint, however, was either misunderstood or willfully distorted by Badran or by its ultimate recipient, Nasser. Nasser, on May 29, stated publicly that Badran had informed him that "the U.S.S.R. supports us in this battle and will not allow any power to intervene until matters [are] restored to what they were in 1956."[80] Nasser's friend Mohamed Heikal asserts, however, that the Egyptian undersecretary of foreign affairs had attended the Moscow meeting with Kosygin and, after hearing Nasser's erroneous account of Kosygin's remarks, sent accurate minutes of the meeting to the Egyptian leader.[81]

The Kosygin remarks were not the only sign of Soviet concern. At

3:00 in the morning, May 27, the Soviet ambassador in Cairo awakened Nasser and, on orders of the Soviet leadership, requested that the Egyptian leader not initiate hostilities. According to American information that was reportedly passed on to Moscow, the Egyptians had planned to launch an attack on the morning of May 27. In spite of Nasser's denial of having any intention to attack on May 27, the Russian ambassador pointed out that if Egypt launched an attack, it would be in an untenable political position and that the Soviet leadership advised Nasser not to commence hostilities.[82]

In the Soviet government's only prewar public statement on the Middle East crisis, issued on 24 May 1967, a line of hostility toward Israel was combined with appeals for restraint. The success of the Soviet campaign to push the Egyptians forward was noted: "Israeli extremists apparently hoped to take Syria by surprise and alone, but they miscalculated. Demonstrating solidarity with the courageous struggle of the Syrian people . . . , the Arab states . . . declared their intention to help Syria in the event of an attack by Israel." Warning the Israelis that any attack on the Arabs would be met by the "united strength of the Arab countries" and "the strong opposition to aggression of the Soviet Union," the statement continued that "it is the firm belief of the Soviet Government that the peoples have no interest in kindling a military conflict in the Middle East."

The Soviet endorsement of peace, rather than the political position of the Egyptians—for example, the Egyptian blockade of the Straits of Tiran was not mentioned—and the qualification placed on Soviet assistance—an Israeli attack would be met, not by the united strength of the Arab countries and the Soviet Union, but rather by the united strength of the Arab countries and "the strong opposition to aggression" of the Soviet Union—indicated that the Soviets were increasingly conditioning their support of the Arabs. The Russian statement concluded that "the Soviet Union is doing and will continue to do everything in its power to prevent a violation of peace and security in the Middle East and to safeguard the legitimate rights of the peoples."[83]

Direct Soviet communications with Israel highlighted the level of moderation that Moscow wished to introduce. In a personal note to Israeli Prime Minister Eshkol on May 26, Chairman Kosygin wrote: "We are concerned that, however complicated the situation on Israel's borders with Syria and the United Arab Republic (Egypt) may be, it is necessary to find ways to settle the conflict by unwarlike means. It is easy to light a fire, but to put out a conflagration may not be . . . as easy. . . ."[84] On June 2, Soviet Foreign Minister Gromyko summoned the Israeli ambassador to the ministry and reproached him for a statement by Israeli Foreign Minister Abba Eban that seemed to indicate that Israel intended to open the blockaded Straits of Tiran with its own forces. After Gromyko's initial reproach, the Soviet foreign minister shifted to a more friendly tone and advised the Israeli government to exercise restraint. In Gromyko's words, "We are working for peace."[85]

Soviet efforts, however, did not cause the Egyptians to lift the blockade of the Straits of Tiran or to withdraw their troops back from the Israeli border.[86] Moreover, to increase Israel's discomfiture, Jordan's King Hussein on May 30 unexpectedly appeared in Cairo to sign a defense agreement. Against this background of a deteriorating security situation combined with strident Arab propaganda calls for the destruction of Israel, the Israeli government decided to launch a preventive attack on its potential Arab assailants.

To summarize, in the weeks before the Six-Day War Soviet diplomacy had played a dangerous game that had backfired. The Soviets had apparently wished to fortify Syria's "progressive" regime and the Arab "anti-imperialist" front by stirring the Arabs into a common stand against the military threat supposedly posed by Israel. The retreat of Israel in the face of Soviet-inspired Arab unity, and particularly in the face of the Soviet-supplied Egyptian army, Moscow apparently thought, would surely improve the prestige and political position of the Soviet Union in the Middle East.

An activist Soviet posture may have seemed particularly desirable as a balance to the relatively passive role that the Soviets had felt compelled to adopt vis-à-vis American action in Vietnam. An immediate event that may have stirred the Soviets to even greater effort was the right-wing anti-Communist coup in Greece on 21 April 1967. Given the conspiratorial world view of the Soviets, the Greek revolt may have been accepted by the Soviets as confirmation of a heightened Western "anti-progressive" campaign that required some kind of response. (Revolts against "anti-imperialist" regimes in Indonesia and Ghana had also occurred in recent years.) Indeed, a *post facto* Soviet account asserts that the Greek coup "helped Israel accomplish its aggression against the UAR (Egypt), Syria, and Jordan."[87]

Once the Arabs had been stirred, however, events acquired dynamics of their own. Nasser, driven either by his longstanding ambitions or by the exhilaration of confrontation, apparently without consultation with the Soviets, expelled UNEF and blockaded the Straits of Tiran. These moves, in the opinion of all the parties concerned (with the possible exception of Nasser), created heightened dangers of war.

After the war, Soviet officials would tell Eric Rouleau of *Le Monde* that Nasser went too far. Of course, he should have reacted to the threats that Israel made against the Syrian regime. But he should have proceeded in a more prudent and especially a more moderate fashion."[88] The expulsion of UNEF and the blockade of the Straits of Tiran, by undermining the desired "moderation," were thus crucial elements that modified the Soviet approach to the prewar 1967 crisis. Another "high Soviet official" told the correspondent of the Paris *Nouvel Observateur* that after Egyptian seizure of Sharm el Sheikh, "we warned Nasser . . . that we would commit ourselves only to neutralizing the United States, that is, we would respond by an escalation equal to any escalation on the part of Washington—and that our support would not go beyond this."[89] While these reports may be self-serving, available evidence indicates that the Soviet posture did in fact become one of restraint after the blockade of the Straits of Tiran.

The Soviets were more aware than anyone that the Arabs had not received appropriate weapons to achieve a quick military victory. (Nasser, however, made several remarks indicating that he believed he had received sufficient weapons.) Moreover, as the result of President Johnson's 22 May letter and the clear pro-Israeli stand that had emerged in Washington, the Soviet government was also increasingly conscious of the possibility of U.S. involvement on the side of Israel. These factors apparently convinced the Soviets that it was imperative to avoid war. The Soviet Union would strive to ensure that the useful Egyptian force demonstration did not become transformed into a disastrous war.

The effectiveness of the Soviet effort to prevent war was hamstrung, however, by the contradictory position into which the Soviet Union had placed itself. The Soviet leadership, in order not to lose its political gains in the Arab world, had to endorse Arab aspirations while at the same time restraining Arab action. Israeli actions had to be condemned; at the same time sufficient good will had to be maintained with Tel Aviv to convince the Israelis of the sincerity of the Soviet peacemaking efforts. In ordinary times such contradictory efforts would have been difficult to maintain; in the white heat of the May–June 1967 events they became impossible.

In sum, the Soviets contributed, perhaps decisively, to the political atmosphere that engendered the Six-Day War. They did, however, engage in substantial efforts to seek to avert the war.

IV   What influence did Soviet weapons have on the course of the new war? As mentioned previously, the large Arab advantage over Israel in terms of interceptor aircraft, as well as the strategic threat posed by Egyptian bombers, provided a strong rationale for Israel to undertake a counterforce strike against Arab air bases at the beginning of any new conflict. On the morning of 5 June 1967, Israel delivered this counterforce strike with devastating success. In less than three hours, nearly three hundred (of a total of some five hundred) Egyptian aircraft were destroyed in attacks on seventeen airfields in Sinai, the Suez Canal Zone, the Nile Delta, along the Red Sea, and in the Nile Valley. Confirmed aircraft "kills" included all thirty of Egypt's TU-16 medium bombers, twenty-seven (of a total of some forty) IL-28 light bombers, twelve (of fifteen to fifty-five) recently delivered SU-7 ground-attack aircraft, ninety (of one hundred twenty to one hundred sixty-three) MIG-21 interceptors, twenty (of forty to eighty) MIG-19 interceptors, seventy-five (of one hundred to one hundred fifty) MIG-17 fighter-bombers, thirty-two transport aircraft, and MI-6 helicopters.[90]

In subsequent attacks on Syria, thirty (of thirty to forty) MIG-21 interceptors, twenty (of thirty to sixty) MIG-17 fighter-bombers, and twenty-one (of forty to sixty) IL-28 light bombers were destroyed. The remaining Syrian aircraft were withdrawn to bases far removed from the Israeli-Syrian zone of conflict. In an attack on the Iraqi forward-based field at location H-3, six MIG-21's and three Hawker Hunter interceptors were destroyed. In Jordan, all twenty of King Hussein's Hawker Hunter fighter-bombers were put out of action.[91]

The Israeli air attack crippled the Arabs and, in one stroke, ensured that Israel would not have to cope with a strategic threat. Most decisively, of course, the destruction of the Egyptian and Syrian interceptor force would give the Israeli air force virtual freedom to attack the Arab ground forces.[92] Thus, the basic model on which the Soviets had constructed the Arab air forces—interceptor superiority coupled with a limited strategic threat—was instantly erased. With these advantages eliminated, the inability of the Arabs to defend themselves was a foregone conclusion. The Arab tank advantage would be meaningless. In the words of a Soviet account, the Israeli air victory would have "fatal consequences for Egyptian tanks maneuvering in the desert and subjected to constant attacks from the air."[93]

The Soviets claim that Israeli air success was achieved because of laxness of the Egyptian air force leadership in maintaining an adequate air alert, as well as various other command shortcomings.[94] According to information from Israeli sources, however, the crucial factor determining Israeli success was primarily good intelligence combined with good fortune—(a) the attack coincided with the return of Egypt's morning air patrol to its bases,[95] and (b) nonalerted bases in Egypt that were not initially attacked did not launch their interceptors against Israeli planes.[96] Other factors that increased the Israeli success were the Egyptian failure to disperse or protect Egyptian aircraft on the airfields and the failure to provide deep rear bases (out of Israeli range) for at least a portion of Egyptian aircraft (particularly bombers). The extent to which Soviet advice was responsible for these shortcomings is not clear.

Egyptian leader Nasser, in the wake of the attacks, was dumbfounded by the Israeli capability to launch massive air strikes against Egypt. Giving some insight into the Soviet decision to provide him with a strategic threat, the Egyptian leader declared after the war: "The enemy attacked, at one go, all the military and civil airfields in the United Arab Republic. This meant he was relying on something more than his normal strength to protect his skies from any retaliation from us."[97] Nasser could not believe that the Israelis would chance leaving their strategic air defense denuded to launch a mass strike against Egypt. Nasser's disbelief in this possibility was one of the foundations of his accusation that American and British aircraft had assisted the Israelis.

In fact, in what could have been a dangerous gamble, the Israeli air force had left only twelve aircraft in a strategic air-defense role—eight airborne and four on the ground at the ends of runways.[98] Had the Arabs not been caught unawares or had their command and control procedures within and between the various countries been better, they might well have turned the Israeli triumph into a Pyrrhic victory.

The vast number of Israeli aircraft that seemed to be over the Arab targets was accounted for by the extremely fast turn-around time (the time required to refuel and rearm aircraft returning from a combat mission) achieved by the Israeli air force. According to one source, the Israelis could achieve the turn-around operation in seven and one-half minutes.[99] The Egyptians, to accomplish the same tasks on their Soviet-built aircraft, required some two hours.[100] The Soviets, of course, if the Egyptians had permitted them to do so, could presumably have improved Egyptian ground-crew performance and equipment. As a consequence of Arab ground-maintenance shortcomings, the Israelis could engage in many more missions over Arab territory than the Egyptian and presumably other Arab air forces.

As the result of the Israeli air attacks approximately one hundred of Egypt's estimated three hundred fifty pilots were killed.[101] Most of those killed were probably in aircraft taxiing or starting their engines upon receipt of warning of the imminent Israeli strike.[102] Because so many qualified pilots remained, however, a Soviet resupply of aircraft during the course of hostilities would have been extremely useful. This resupply was never forthcoming.[103]

Because of the surprise nature of the initial Israeli air attack, only eight Egyptian MIG's were able to take off during its course. These eight aircraft reportedly downed two Israeli jets before they all were shot down.[104] This initial air-to-air encounter very much reflected

Arab air-combat performance during the entire war. The Israelis claim that during the course of the six days of fighting, out of a total of some 338 Egyptian, 61 Syrian, 29 Jordanian, and one Lebanese aircraft destroyed, about 59 were shot down in the air.[105] According to Israeli air force chief Hod, in actual dogfights some 50 Arab aircraft were downed in 64 air engagements with no Israeli losses.[106]

Most of the air-to-air engagements took place when Arab planes that emerged unscathed from Israeli attacks sought to fly ground-support missions. While total sortie/loss figures were not available for these Arab missions, in one sample, in the northern Sinai sector on June 8, the Egyptians flew thirty-two sorties. Twenty-one Egyptian aircraft were shot down, most of them in air-to-air combat.[107]

The eloquent statistics testifying to the poor combat performance of Arab pilots would influence the Russians in planning for future Middle Eastern wars. Interceptor numerical superiority alone would no longer be a sufficient recipe for Arab air superiority.

The Israelis during the course of the war lost some forty aircraft, of which perhaps twelve were shot down by enemy planes.[108] The Israeli air force apparently maintains that those shot down from the air were surprised while engaged in ground attack and therefore did not constitute air-to-air combat losses.[109] Most of the remaining Israeli losses were inflicted by antiaircraft fire. Though the Egyptians and Syrians possessed SAM-2 surface-to-air missile systems, they were almost completely ineffective because most of the Israeli air attacks were at very low levels. The SAM-2's with a low rate of acceleration were fairly easy to evade at minimal altitudes.[110] According to the Israeli air force, only one aircraft *may* have been shot down by a SAM-2.[111]

With regard to penetration of Israeli air space, the Arabs were singularly lax in their efforts. Part of the reason for the Arab failure, as noted earlier, was the lack of effective coordination between the various Arab countries. Several hours passed between the initial Israeli attacks on Egypt and the attacks on airfields in Syria, Jordan, and Iraq. During that period, Israel was quite vulnerable to an Arab attack. In fact, the few Arab aircraft that did attack Israel on the morning of the first day of combat apparently were able to penetrate to civilian and military targets, though they caused little damage. (In addition to air attacks, Jordanian long-range artillery hit the Tel Aviv environs, and Syrian artillery hit border settlements.) On the morning of June 5, several Jordanian fighter-bombers attacked Israeli airfields at Natanya, Kfar Sirkin, and Kfar Sava. Most Jordanian aircraft were destroyed, however, by the Israelis after the attacking planes had returned to their bases.[112] Later in the day, about a dozen Syrian MIG's dropped bombs near the Haifa oil refinery and near Tiberias and attacked the Israeli airfield at Megiddo.[113] On June 6, an Iraqi TU-16 bomber dropped three bombs on Natanya but was shot down after the attack by antiaircraft fire over the Jezreel Valley.[114]

Though the attempts at penetration were relatively few and were considerably eased by the proximity of Arab airfields to Israeli targets (in the pre-1967 borders), confident Israeli official assertions to the effect that "all planes which entered Israeli air space were shot down" may be too facile. Had the Arabs planned a coordinated air strategy and alert procedure, better identified potential targets, and struck at civilian centers, the Israelis would have paid dearly for their first strike on Egypt.[115] One can assume, therefore, that the Russian failure to spur improved and integrated defense planning, at least among the "progressive" Arab states, constituted a limitation on the effectiveness of Arab action. The Soviet possibilities in this regard, of course, were strongly inhibited by the jealousies and suspicions prevailing among the Arabs.

The decisive success of the Israeli air strike in good measure predetermined the results of the land battle. In the desert environment, with little cover and relatively primitive antiaircraft protection, the Arab forces were quite vulnerable to Israeli air strikes. The Israelis point out that two-thirds of the air sorties flown during the six days were directed against ground forces.[116] Although it is not known for certain, one assumes that the vast majority of the five hundred Egyptian tanks destroyed by the Israelis[117] were eliminated by aircraft attack. The Israelis in the Sinai were hence able to advance progressively increasing distances on each day of their attack, not only because of the collapse of Egyptian command and control but also because of the increasing availability of air support. In addition, Israeli forces, except in a few isolated cases, were not subject to air attack.

As regards tank-to-tank combat, the Israelis' modified Centurion tanks were able to fire from outside the range of the guns of Russian-supplied T-54/55 tanks.[118] This qualitative advantage and the substantially better accuracy and firing speed of Israeli crews in all types of tanks were decisive in confronting and destroying the Arab tank forces on the ground. Though Arab antitank gunners were quite good, the fixed positions and limited numbers of their guns limited their effectiveness. The Soviet *Shmel* (*Snapper*) antitank missile was used on few occasions by the Arabs and was largely ineffectual.[119]

On neither side did naval forces play a crucial role in the war. Aggressive Israeli naval commando and patrol-boat attacks caused the Egyptians to withdraw their potentially dangerous Russian-supplied missile boats out of range of Israel. Several of Egypt's dozen submarines were operationally deployed near Israel's coast, presumably to interfere with Israel-bound shipping, but on several occasions the Israeli navy detected these vessels and dropped depth charges on them, causing the submarines to flee. Two of the submarines were believed damaged.[120] Thus, the Israeli navy nullified any possibilities the Arabs might have had for striking Israel from the sea and interfering with Israeli sea-borne commerce.

On all fronts, besides the factor of better Israeli personnel and, to a certain extent, equipment, the possession of absolute air superiority was key. In the crucial ground theater, had the Arabs possessed the capability to attack the trucks that carried fuel and supplies in the wake of rapidly advancing Israeli tanks on the few available roads in Sinai, the Israeli attack would never have been as rapid and deep as it turned out to be. The maneuvering of Israeli ground forces could have been inhibited, and the battle would have become much more the set-piece affair for which the Egyptians had been preparing.

The Israeli capability to shock the Arab defenses with rapid tank advances, coupled with the ever-present air strikes, first destroyed the Egyptian capability of resistance and then transformed the Egyptian withdrawal into a disorganized rout. On the Syrian and Jordanian fronts, air support was also crucial. According to Israeli sources, more sorties were flown against the fortified positions on the narrow Syrian front than against the other fronts combined.[121] Aviation on all fronts had indeed served as Israel's artillery. Its decisiveness would not be forgotten by the Arabs' Russian tutors.

Questions of equipment aside, what was the impact of Russian training and military advice on the course of the war? Russian instruction to both the Egyptians and the Syrians had been relatively simple. Egyptian prisoners told the Israelis that the Russians had told them to organize a strong three-echelon defense along the front and to forget about their flanks.[122] Such advice might have been ideal if the Egyptians had been manning a solid front or if their flanks were physically impassable; however, neither condition obtained, and Israeli armored units were able to envelop the Egyptian forces and to subject them to fire from several directions. If the Egyptians had been able to call for air support or to engage in strategic maneuver, all might have been saved, but due to Israeli aerial mastery and the breakdown of Arab command and control capabilities, this was not possible. The Syrians also had been tied to rather rigid tactical concepts. The lack of flexibility apparently introduced by the Russians into their clients' plans, though perhaps suited for their limited capability to engage in complex actions, doomed the Arabs in the quickly changing situation introduced by the swift Israeli strikes. Once subjected to attack, the Arab defenders were faced by the necessity of either resisting in place or dispersing in a disorganized manner. Under the shock of Israeli attack, the Arabs in their scattered points of concentration would more often than not retreat in disorder when further resistance seemed hopeless.

With regard to Russian advisers, the Israelis, in spite of some preliminary claims to the contrary, did not capture or recover the bodies of any Soviet personnel.[123] Apparently, no Russian advisers were present in Sinai, and those serving with Syrian forces reportedly were withdrawn to Damascus on the first day of the war.[124]

To review, then, the Russians had designed the Arab armed forces in such a way as to enable their ground elements to operate with minimal interference from Israeli air attacks, the key factor that had broken Egyptian ground resistance in 1956. By providing the Egyptians with the means to threaten Israel proper and by giving the Arabs a significant interceptor advantage, the Soviet's hoped to tie the Israeli air force down in air defense and air-to-air combat so that it would not be able to intervene on the ground. On the other hand, the Russians must have considered that once the decision had been made to launch a war and inflict a military defeat on the Arabs, the Israeli air force would seek to reduce or eliminate the Arab advantages. The Russians and Arabs, considering the 1956 Egyptian experience, should have been aware of the dangers of a preemptive Israeli air strike.

Nonetheless, whether because of Arab command shortcomings or because of poor or insufficient Soviet advice, the Arab air forces were allowed to remain extremely vulnerable to Israeli attack. Even if vulnerability had not been reduced by better alert and patrol procedures, dispersion and protection of aircraft on airfields, and other such measures, the introduction of improved command and control procedures within Egypt (to allow nonalerted aircraft to be quickly launched) and between Arab countries might have contributed to partially frustrating the Israeli attack and inflicting some damage on Israeli targets. In any case, given the substantial quantitative aircraft superiority provided to the Arabs by the Soviets, the vulnerability of these planes made them in times of crisis prime, and indeed almost required, targets for an Israeli surprise attack. By providing numerical superiority and not reducing vulnerability, the Soviets thus introduced a disastrous instability into the Arab-Israeli strategic equation. (The Soviets, of course, held the Arabs responsible for the vulnerability of their aircraft in the Six-Day War.)

The elimination of Arab air advantages predetermined the course of the war in the desert environment. Not only did Israeli tank forces outperform their Arab counterparts, but the added rapid, mobile firepower provided by Israeli aircraft made Arab ground resistance an impossibility. These Arab disadvantages were heightened by the application of

Russian-introduced tactical models that were ill-suited for the fluid situation created by Israeli deep-penetration tactics. These Israeli tactics were, in large measure, possible only because of Israeli air superiority. Moreover, Arab capability to cope with the fast-changing situation was significantly reduced because of the inability of the Arab commands to maintain communications and organization among subordinate echelons. The Soviets presumably could have remedied these deficiencies before the war by providing more extensive command training as well as better and more secure communications systems.

In sum, the Russian design for limited Arab military superiority had been ruptured by the Israeli surprise attack. One can only assume that the Soviet failure to introduce (or convince the Arabs to introduce) means or procedures to cope with, or minimize the damage of, such a surprise attack was the result of oversight or resistance within the Arab military establishments. (Soviet published comments seem to imply that the latter was the case.) For whatever reason, however, the failure to reduce the vulnerability of the Arab air force made an Israeli decision to strike first a most attractive alternative.

We shall now turn to the question of the influence of Russian diplomacy on the extent and limitations of military activity in the course of the Six-Day War.

V On the morning of 5 June 1967, the Israeli air force launched its attack on Egyptian and, later, other Arab air bases. The Soviet public response to the Israeli attack, in contrast to the response in 1956, was immediate. As in 1956, however, the initial Russian reaction was not exceedingly menacing. Moscow's first public declaration, a statement of the Soviet government issued on June 5, labeled the Israeli offensive an "aggression" that could "undermine . . . the foundations for the development and very existence of the state of Israel. . . ." The Soviet statement pointed out that the Soviet Union had called upon Israel to avoid war and had warned of the consequences of "aggression." The Soviets expressed "resolute support" for the Arabs and demanded an immediate and unconditional Israeli ceasefire and a withdrawal of Israeli troops beyond the 1949 truce line. Hope was expressed that the governments of other states, "including the great powers," would seek to end the war. In conclusion, the statement declared: "The Soviet Government reserves the right to take all steps which may be required by the situation."[125]

Aside from the implied threat to the existence of the state of Israel, this initial Soviet public reaction made no concrete suggestion of any specific Soviet actions against Israel, nor were any U.N. collective sanc-

tions (other than condemnation and unspecified "appropriate" steps)
proposed. Moreover, the Soviet statement did not specify the nature of
Russian support that would be given the Arab states. The reserved
nature of Soviet threats and promises suggested that Moscow had been
caught unawares by the Israeli attack, probably due to concentration on
prewar Egyptian "adventurism." Moreover, because of the lack of
specificity of Soviet commitments to action, one can conclude that no
previously decided Soviet position existed that would immediately legit-
imize direct actions in favor of Egypt and Syria and against Israel.
Moscow had not obligated itself to full support of the Arabs, and its
hesitancy to do so would mark its entire approach to the war.

The initial June 5 communication from Chairman Kosygin to Israeli
Prime Minister Eshkol, like the Soviet public statement, was also quite
vague. Though the Israeli attack was labeled a "treacherous aggression"
and an "adventurous act," Soviet threats were limited to the stock
formulation that if the Israelis did not cease fire and withdraw their
troops, the Israeli government would "bear the responsibility for the
outbreak of war and for all its possible results."[126]

In the first use of the Moscow-Washington hot line in the four years
of its existence, Chairman Kosygin on the morning of June 5 communicated to President Johnson that the Soviet Union was concerned with
the outbreak of fighting in the Middle East. Kosygin expressed hope
that the United States would exert influence on Israel in favor of a
ceasefire. Johnson agreed with Kosygin that it was desirable for hostilities to end and expressed pleasure that the Russians shared the American point of view.[127] Kosygin's message suggested that the Soviets
were in favor of a prompt ceasefire.

On June 5, the Egyptian ambassador to the Soviet Union, Mohamed
Ghaleb, called on Kosygin. In reply to Ghaleb's request for assistance,
Kosygin, according to one source, stated that the Soviet Union supported the Arabs and that arms would be supplied to replace Arab
losses. Though the Soviet Union would seek to stop the fighting and
press Israel to abandon the territory it had seized, Moscow probably
would not militarily intervene in the war.[128]

Though the contents of Ghaleb's conversation with Kosygin cannot
be verified, the substance of the reported remarks of the Soviet leader
seems accurate enough. Nasser, after the end of the war, was clearly
disappointed by the extent of support received from the Soviet Union.
He told his associate Abdel Latif Boghdady that after the Israeli attack,
the Russians had been "frozen into immobility by their fear of a confrontation with America." Nasser allegedly told Boghdady that the Soviets had not sent replacement aircraft to Egypt because of their
hesitation to become involved with the U.S. Sixth Fleet (presumably for

fear of clashing with U.S. carrier aircraft). At one point, after several desperate appeals from Nasser, the Soviets had agreed to send aircraft to Egypt via Yugoslavia, if Yugoslav leader Tito agreed. Though Tito concurred, the Soviets then reversed their position and stated that aircraft could not be supplied for several weeks. Additionally, according to Boghdady, Nasser stated that the Soviets had sent a ship to Egypt just before the outbreak of war with a cargo of weapons. The captain of the Soviet ship supposedly turned back within sight of Alexandria because of Soviet fears of Israeli bombing.[129] Though Boghdady or Nasser might well have been exaggerating, the Soviets did not in fact resupply the Arab belligerents in any major way during the course of hostilities.

Soviet reluctance to resupply the Arabs during the war was a factor of utmost importance, especially because of the destruction of the Arab air forces on the ground. Because of the ground destruction, many qualified Arab pilots would have been available for combat if Soviet replacement aircraft had been provided. The aircraft, of course, would have had to be ferried to the Middle East by Soviet pilots, thus opening the possibility for direct confrontation with U.S. forces in the Mediterranean. The Russian failure to deliver aircraft or other weapons demonstrated the continued Soviet concern over a possible clash with the Americans. It may also have indicated practical difficulties in arranging a massive resupply on short notice. In this regard, it should be pointed out that Russian replenishment of Arab losses did not begin on a large scale until June 23, some two weeks after the war had ended.

At the United Nations, the United States attempted on the first day of the war to achieve a ceasefire as well as a lifting of the blockade of the Straits of Tiran and a withdrawal of both Egyptian and Israeli forces from Sinai. The Egyptian position, which was supported by the Soviet Union, called for only a ceasefire and a withdrawal of Israeli forces. Because of the impasse between the two positions, no progress toward halting combat was achieved in the United Nations on the first day of the fighting.[130] It thus appeared that though the Soviet Union was not prepared immediately to offer the Arabs military support, Moscow was ready to back fully the Arabs' political position, notwithstanding the risks of prolonging the war.

On June 6, Kosygin and Johnson again communicated on the hot line. One of the subjects raised was the false Arab accusation that American aircraft had participated in the Israeli air attacks on the Arabs. (Egypt, Algeria, Syria, Iraq, the Sudan, and Yemen broke diplomatic relations with the United States on the basis of this accusation.) Though the matter apparently was not mentioned on the hot line by Moscow, Johnson raised it and reminded Kosygin that Soviet intelligence knew where American ships and planes were located. Johnson suggested that Moscow pass this information on to Cairo.[131] According to one account, on June 6, Kosygin, in justifying Soviet noninvolvement in the war, informed the envoys of Egypt, Syria, and Jordan that the Arab accusations were false.[132]

On the basis of reports detailing the drastic deterioration of Arab military fortunes, late on June 6 the Soviet government instructed the Soviet delegation at the United Nations to vote for a resolution calling simply for a ceasefire, not a withdrawal of Israeli troops. Though there were some initial indications that the Arabs were ready to accept the ceasefire, on the day following the affirmative vote only Jordan clearly acknowledged acceptance of the halt in hostilities.[133]

In spite of the Egyptian and Syrian reluctance to accept the ceasefire, the Soviets were still clearly disappointed by the Israeli failure to halt military operations. The Soviets had apparently hoped that the Israelis would cease their attack in response to the U.N. resolution, thereby obviating the need for a humiliating Arab acceptance of the ceasefire. Possibly in response to Arab pressure, the Soviet government on June 7 delivered a written statement to the Israeli embassy in Moscow. The statement declared that Israel was not adhering to the U.N. ceasefire resolution. If Israel did not cease fire, the statement continued, "the Soviet Union will revise its attitude concerning Israel and will make a decision regarding the further maintenance of diplomatic relations with Israel . . . ."[134]

Though Moscow's suggestion of a break in diplomatic relations with Israel was the most specific action yet threatened against Tel Aviv, it was hardly a move which might give significant pause to Israeli leaders. Rather than a legitimate threat against Israel (which was hardly called for in any case since the Israelis had indicated that they would accept the U.N. ceasefire when the Arab belligerents did), the Soviet declaration was probably an effort to show solidarity with the Arab states that had just broken diplomatic relations with the United States. If the Soviet Union would not act against the powerful United States, Arab thinking probably went, the Soviets could, at the very minimum, take some kind of action against tiny Israel.

Faced by an Arab military disaster of geometrically increasing magnitude, the Soviets on June 7, on the basis of an urgent Egyptian request,[135] asked for immediate convocation of the U.N. Security Council. The Security Council unanimously adopted a Soviet draft resolution again calling for a ceasefire to take effect at 8 P.M. GMT, June 7. The Soviets did not insist on former demands of U.N. condemnation of Israel and withdrawal of Israeli forces. The only Soviet demand was that the Security Council immediately vote on the ceasefire resolution.[136] Halting of the progress of Israeli armed forces had clearly become a matter that, in Soviet eyes, would brook no further delay. Egyptian acceptance of the ceasefire quickly followed on June 8, and by the close of that day, hostilities for the most part had ceased between Israel and Jordan and Israel and Egypt.

Moscow's initial reluctance to agree to a ceasefire without condemnation of Israel and Israeli troop withdrawal, a position which was dropped after two days, was indicative of the degree to which Soviet desire to limit the prolongation of the conflict was keyed to the degree of Arab success. While apparently unwilling to risk any type of direct involvement in the conflict for fear of escalation, the Soviets seemingly had no qualms about permitting the local war between the Arabs and Israelis to continue as long as the "progressive" Arab regimes were not endangered.

On June 8, in addition to the ceasefire, another significant event took place. As the result of a grievous error, the American electronic intelligence-gathering ship *Liberty* was torpedoed by Israeli gunboats and attacked by Israeli aircraft in international waters off the Sinai coast. There were ten Americans killed and one hundred wounded as a result of the attack. (A Soviet account claims that the *Liberty*, in addition to monitoring Arab communications, was supposedly jamming Egyptian radar and providing Tel Aviv with Egyptian codes, which, in turn, were used by the Israelis to transmit counterfeit orders of retreat to Egyptian units.)[137] President Johnson ordered U.S. carrier aircraft to proceed to the location of the *Liberty* to investigate the incident. In order to avoid misunderstandings, the president informed Kosygin on the hot line of the American action, pointed out that the only purpose of the flights was to investigate the *Liberty* incident, and requested that appropriate parties in the area be informed. Kosygin acknowledged Johnson's message and stated that the information had been immediately passed on to the Egyptians.[138] According to the American ambassador in Moscow, the *Liberty* exchange made a favorable impression on the Russians, presumably because the Americans had implicitly recognized the legitimacy of the Soviet role in the Middle East by informing the Russians of a unilateral American military action and by allowing them to act as an intermediary with the Egyptians. The Egyptians, however, saw the Kosygin message regarding the *Liberty* as part of an American double-cross effort. Nasser felt that because the message was transmitted through Kosygin, "it was directed at the Russians in an effort to neutralize the Soviet Union, blinding them against an operation being conducted against Egypt."[139]

By June 9, hostilities had ceased on all Arab-Israeli fronts but the Syrian combat zone. On June 9, Syria announced acceptance of the U.N. ceasefire resolution, but Israel and Syria charged each other with massive truce violations. Heavy fighting continued, and Israeli forces began to make serious inroads into Syrian positions on the Golan Heights. On June 9, the U.N. Security Council adopted a third ceasefire resolution, this time calling for an end to hostilities between Israel and Syria. Though both Israel and Syria accepted the resolution, fighting continued as each side accused the other of ceasefire violations.[140]

Given the dramatic Israeli victories in the previous few days of military activity, combined with Syrian accusations of continued Israeli ceasefire violations, the Soviets apparently drew the conclusion that Israel, intoxicated by its triumphs, would not stop until the "progressive" Syrian government was liquidated. As a consequence of the probable assessment of Israeli aims as unlimited, the Russians adopted a basic change in their reasonably moderate posture of the previous days and began to escalate their vituperation and threats against Israel and its Western supporters. In the Security Council on June 9, Soviet representative Fedorenko, adopting an extremely vicious rhetoric, asserted that the Israelis "take their arguments from the garbage heap of history and from the arsenal of the most famous criminals in history. They follow the bloody footsteps of Hitler's executioners who always accused the victims of their own aggression."[141]

More significantly, on June 9, Communist leaders of the Soviet Union, Hungary, East Germany, Poland, Czechoslovakia, and Yugoslavia met in Moscow to discuss joint action regarding the Middle East. In a statement issued at the conclusion of the meeting, for the first time the United States was explicitly accused of being part of a "collusion of imperialist forces" that caused Israeli "aggression." Drawing the "appropriate conclusions" from the alleged Israeli ceasefire violations, the statement asserted that Israel would use occupation of Arab territory "for restoration of the foreign colonial regime." In a menacing gesture aimed at the Western powers, the declaration added that if the U.N. Security Council did not take appropriate measures, "a grave responsibility will rest with those states which failed to fulfill their duty as members of the Security Council." Finally, in the most specific threat of action yet leveled against Israel, the joint declaration stated: "If . . . Israel does not stop its aggression and withdraw its troops behind the truce line, the socialist states which signed this declaration will do everything necessary to assist the peoples of the Arab countries to deliver a resolute rebuff to the aggressor. . . ."[142]

At the United Nations, in a change from former postures, some Eastern European diplomats began hinting that "volunteers" might be dispatched to the Arab countries.[143] The limited nature of this first Soviet–East European commitment to direct action was highlighted, however, by the joint declaration which declared that assistance would be offered to the Arabs to defend "their national independence and territorial integrity," thus implicitly dissociating the Soviets from maximalist demands to eliminate the state of Israel.

On June 9 and 10, as fighting continued on the Syrian front, Syria's U.N. representative, playing very much on Russian sensitivities, declared that the Israelis were seeking to overthrow the Syrian government and had embarked on a bombardment of Damascus, Syria's capital.[144] The accusation of the Damascus bombardment and a concurrent Egyptian claim that Cairo was being bombarded were never substantiated.[145]

Nonetheless, Moscow's anxiety over the failure to halt the Israelis became increasingly clear. On June 10, Israel's ambassador to the Soviet Union was summoned to the foreign ministry, where he was handed a note which declared that, because of Israel's "continued aggression," the Soviet Union had decided to break diplomatic relations with the Jewish state. The note added: "Unless Israel immediately halts its military actions, the Soviet Union, jointly with other peace-loving states, will adopt sanctions against Israel, with all the consequences flowing from this."[146] Unlike the six-power declaration of the previous day, the Soviet note made no demand for Israeli withdrawal from occupied territory. The dropping of this demand, like the earlier change in the Soviet stance on the various ceasefire resolutions, probably reflected the degree of urgency which the Soviets attached to a halt of Israeli advances. The rupture of diplomatic relations, while not a sanction of great magnitude, was probably meant to convey to the Israelis that more serious moves could be expected if fighting did not immediately cease. The Soviet message was fortified by a most decisive threat transmitted to Washington on the hot line.

On the morning of June 10, while fighting continued in Syria, the Soviet leadership, emulating Khrushchev's 1956 example, made a major turn in its position and threatened unilateral action in the Middle East. The Soviet message to the American president stated that "a very crucial moment" had arrived and that the possibility existed for an "independent decision" by Moscow. The Russian communication envisaged the possibility of a "grave catastrophe" and said that unless the Israelis halted military operations within a few hours, the Soviet Union would take "necessary action, including military."[147]

The Soviet threat of direct action, like its 1956 predecessor, came at the end of the crisis. Because the situation seemed to be moving toward a ceasefire, the Soviet threat was a surprise to U.S. officials. In President Johnson's words, in the period just before arrival of the Soviet message, "we thought we could see the end of the road."[148] Due to the apparently successful progress being made toward a halt in fighting (both

Syria and Israel agreed that the ceasefire would take place at 4:30 P.M. GMT, June 10), the Soviet threat, like its 1956 precedent, may have been largely a gratuitous gesture to regain Arab political support. In addition, however, it is probable that the Soviets legitimately desired that the United States inject itself into the crisis to restrain Israel from upsetting the Syrian regime. President Johnson did, in fact, reply to Kosygin's message stressing the progress that was being made toward a ceasefire.[149] Moreover, the State Department reportedly instructed the American ambassador to Israel to intervene urgently with the Israeli government to insist on a termination of hostilities.[150] As a demonstration of concern, the Soviet threat could thus be judged successful.

The American actions taken vis-à-vis Israel were not based on a sense of weakness relative to the Soviets. General Earl Wheeler, chairman of the Joint Chiefs of Staff, purportedly stated: "We have nothing to fear from Soviet action. The Soviets have no large mobile units to put into action at once in the Middle Eastern war. They have alerted their paratrooper divisions, but they know how dangerous it would be to put them into action."[151] Concerning the Soviet naval forces, during the course of the Six-Day War, in an unprecedented move, the Soviet Union had sent a steady stream of Soviet warships into the Mediterranean from the Black Sea. The approximately seventy Soviet naval vessels that were eventually dispatched to the Mediterranean, however, had little amphibious-landing or nonnuclear-war-fighting capabilities.[152]

Because of these Soviet military deficiencies, President Johnson felt free, upon receipt of Kosygin's threat, to alter the course of the Sixth Fleet toward the Syrian mainland and to reduce the previous restriction on proximity of the fleet to the coast from one hundred miles to fifty miles. In Johnson's words, this signal was meant to indicate that "the United States was prepared to resist Soviet intrusion in the Middle East."[153] In spite of Johnson's bravado, the American pressure placed on Israel probably convinced the Russians that the presence of their naval force and their intervention threat were highly useful diplomatic instruments.

While the tone of Soviet comments on the hot line became more moderate as the ceasefire took hold in the Middle East (the fourth and final U.N. Security Council ceasefire resolution was adopted on June 12), it was clear that the Russians, as in 1956, claimed credit, by their threats, for containing the Israelis. Chairman Kosygin, speaking at the special session of the U.N. General Assembly convened one week after the termination of hostilities, asserted that Israeli forces had intended to break through Syrian lines to Damascus. He added: ". . . a number of states had to sever diplomatic relations with Israel and give a firm warning about the use of sanctions before the Israeli troops stopped military actions."[154]

While Kosygin's General Assembly speech might have been particularly calculated as a public relations gesture to advertise the resolute nature of Soviet support to the Arab cause, the results of a highly unusual Central Committee plenum held in June 1967 to discuss the Middle Eastern crisis demonstrated that the line of decisive, though measured, Soviet threats had been deemed successful by the Soviet political elite. The concluding communiqué of the Central Committee plenum asserted that "the speedy, resolute actions by the Soviet Union and other socialist states have played an important role in stopping the military operations in the Middle East."[155] When judged against the background that prompted the convening of the Central Committee plenum, this statement is highly significant.

According to some reports, the plenum was called to endorse the Soviet leadership's policy during the Six-Day War. This policy had been criticized by the Chinese and, ostensibly, by certain members of the Soviet political elite. The removal shortly after the plenum of Nikolai Yegorychev, first secretary of the Moscow City Committee of the Communist Party, who had made a trip to Cairo in early 1967, raised speculation that Politburo's conduct had been criticized by Yegorychev and others as a faint-hearted betrayal of the Arab clients.[155] The plenum's resolution implicitly gave credence to this view by raising, for the first time in the crisis, the specter of hard-line opposition emanating from the Chinese. The resolution stated that it was necessary to "resist the slander campaign and splitting activities of Mao Tse-tung's group aimed at disuniting the anti-imperialist forces and undermining the trust between the peoples of the Arab states and the peoples of the socialist countries."[157] The criticism of Mao also, of course, could be equally applied to Soviet political figures who may have questioned the strength of Soviet reactions on behalf of the Arabs.

Given the possibility that criticism of the Soviet leadership's policy had come from the hard-line direction as well as from the Soviets' Arab clients, it is easy to understand why the Soviets, as in 1956, again threatened direct intervention in the Middle East crisis. Continuing the leadership's possible "defensive" responses to such complaints, a massive and extremely expensive Soviet airlift (and later sealift) of weapons to the Arab belligerents began on June 23.[158]

How can we interpret Russian diplomatic moves before and during the Six-Day War? Moscow, in the weeks before the war, initially had sought to preserve the perceived favorable "anti-imperialist" situation in the Middle East by weakening Israel. Tel Aviv's successful military actions, in Moscow's view, threatened to discredit the value of the links among the "progressive" states of the area as well as the ties between the "progressive" states and the Soviet Union. In order to communicate to Israel that it could no longer undertake military actions against the "progressive" states with impunity, Moscow stirred the Egyptians into making a militant gesture against Israel. Once stirred, however, the Egyptians got out of hand and began pursuing the threat of war in a far too serious manner. The Russians, feeling that an Egyptian-initiated war would not be in their interest, spent much of the two to three weeks before the outbreak of hostilities seeking to calm the situation. Attempts were made to restrain the Egyptians and to ensure the Israelis that the Soviet Union was acting to preserve peace.

Against this background, war broke out in the Middle East. Though Israel had attacked first, the Russians apparently felt that the Egyptians, by their immoderate prewar posture, had done much to bring about the war. The Soviets, because of their initial resentment of Egyptian irresponsibility, coupled with a desire not to risk a clash with the United States, declined to offer immediate military assistance to the Arabs and limited themselves to provision of political support.

By deciding to provide backing, however, the Russians had to forgo seeking an immediate end to hostilities (which Kosygin's initial message to President Johnson seemed to indicate was a Soviet desire). The Soviets, in deference to the Arabs, had to allow the war to continue until the Arab states felt compelled to cease hostilities. Continuation of the war, of course, increased the possibility of an American clash with the Soviet Union, a turn of events which Moscow wished to avoid.

Once the Arab states had indicated that they were ready to terminate hostilities, the Russians pressed immediate ceasefire resolutions through the United Nations. Though the Israelis had driven for and reached salient geographical objectives on the Jordanian and Egyptian fronts (the Jordan River and the Suez Canal, respectively), Israeli goals on the Syrian front were not so clear. When Syria announced acceptance of the U.N. ceasefire (9 June), and the Israelis continued to advance, the Russians undoubtedly recalled the concern that had started the whole crisis—the purported Israeli threat to overthrow the "progressive" Syrian regime. At this point Soviet policy turned from sideline political support of the Arabs to direct involvement on their behalf. While the Soviet threat of military intervention probably did not reflect a genuine intention to undertake full-scale military efforts in the Middle East, it did serve to highlight effectively Soviet concern over the perceived threat to Syria. The apparent success of the Soviet intervention threat in hastening a positive political solution of a Middle East conflict for the second time since 1956 would likely establish this technique as a constituent element in future Soviet Middle East crisis repertoires.

Another aspect of the Six-Day War politics that would have an impact on the future would be the leadership's sensitivity to charges of having let down the Arabs. The postwar attack on "Maoist splitters," the quick replenishment of Arab military supplies, and accusations that "anti-Soviets" had been responsible for Arab defeats all may have reflected overt or subconscious Soviet guilt feelings that, perhaps, Moscow had not been sufficiently forthcoming in a time of its clients' greatest need.[159] There may have been a sense that Moscow's caution had darkened the Soviet reputation with other antiimperialist forces. This sense of contrition may have had impact on Soviet decisionmaking in later years.

VI The Soviet role in the events during and preceding the Six-Day War is illustrative of the differing burdens placed on an established, as opposed to an aspiring, power. In the two years before the 1956 Suez War, the Soviet Union, seeking to weaken the influence of the West in the Middle East, was cast in the role of a spoiler. Any breakdown in the Western-dominated status quo could only redound to its benefit. In the years after Suez, however, other states besides Nasser's Egypt began reorienting their policies in an anti-Western direction. The Soviet Union began supplying military equipment to these countries and assumed at least a moral commitment to help protect the security of these new clients. Rather than simply deriving benefit from any breakdown of the status quo, as formerly, the Soviet Union was placed in the position of being a partial guarantor of the existing order.

The new Soviet position was, at once, helped and hindered by political changes that were taking place in the Arab states. On the encouraging side, from the Soviet perspective, not only were the foreign policies of several states of the area becoming decidedly anti-Western, but domestic socioeconomic changes were also taking place. In several of the "progressive" Arab states, the sphere of nationalized industry and commerce was becoming more broad. Formerly powerful foreign interests and "landlord and bourgeois" elements were being increasingly dispossessed and politically weakened. These developments offered promise, in Soviet eyes, of permanent conversion of the "progressive" states into reliable associates of Moscow. In the Soviet judgment, "progressive" domestic structural changes, unlike simple foreign-policy realignment, would be much less subject to possible future reversal.

The basic transformations that were taking place in the Middle East offered not only opportunities but also threats to Soviet interests. Moscow anticipated that its Middle Eastern clients would face serious challenges from forces in the West whose political and economic positions were being jeopardized. The "imperialist" powers would turn to Middle Eastern subordinates, such as Israel and the traditional Arab monarchies, as well as to disestablished members of the old power elite inside the "progressive" Arab states to attack and subvert the anti-

Western regimes. These threats from the Right would be augmented by dangerous new alternatives available on the Left as a consequence of China's emergence as a challenger to the Soviet Union.

The Soviet Union would thus have to find a way to both protect and maintain the loyalty of the "progressive" Arab states. Conceivably, some type of formal or declaratory security guarantee could have been offered to these states, but Moscow had shown itself reluctant to intervene directly on behalf of the Arabs. In both the 1956 Suez War and the 1958 Iraqi crisis, the Soviet Union, because of fears of clashing with the Western powers, had desisted from taking any direct action on behalf of the "progressive" Arabs. The Soviets, thus, continued to rely on the tried and tested recipe of the past—the delivery of modern weapons—which would provide a measure of protection to the "progressive" states and serve as a graphic illustration of Moscow's goodwill and yet, simultaneously, would not cause the Soviet Union to clash directly with the Western powers.

By carefully structuring the contents of the weapons deliveries, the Soviet Union provided the Arabs with suitable armed forces for self-protection and limited offensive action but did not provide them with the capability to undertake a decisive offensive effort with any high degree of confidence. Arab armed forces were designed to serve a deterrent rather than a war-fighting function. The Soviet leadership had no wish to have the "progressive" Arabs involve the Soviet Union in a catalytic war.

Moscow thus faced the following dilemma in the early 1960s: the viability of the increasingly appealing "progressive" Arab states was being threatened, but the Soviet Union wished to avoid direct participation in their defense. The solution to this dilemma, in Moscow's view, would be not only to provide weapons to the individual "progressive" Arab states but also to spur the unity of these countries. Increased unity would allow them to confront external enemies more strongly and, by providing a shared platform and cause, would contain possible pro-Western or pro-Chinese deviance in individual countries. Moreover, a unified bloc of "progressive" Arab states would serve as a magnet for radical elements seeking transformation of the conservative Arab states.

Common hatred for Israel was the most likely basis of "progressive" Arab unity and, since Moscow had no special affection for the Jewish state, which it regarded as a tool of the West, the Soviets quite readily endorsed collective arrangements directed against Tel Aviv. The 1966 defense agreement between Egypt and Syria, largely aimed against Israel, reflected a desirable move, from Moscow's point of view, toward necessary joint Arab efforts.

After the Egyptian-Syrian pact, tension generated by terrorist incidents grew on the Arab-Israeli borders, and Israel began to lash out in increasingly severe reprisal raids. From Moscow's perspective, Israel's actions and the militant declarations of Israeli political and military leaders seemed to portend a decisive "imperialist" attempt to disrupt evolving Arab unity and to unseat the "progressive" Syrian government. With this in mind, Moscow encouraged the Egyptians to make a decisive stand on behalf of Syria and against Israel.

Unfortunately for Moscow, however, once the Egyptians were stirred, they could not be contained. What was to have been a show of strength, a display of deterrence, was transformed into an incipient war. While Moscow tried to calm the situation, the combination of high tensions coupled with the tremendous advantage that would accrue to Israel by striking first at the Arabs' large but vulnerable air arsenal undercut Soviet peace efforts.

With the outbreak of war, the Soviets were again confronted with the contradictory urges to end the war promptly in order to avoid a clash with the West and to support the "progressive" Arabs' political objectives. Though the Soviets opted for the latter, the contradiction between the two desires quickly faded as the Arabs rapidly suffered disastrous military defeat. By virtue of the Israeli surprise attack, the various military superiorities which the Soviets had given the Arabs were destroyed in one stroke. The Soviet Union endeavored to spare the "progressive" Arab states further humiliation by driving an immediate ceasefire resolution through the United Nations. However, to the acute discomfiture of the Soviets, the Israelis would not halt their actions in Syria.

The Russians were faced by what they apparently conceived as a fundamental challenge to their entire political position in the Middle East. As a consequence, the Soviets reversed their previous policy of avoiding direct involvement and threatened intervention. The Soviet gesture was effective in prompting American pressure on Israel. Tel Aviv, either because of American pressure or for its own reasons, stopped moving forward in Syria.

American decisionmakers in 1967 did not consider that the Soviet Union had an effective capability to intervene in a combat role in the Middle East. Nonetheless, presumably as a hedge and warning against an irrational Soviet decision in favor of military intervention, President Johnson moved the American fleet toward the Syrian coast. The Russians, of course, whatever their original intentions, did not directly intervene in the Middle East.

The key element, then, that determined the evolution of events before and during the Six-Day War was the Soviet desire to support the "progressive" Arab states and yet to avoid clashing with the West. Soviet reluctance in this period to confront the West, particularly the United States, was not due to any sense that good political relations would be spoiled. Though the Soviet Union would make some conciliatory gestures toward the United States later in 1967, such as the Johnson-Kosygin Glassboro Summit, because of Vietnam, relations between the Soviet Union and the United States were hardly cordial. Moscow's disregard for the consequences of damaging East-West relations would be demonstrated by the invasion of Czechoslovakia one year later.

Military factors, on the other hand, probably played an important role in Moscow's decision to avoid confrontation with the West. Though the Soviets clearly had the capacity to threaten the United States with substantial strategic nuclear damage (they had not yet, however, achieved the symbolically important level of strategic parity), and though they maintained a formidable tactical threat in the form of massive Soviet forces poised on the West German frontier, the Soviet Union did not have the capability to project quickly and safely a force viable for long-term local combat into the Middle East.

In addition, and perhaps most importantly, the Soviets apparently did not feel confident that they could contain any contest in which they were involved to the local level. In view of the programmatic American hostility to Communist expansion, as reflected in the Dominican Republic intervention and the Vietnam War, any Soviet action would likely spur a serious American response. From the Soviet perspective, the risks involved in confronting the Americans were not commensurate with the gains that could be achieved for the Arab states. It was better to "roll with the punches" during the war, massively rearm the Arabs, and undertake diplomatic and military moves in future years that would place the Soviet Union in a better position to protect its clients' interests. Above all, the Soviets would have to develop means to assist its clients quickly and visibly with military aid while at the same time neutralizing American actions.

CHAPTER FOUR † PRELUDE TO YOM KIPPUR: THE "WAR OF ATTRITION" AND ITS AFTERMATH

The Soviet military presence in the Arab world, particularly in Egypt, increased dramatically after the 1967 Six-Day War. Confronted by Israeli occupation of the Sinai Peninsula, the Golan Heights, and Jordan's West Bank, the "progressive" Arab nations turned to Moscow for diplomatic and military succor. For Egypt, the need for Soviet help became extremely acute as the result of reverses suffered in the 1969–70 "war of attrition," a campaign of military pressure launched against Israeli forces on the east bank of the Suez Canal.

By the end of 1970, the Soviet Union, in response to Cairo's pleas for assistance, had occupied military bases and was operating high-performance fighter aircraft and surface-to-air missiles in Egypt. However, in July 1972 this operation, staffed by well over ten thousand Soviet personnel, was suddenly liquidated at the request of the Egyptian government.

Many observers in the West gloated over the Soviet expulsion. To the surprise of these analysts, in little over a year after the dramatic Egyptian-Soviet break, Moscow was again closely involved in support of an Arab military venture—the 1973 Yom Kippur War. The growth, decline, and resurgence of Soviet military participation in the Middle East from 1967 to 1973 was at once paradoxical and revealing. How did it come about?

From the end of the Six-Day War, the Soviet Union had displayed uniform hostility toward Israeli policy. Israel's continued occupation of conquered Arab land was viewed by Moscow as both an irritating reminder of the inability of the Soviet Union to defend its Arab clients and a convenient means to spur the unity of the "progressive" Arab states. Both considerations militated in favor of strong Soviet support for efforts to expel Israel from the occupied territories.

At the United Nations, after the failure of initial attempts to condemn Israel, the focus of Soviet diplomacy in 1967 shifted toward "elimination of the consequences of Israeli aggression." While the Soviet Union pronounced itself in favor of the continued existence of Israel as a state, the principal thrust of Russian efforts in the United

Nations and other forums was directed toward securing a total and complete withdrawal of Israeli forces from the conquered territories.[1] The Soviet U.N. delegation voted in favor of Security Council Resolution 242, a compromise proposal calling for both the withdrawal of Israeli forces from unspecified occupied territories and the acknowledgment of Israel's right to exist within secure boundaries. However, Soviet Deputy Foreign Minister Kuznetsov, in justifying the Russian vote in favor of Resolution 242, stated that from the Soviet perspective, implementation of the Security Council decision required first of all withdrawal of Israeli troops from the occupied zones.[2] The other aspects of Resolution 242 could be implemented only after a complete Israeli pullback.

Soviet political support for Arab territorial claims was accompanied by a replenishment of military equipment destroyed during the Six-Day War. On June 21 (ten days after the conclusion of the 1967 war), Soviet President Nikolai Podgorny arrived in Cairo. He was preceded on June 20 by Soviet Army Chief of Staff Marshal Matvey Zakharov and a large military delegation.[3] As a result of the Podgorny-Zakharov visit, substantial quantities of Soviet military equipment were rushed to Egypt. Within one week of the visit, in a most dramatic move, a reported 130 combat aircraft had already been delivered. By mid-1968, Egypt had almost reached its prewar combat-aircraft strength.[4] Meanwhile, other Soviet replacement weapons were rapidly dispatched to Egypt by air- and sealift. President Podgorny visited Damascus on July 1,[5] and Syria, like Egypt, was subsequently resupplied with weapons and equipment. Iraq's small aircraft losses were also replaced.

During Podgorny's visit to Cairo, in a departure from previous policy, Egyptian leader Gamal Abdel Nasser requested that the Russians dispatch military advisors and instructors to Egypt. Nasser apparently recognized that Egypt's defeat in the Six-Day War had been due as much to command malfeasance as to military-equipment deficiencies. The Egyptian leader, as a consequence, asked that Russian advisors be sent to join his forces down to the battalion level. (Previously, only relatively small numbers of Soviet weapons instructors and teachers in military academies had been present in Egypt.) The Soviets were reportedly reluctant to accede to Nasser's request because of the perceived danger of confrontation with the United States. However, after some further consideration, the Soviet leadership agreed, and several thousand military advisers and instructors were dispatched to Egypt.[6]

One account of the Podgorny Cairo visit asserts that Nasser, after comparing Egypt's position to that of the Soviet Union in the darkest days of World War II, asked that the Soviet Union enter into a mutual-defense agreement with Egypt. The Russians, under the terms of Nasser's proposed agreement, would provide Egypt with air support, which would allow Egyptian ground troops to counterattack and liberate the occupied Arab territories.* Podgorny, according to the report, declined Nasser's proposal and indicated that a mutual-defense pact could not yet be signed. He added that the Soviet Union would assist Egypt in rebuilding its armed forces, but only on the condition that incompetent and undesirable officers be removed from the Egyptian military establishment. Podgorny also promised diplomatic support for Egypt's efforts to recover the lost territories but cautioned Nasser against immediate use of force for such a purpose.[7]

Whether or not the Soviets were reluctant, in fact, to accept Nasser's request for advisers or to associate themselves more closely with Egyptian designs for military reconquest of the occupied territories, it is clear that, at least in retrospect, the Russians attributed much of the blame for Egypt's Six-Day War defeat to the military and political shortcomings of Egyptian command personnel. According to one Soviet source, "individual Generals and high officers . . . were not ready for fulfillment of their . . . duty. They were opposed to the main line of the government's policy directed toward conducting deep social transformations in the country. Using their official position, many of them actively opposed any kind of political work among the soldiers and non-commissioned officers which lowered the combat capability of the Egyptian army."[8]

Presumably, then, on the basis of such conclusions, the Russians felt that if defense of the "progressive" Arab regimes was to be realized, the Soviet Union would be required to provide more than technical instruction. A reshaping of the Egyptian officer corps would also have to be encouraged. This conclusion regarding the need for a basic reorientation of the Egyptian armed forces, combined with the high value placed on maintaining the loyalty of the "progressive" Arab states, apparently convinced the Soviet leadership to take the risky step of introducing Soviet armed forces personnel in substantial number into Egypt.

The purported Soviet insistence on the improvement of Egyptian command personnel complemented Nasser's own evaluation that Egyptian social inadequacies had been a prime cause of the Six-Day War setback. In a 23 July 1967 speech, the Egyptian leader declared that before the Six-Day War the "army class" and the bureaucracy had acquired "unjust" privileges. Nasser concluded that the Egyptian social revolution must be pressed forward because "imperialist Zionist aggression" was aimed not only at the occupation of territory but also at

---

* Egyptian President Sadat, in an interview with *Al-Hawadith* (Beirut), claimed that the Egyptians offered to give the Russians command of the Egyptian air defense and air forces. The Russians reportedly refused (quoted by Cairo Middle East News Agency [MENA], 19 March, 1975).

"liquidation of the Arab revolution. . . ."[9] In Nasser's view, salvation from the debacle of June 1967 was to be found in the accelerated transformation of Egyptian society, particularly the army and the officer corps. Nasser's determination to achieve the reshaping of the military hierarchy was both mirrored and encouraged by the cashiering for incompetence of former Egyptian Commander-in-Chief Amer and ten other senior generals and the later arrest of Amer and fifty other officers for conspiring to overthrow the regime.[10]

In the years following the Six-Day War, presumably at least partially under Soviet encouragement, the Egyptian officer corps significantly improved, as did relations between officers and enlisted men. More educated people were introduced into the armed forces, and all military officers became career personnel. Pay was improved and discipline was tightened at all levels of the military. Most importantly, the previously existing sharp cleavage between officers and enlisted men was significantly eroded.[11]

Because of Nasser's renewed commitment to press forward "progressive" socioeconomic and military changes within Egypt, the Russians were strongly drawn toward providing support that would confirm these highly positive moves. Elements of the Soviet leadership must have feared that faint-hearted support for the Arabs during the Six-Day War would redound badly for the "progressive" cause in the Arab world. Now that peace had returned and Nasser had pronounced his desire to continue down the "progressive" path, there were powerful incentives to reverse the Russian image of weakness and to demonstrate graphically Soviet support for the "progressive" states. Occasions for the manifestation of Soviet support would be provided in the years ahead.

The first display of Russian concern came only a few months after the conclusion of the Six-Day War. Following a rash of artillery and small-arms duels across the Suez Canal, on 21 October 1967, Egyptian *Komar*-class patrol boats utilizing *Styx* ship-to-ship rockets sank the Israeli destroyer *Eilat* off Port Said. In retaliation, Israeli forces shelled and destroyed the second largest Egyptian oil refinery, at the city of Suez. When Israeli leaders rhetorically threatened the Egyptians with the renewal of hostilities, Russian ships that had departed Egyptian ports in previous days returned to these ports, presumably to underline Russian support for Egypt.[12] In the following years, Soviet ships would maintain an almost permanent presence in Egyptian ports.

Against a background of substantial weapons deliveries and the introduction of some four thousand military advisers,[13] Soviet efforts through the end of 1969 focused on the rebuilding of the crushed Arab armed forces. Nasser, in the interim, in July 1968, visited Moscow to sound out the intentions of the Soviet leadership. He reportedly found that the Russians did not wish to risk "a hot confrontation with the United States." The Soviet leadership indicated, presumably in response to requests for support for military liberation of the occupied lands, that their attitude toward the final resolution of the Middle Eastern problem would ultimately rest on "the question of Arab will and ability to struggle." Nasser reportedly told the Soviet leaders that there would be "no negotiations, no peace treaty, no recognition of Israel and no ceding of Arab territories to Israel." The Soviets supported Nasser's demands.[14]

The Russians were apparently willing to back the Arabs' harshest political claims, but at the same time, they were anxious to avoid clashes with the United States. They also seemingly wished to see more evidence of their clients' mettle before endorsing a course aimed at military removal of Israeli forces from the occupied territories. The Arabs, meanwhile, because of their partially restored strength, were becoming impatient with Israeli occupation. Plans for new forms of military pressure on the Israelis were being aired and would soon be implemented. Impetus for these new plans would come, at least partially, from the activity of Palestinian guerrilla organizations.

In the wake of the Six-Day War, membership in Palestinian terrorist groups swelled, and commando raids across the new Jordanian and Syrian ceasefire lines became commonplace. These Palestinian guerrilla actions received broad support in the Arab world, at least in part because of the failure of Arab conventional war strategy in 1967.[15] The established "progressive" Arab regimes, in order to demonstrate their legitimacy as defenders of radical Arab aspirations, felt called upon to display an activism at least equal to that of the Palestinians and to find a means to apply their conventional military power effectively.

Egyptian leader Nasser in mid-1969 responded to the perceived need for greater action by proclaiming a "war of attrition" against Israel. The "war of attrition" consisted of applying continuous pressure on Israeli forces on the east bank of the Suez Canal by means of artillery bombardment and commando raids. These methods were designed to inflict high casualties on the Israelis and to compel them to maintain a prolonged mobilization of forces—both highly significant costs for a country with a small population.

Nasser's confidant, *Al Ahram* editor Mohamed Heikal, justified the Egyptian decision in favor of the "war of attrition" in the following manner.[16] The Israelis, first of all, according to Heikal, had no incentive to advance further into the Arab countries because they would then have to cope with the bulk of the Arab population. The Arabs, therefore, were reasonably safe. In order to expel the Israelis from the occupied territories, however, positive action would have to be taken by the Arabs. A number of alternative possibilities for action were conceivable:

(a) a massive broad frontal assault across the ceasefire lines, (b) a disarming aerial first strike against the Israeli air force, and (c) a blitzkrieg spearhead thrust into the occupied territories. While these alternatives certainly were not mutually exclusive, they did represent different possible emphases of effort.

Regarding a broad frontal assault across the ceasefire lines, Heikal continued, traditional military doctrine called for a two-to-one or three-to-one force advantage over the defenders for such an attack. It was clear that Arab forces would have to build up their forces to handle such an effort. Coordination between the Arab countries would also have to be improved in order to gain greater manpower and equipment advantages. Additional military hardware would have to be obtained to ease the crossing of the various natural barriers in the path of attack (the Suez Canal, the Golan Heights, and the Jordan River). In short, the Arabs would have to wait some time before launching a frontal attack.

With regard to a disarming air strike on the Israeli air force, Heikal noted that there were a number of reasons for assuming that such a strike would not be successful: (a) the Israeli air force, unlike its Egyptian counterpart in 1967, was constantly on full alert; (b) after the Six-Day War, the Israelis had many more airfields on which to disperse their aircraft;[17] (c) because of the broad expanse of the occupied territories, Israeli strategic aircraft were virtually inaccessible to Arab planes,[18] due to the short range of the MIG-21 interceptors, which would have to escort Egypt's slow and vulnerable bombers; and (d) the Israeli air force had a very capable air defense and was well aware of the strengths and vulnerabilities of Arab aircraft.[19]

As Heikal saw the problem, the root of Arab air difficulties was the lack of a capability to safely deliver a strategic air blow to the Israelis. The Egyptian editor, therefore, concluded that "it would be no use limiting the blows of our Air Force to enemy targets which are near us. The blows should extend to the enemy's strategic centers. . . ." Presumably, the Arabs would have to obtain either longer-range interceptor escort aircraft to accompany their bombers or assured-penetration vehicles, such as missiles, before a disarming air strike could be contemplated.

The third alternative, a "lightning war" against the Israelis, was also unthinkable for the Arabs in the short run. Such a war required great planning and technical efficiency. The Arabs, in Heikal's view, were not yet ready for such a complex action.

The only alternative available to the Arabs, therefore, was a protracted struggle. This option was favored by a basic difference that Heikal saw between the Arabs and the Israelis. For the Israelis to win the military conflict against the Arabs, they would have to deal the Arabs a "fatal blow." For the Arabs to vanquish the Israelis, however, only "significant losses" would have to be inflicted. These losses could be generated by compelling the Israelis to maintain their forces near full mobilization and by inflicting high casualties on them.

The flaw in Nasser's plan (as explained by Heikal), of course, was that it did not take into account Israeli capabilities of inflicting substantial damage on the Egyptians. In the months following the inauguration of the "war of attrition," the Israeli air force steadily pounded the Egyptian positions along the Suez Canal. In a fifty-day period, Israeli aircraft flew one thousand missions over the Canal.[20] By November 1969, all Egyptian surface-to-air missile sites along the Canal were destroyed,[21] Egyptian interceptors were virtually banished from the skies,[22] and Cairo's troops on the ground were open to punishment from the air.

Moscow had apparently warned Nasser that the time was still not ripe for Egyptian offensive action. In an apparently authoritative article that appeared in *Pravda* in June 1969, the Egyptians, and possibly Soviet partisans of the Arab cause, were told that the forces encouraging offensive action were seeking only to destroy the "progressive" social changes in Egypt.[23]

According to this analysis, certain social groups in Egypt, such as the propertied classes, the village elite, businessmen, certain bureaucrats and army officers, and religious circles, had viewed Egypt's defeat in the Six-Day War as a splendid opportunity to overthrow Nasser's "progressive" government. Having thus far failed, these groups "fan up nationalist and revanchist moods in the people and army calculated to push the UAR (Egypt) on an adventurist course. As a result, according to their calculation, the existing regime will not be able to hold together." The *Pravda* article suggested that the Egyptian government would be better served by consolidating internal sociopolitical changes and continuing the build-up of the armed forces than by embarking on premature military efforts.

In spite of Soviet cautions, however, the Egyptians continued their "war of attrition," and the Israelis heightened their reprisals. In June and August 1969, Israeli commandos raided Egyptian installations in the Nile Valley; also in June, Israeli aircraft flew reconnaissance flights over Cairo; in the fall of 1969, bombing was moved from the Canal progressively closer to the capital; and in September 1969, an Israeli armored unit crossed the Canal and penetrated some fifty miles into the Egyptian interior.[24] After the Egyptian SAM sites were destroyed, Israeli forces and aircraft were able, because of the weakness of the Egyptian air force, to penetrate across the Canal virtually at will. In the aforementioned September 1969 Israeli armored incursion, for example, not one Egyptian aircraft intervened against the Israelis.

Helpless in the face of the Israeli attack, the Egyptians began to search for scapegoats. Nasser, focusing on the September 1969 American decision to ship Phantom fighter-bombers to Israel, said that the Americans were "fighting behind" Tel Aviv. Becoming more shrill, the Egyptian leader asserted that peace was impossible and there was "no longer any way out except to use force to open our own road toward what we want—over a sea of blood and under a horizon of fire."[25]

The Russians, presumably both to restrain Nasser from any act of desperation and to identify themselves more closely with the militant Egyptian posture, began to take a more conciliatory view toward Nasser's military ambitions. Soviet commentator Igor Belyayev, for example, writing in *Pravda* at the end of August 1969, stated that "millions of simple Egyptians are full of decisiveness to defend the freedom and territorial integrity of the Arab countries. . . ."[26] This observation seemed to contradict Rumyantsev's assertion only three months previously that only the Egyptian bourgeoisie were interested in renewing hostilities. On 19 September 1969 Foreign Minister Gromyko, speaking at the U.N. General Assembly, stated that American proposals to reach a Middle Eastern arms-control agreement were clearly unacceptable while Israel continued to occupy Arab land.[27]

Finally, indicating that the Soviet leadership had seized on the problem, an article signed "Observer" (generally indicating high-level authorship) appeared in *Pravda* on 2 October 1969.[28] The article condemned American arms shipments to Israel and stated that the United States was seeking to use Israel to overthrow "progressive" and nationalist regimes in the Middle East. Seeking to head off further American shipments of aircraft and surface-to-air missiles to Israel, "Observer" pointed up the supposed contradiction between the U.S. proclaimed policy of peaceful settlement and the U.S. shipment of arms to the Middle East. On the threatening note, "Observer" concluded that Israel "tries the patience of the peoples" and that "the Soviet Union . . . will do everything necessary to achieve the liquidation of the consequences of Israeli aggression. . . ." The Soviets, in spite of initial reservations about the "war of attrition," were moving toward providing support, perhaps not to assure its success but at least to avert its defeat.

TASS transmitted from Cairo only a few days later an extremely detailed account of *Al Ahram* editor Heikal's most recent discussion of the Egyptian military situation. The printing of this detailed political-military analysis in the Soviet press probably indicated that the Soviet authorities had no quarrel with Heikal's basic frame of reference.[29]

Heikal explained that once Egypt opened fire in the "war of attrition," Israel faced two choices: either to conduct partial mobilization or to construct a line of fortifications. The Israelis had chosen the latter course and established the Bar-Lev Line. Now the Israelis were relying on their air force and conducting a "dialogue by fire" with the Egyptians.

The Israeli air force, in Heikal's view, was engaging in four modes of operation against Egypt: (a) mass application of aircraft against Egyptian positions along the Canal, (b) daily strikes along the Canal to break holes in Egypt's antiaircraft defense, (c) exploitation of those breaks to conduct operations in northern Egypt, and (d) propaganda and psychological-influence operations.

Using these tools, the Israelis, according to Heikal, wanted to accomplish the following goals: (a) to force Egypt to disperse its forces away from the Suez Canal, (b) to convince Egypt that war would not take place only along the Canal, where Egypt was striving for military superiority, (c) to force Egypt to respond to secondary Israeli operations, thereby wearing out Egyptian forces, (d) to influence Egyptian public opinion that after the passage of two years Israeli military superiority could not be broken, and (e) to demonstrate to the other Arab countries that Egypt, the strongest Arab state, was not ready for confrontation.

The Soviets, while not wishing to encourage a rash Egyptian cross-Canal attack, which might bring down Nasser's regime, simultaneously did not want to see their efforts to rebuild Egypt's defenses discredited by Israeli air operations. It would be far too easy for Nasser's opponents to blame Egypt's vulnerability on its ties with Moscow. The Soviets, therefore, had strong incentives to frustrate Israel's air campaign.

Thus, on 9 December 1969 Nasser's personal emissary Anwar Sadat, accompanied by Egyptian War Minister Fawzi, arrived in the Soviet Union for talks with the Politburo leadership. Any doubt about what the meeting was intended to discuss was dispelled by a small TASS item that appeared next to Sadat's arrival notice. Under the heading "Account Opened" the TASS story related that the first American-produced Phantom jet had just been shot down over the Suez Canal.[30]

Sadat met on December 10 with Soviet leaders Brezhnev, Kosygin, and Podgorny in an atmosphere that was described as "full of mutual understanding and friendship." In Kosygin's speech in honor of the Egyptian visitor, the justification for the Soviet Union's new policy of added support for Egypt was clearly spelled out. In the words of the Soviet leader, "Israel believes that extension of the conflict will lead to the breakdown of internal stability in the Arab countries and to the rupture of friendship between the Arabs and the Soviet Union. . . ." In order, therefore, to preserve the "progressive" regimes and to maintain their allegiance to Moscow, the Soviet Union felt obliged to counter Israel's air attacks on Egypt.

The Soviet Union, Kosygin said, would take "active measures in strengthening the defense capability of the UAR (Egypt) and the other Arab states." The Soviet Union would not allow the Israelis to use military superiority to dictate either a peace settlement or the domestic- and foreign-policy orientation of its client. According to Kosygin, "We consider it impermissible for an aggressor to receive any kind of advantages as the result of his criminal activities. That is the position of our Communist Party, the Soviet Government, and the whole Soviet people."[31]

The Russian leadership had made a decision, therefore, to blunt the Israeli retaliatory sword. Implementation of this decision was made more urgent by the Israeli move in January 1970 to extend bombings to the urbanized areas of the Nile Valley and Delta. As Israeli Minister of Defense Moshe Dayan declared on January 24, because Egypt wants neither peace nor a ceasefire, "all of Egypt is the battlefield."[32] Israel's decision to extend the air war to Egypt's heartland was prompted at least in part by a Soviet note to the United States dated 23 December 1969, which rejected the American-sponsored Rogers Plan for an Egyptian-Israeli settlement based on a partial Israeli pullback along the Suez Canal. It was generally felt that the Soviet rejection of the Rogers Plan was made under Egyptian pressure because of Nasser's desire not to negotiate from a position of inferiority.[33]

Once the areas around Cairo were subjected to bombing, Nasser, recognizing Egypt's complete vulnerability, hastened to Moscow in late January 1970 on a secret, unannounced visit.[34] His goal was to accelerate deliveries of the air-defense equipment promised to Sadat in December. Though the Egyptian leader did not receive the commitment of advanced Soviet MIG-23(25) interceptors that he desired,[35] the Russians agreed to supply SAM-3 surface-to-air missiles, which were effective at low altitudes. (The early SAM-2 antiaircraft missiles were only very minimally effective against Israeli aircraft and then only at high altitudes. The SAM-3's, incidentally, in early 1970 had not even been provided to embattled North Vietnam.) Most significantly, the Russians agreed either in January or February to dispatch Soviet crews to Egypt to operate the SAM-3's.[36]

The commitment of Soviet personnel in a combat role against the Israelis must have caused the Kremlin leadership considerable pause.[37] No analogous move had ever been made by the Soviet Union outside the Communist camp. Before taking this radical step, the Soviets first tested American reactions to Soviet involvement, as well as Washington's willingness to curb the Israelis. Chairman Kosygin, on 31 January 1970, sent a first-person note to President Nixon in which he reportedly pointed out that Egypt was virtually defenseless. If the United States could not restrain Israel, Kosygin said, the Soviets would feel forced to provide new arms for Nasser.[38]

According to one source, in either the January 31 note or some later communication the United States was told that the introduction of Soviet fighting personnel was essential to defend Egypt. The new SAM-3 batteries, the United States was informed, would be emplaced only in the developed areas of central Egypt—around Cairo, Alexandria, and the Aswan Dam.[39] The Soviets were thus careful to distinguish that their involvement was only defensive—to curb the deep-penetration raids rather than to support the "war of attrition" along the Canal.

While some observers have speculated that the Israeli initiation of deep-penetration raids against the urbanized areas of Egypt was the precipitating cause of the Soviet decision to supply SAM-3's with Russian personnel, Israeli intelligence reportedly indicates that the simple physical breakdown of Egyptian air defense was the key motivating factor.[40] The eventual extension of the SAM-3 deployment beyond the urbanized areas of central Egypt (outside the area of deep-penetration raids) tends to give credence to the Israeli assertion.

TABLE 1. ESTIMATED SOVIET MILITARY INSTALLATIONS IN EGYPT, 1970

	Personnel			Soviet-manned SAM Sites	Soviet-manned aircraft	Soviet-controlled airfields
Date	Pilots	Missile Crew	Others			
Jan. 1	0	0	2,500–4,000	0	0	0
Mar. 31	60–80	4,000	2,500–4,000	22	0	1 (?)
June 30	100–150	8,000	2,500–4,000	45–55	120	6
Sept. 30	150	10,000–13,000	2,500–4,000	70–80	150	6
Dec. 31	200+	12,000–15,000	4,000	75–85	150	6

SOURCE: *Strategic Survey, 1970* (London: Institute for Strategic Studies, 1971), p. 47.

In any event, after Nasser's visit to Moscow, commentaries in the Soviet press indicated that a basic decision had indeed been made to extinguish any of Tel Aviv's hopes for achieving Egyptian acquiescence to peace through application of Israel air power. *Pravda*, in an important commentary on 27 January 1970, adopted a new line proclaiming that a political solution for the Middle Eastern conflict would be expedited by eliminating Israel's military advantages. According to *Pravda*, "the growth of the combat capability of the Arab armies, especially the army of the UAR (Egypt), works in favor of a political solution because it destroys Tel Aviv's illusions and calculations that the Arab world will remain forever for Israel a kind of 'open zone' from the military point of view."[41]

Soviet adherence to the new policy view was accented by a massive propaganda campaign launched after the February 12 Israeli bombing of the Abu Zaabal metallurgical plant at El Khanka, Egypt. The Israeli attack, which killed some seventy to eighty workers and injured an additional one hundred, purportedly resulted from an electrical failure on an Israeli Phantom fighter-bomber. The mechanical breakdown caused the Phantom's bombload to be dropped one mile from its intended target, the Egyptian air force supply base at El Khanka.[42] Egyptian leader Nasser believed, however, that the attack was another calculated Israeli attempt to "teach [Egypt] a lesson."[43]

The Soviets, who probably shared Nasser's assessment of the Abu Zaabal strike, seized on the incident both to justify their greater involvement in Egypt's defense and to indicate to the United States and Israel the depth of Soviet concern with the Israeli air offensive. Tied to the latter question was the Soviet desire to stop the reported imminent U.S. decision to ship additional American Phantom and Skyhawk jets to Israel. As additional side benefits, the Soviets also linked their continuing campaign against Zionism (that is, against Soviet Jewish emigration) into the propaganda sallies against the Israeli attack.[44]

Beginning on February 17 and continuing until the end of March 1970, the Soviet press day after day carried resolutions of factory workers, letters of "concerned citizens," and statements of Soviet Jewish "spokesmen" condemning Israeli bombardments and various and sundry other "Zionist outrages." On March 3, in a front-page editorial, *Pravda* stated that the purpose of the Soviet protests was to "force Israel to cease armed provocations."[45]

Writing from Cairo, in the midst of the anti-Israel propaganda campaign, Soviet correspondent Yuriy Glukhov pointed up one of the factors that in the minds of the Soviet leadership may have legitimized the new level of commitment on Egypt's behalf. According to the correspondent, Israel was using the occupied lands as a "trampoline to expand aggression." Because of the propinquity of Israeli air bases in Sinai, Israeli aircraft were capable of penetrating at a low altitude to the depths of Egypt in only a few minutes.[46] This geographic advantage, which was nothing but a "benefit of aggression," was thus balanced by Soviet intervention. Correspondent Glukhov, in addition to pointing up the Israeli advantage, implicitly revealed the next Russian counter to Israeli actions. In a commonly used ploy to justify Soviet involvement, he accused the United States of sending American pilots to Israel.

The false accusation, repeated on several occasions, of the American dispatch of pilots and other combatants to Israel coincided with the Soviet decision to send a limited number of Russian pilots to Egypt.[47] The approximately one hundred pilots were ostensibly sent to protect the new SAM-3 missile sites from Israeli attack. Unlike in the case of the decision to deploy Soviet-operated SAM-3's, the Russians did not see fit to inform the United States of the dispatch of combat pilots to Egypt.[48]

The end of both Soviet consideration for American sensitivities and the perceived need to test American reactions may have been tied to the hesitation that had appeared in Washington concerning the supply of additional aircraft to Israel. Though President Nixon in mid-February had warned that the United States would "maintain careful watch on the balance of military forces" in the Middle East and would "view any effort by the Soviet Union to seek predominance . . . as a matter of grave concern,"[49] on March 23, in spite of accelerated Soviet arms deliveries to Egypt, the United States postponed further shipments of Phantom and Skyhawk aircraft to Israel.[50]

The American decision to delay further aircraft deliveries may have been motivated by the desire to pressure Israel to terminate the deep-penetration raids as well as to signal the Russians that the United States was prepared to exercise restraint in the Middle East.[51] If these, indeed, were its purposes, the former goal succeeded admirably, though the latter proved to be an inappropriate signal. Again, as on several other occasions during the Arab-Israeli conflict, the United States took a decision which on its own merits was sound (the application of pressure to end the deep-penetration raids) but which conveyed a dangerous message of temerity and vacillation to the Russians.

In early April 1970, partially in response to the American halt in aircraft shipments and partially due to new Soviet air-defense deployments, the Israelis terminated deep-penetration raids into Egypt. Upon suspending deep penetration, the Israelis sought to establish a clear dividing line between what they were now prepared to regard as a legitimate sphere of Russian air-defense activity (protection of the populated areas of central Egypt) and what they considered to be illegitimate Soviet activity—the blocking of Israeli air operations over the zone of immediate military confrontation on the Suez Canal. Israeli Minister of Defense Moshe Dayan, in announcing the decision to end deep raids on April 6, stated that Israel would not "exhaust" itself flying over Cairo, Alexandria, and Aswan but would continue strikes "to ensure that we keep our hold on the Canal." Dayan added that he hoped "this distinction exists with the Russians." In line with these statements, Israeli Air Force Chief Peled commented on March 29 that as long as Soviet SAM-3's were not installed within twenty to thirty kilometers of the Canal, there was a minimal chance of involvement with the Russians.[52]

The suspension of Israeli deep-penetration raids brought in its wake an increase in combat activity along the Canal. Egyptian air, artillery, and commando assaults increased to levels higher than in any previous months. In reply to the increased Egyptian activity, the Israelis pursued a dual policy of diplomatically highlighting the new Russian operational role (primarily for Washington's benefit) and increasing their air strikes on the Canal area.

On 29 April 1970 the Israelis publicly disclosed for the first time that Soviet pilots were now "flying operational missions from military installations under their control in Egypt." The Israelis pointed out, however, that the Russian operations had not yet extended to the ceasefire line.[53] Israeli Defense Minister Dayan, possibly in response to the new Russian moves, on May 3 offered the Egyptians an immediate and unconditional ceasefire. Dayan, however, signaled Israel's determination "to fight physically" to hold its lines on the Canal "even against Soviet aid."[54]

In May–June 1970 the Egyptians, far from accepting a ceasefire, began reconstruction work on the SAM sites along the Canal that had been destroyed by Israel. In response the Israeli air force sharply stepped up its air strikes to massive levels. It soon became apparent, however, much to the Israelis' discomfiture, that Soviet-manned SAM-3 units were being added to the Canal air defenses. These new SAM-3 installations, coupled with improved SAM-2 models, which were being installed, began to take a heavier toll of attacking Israeli aircraft. Moreover, Russian-piloted interceptors, which, during their first weeks in Egypt, had restricted their patrols to the Nile Valley, now extended their operations forward to areas on the flanks of the Canal front.[55]

It is not clear in retrospect whether the extension of the Soviet involvement to the Canal area represented a new decision or was only a further step in implementing the policy decided in December and January of depriving Israel of military advantages. The Soviets undoubtedly noted the Israelis' distinction between central Egypt and the Canal battle area. Nonetheless, in the mind of the Soviets, Israeli determination to have a free hand over the Canal Zone meant only that Tel Aviv wished to maintain its hold on the conquered territories through application of military pressure on the Egyptians.

While the Soviets were not yet ready to encourage Nasser to undertake a cross-Canal offensive, at the same time they were not prepared to concede the legitimacy of Israel's hold on the occupied territories. As Soviet Communist Party General Secretary Brezhnev stated in Kharkov on 14 April 1970, "No one should have any doubts that the Arab people will capitulate to the permanence of occupation of their lands." Brezhnev added: "The Arab peoples have true friends—the socialist countries—ready to render the necessary assistance for wrecking the plans of the aggressors in the Near East."[56]

The Soviets probably viewed their move into the Canal area as one involving a calculated minimal risk. If a relatively small quantity of aircraft losses could be inflicted on the Israelis, they probably thought, Tel Aviv could soon be brought to heel, especially given the demonstrated American reluctance to resupply Israeli losses. As a Soviet commentator indicated, "It would be a mistake to assume that a small country such as Israel . . . is capable of maintaining its military advantage for long. . . ."[57]

Improved results in the aerial war against Israel became evident in June and July of 1970, as the Soviets and Egyptians in rapid order reestablished SAM positions along the Canal in spite of very heavy Israeli attacks. In contrast to previous months, when Israeli aircraft losses were virtually nonexistent, Tel Aviv's air force lost a substantial total of one Skyhawk and five Phantoms during largely futile June and July attacks on the Canal SAM sites.[58]

The Soviet-Egyptian success in reestablishing the SAM defenses was achieved by setting up the SAM sites often overnight with minimum consideration for reducing vulnerability and making fine adjustments for accuracy. By this technique, Israeli raiders were frequently surprised by new SAM installations.[59] Moreover, new weapons were introduced, such as the SAM-3 and improved models of the SAM-2. The new SAM-2's possessed better computer fire control and a capability of launching salvos of six rockets in an integrated time sequence.[60] This technique of so-called ripple firing was, of course, extremely expensive, but it did compensate for accuracy losses because of speedy installation, and it also better assured the imposition of high Israeli losses, which was the goal of the Soviet campaign.

As an additional warning to the Israelis, on July 25 Soviet-piloted MIG-21's attacked two Israeli Skyhawks on a bombing run near the Canal. The Israeli aircraft jettisoned their ordnance and fled the scene. On July 30, presumably in retaliation, the Israelis baited Soviet-piloted aircraft into action, ambushed them, and downed four MIG-21's with Soviet pilots.[61] This incident, never reported in the Soviet media, probably accented to the Russians the risks involved in further hostilities on the Canal.

During the course of the Suez aerial battles (and prior to the Israeli-Soviet air confrontation), Nasser visited the Soviet Union from June 30 until July 18. During the visit, the Egyptian leader received medical treatment and held consultations with the Soviet leadership. During the course of the discussions, a tentative agreement was presumably reached looking toward acceptance of a ceasefire once Israeli air superiority had been eliminated. (American Secretary of State Rogers had launched an initiative in favor of a temporary ceasefire in the Middle East in March 1970.)

In the face of high personnel losses along the Canal[62] and probable Soviet pressure, the Egyptians had curtailed the ambitions of the "war of attrition." Rather than striving for the expulsion of the Israelis from the occupied zones, Nasser was now ready to accept the more moderate Soviet-endorsed objective of eliminating Israel's military (that is, air) advantages. The Soviet endorsement of the shift in Egyptian goals was highlighted in an interview with Vice-President Sadat by a Soviet correspondent in Egypt on May 30. As Sadat was quoted, "Our task is to counter the (Israeli) air war. As you observe we are succeeding. And on the more general plane, (our goal is) to create all the conditions for . . . reflection of any air aggression."[63]

At the conclusion of Nasser's Russian visit, a communiqué was issued that stated, in part: "The earlier the peace-loving forces make Israel turn away from the hopeless 'policy from a position of strength' . . . , the quicker a just and firm peace in this region will be guaranteed."[64] By the end of July, rising Israeli air losses along the Canal, coupled with Soviet diplomatic pressure, apparently convinced Nasser that Israel's "position of strength" had indeed been eroded.[65]

The Soviet press strived to reinforce the impression that a new situation had been created. Pravda's Igor Belyayev, with obvious satisfaction, noted that by late July, Israeli air losses had dramatically risen. In the West, Belyayev indicated, there was considerable appreciation that a fundamental change had taken place in the balance of forces along the Canal.[66]

As a result of the perceived loss of Israel's aerial free hand, Nasser, by July 30, was ready to accept the ceasefire. The Soviet press, reporting the Egyptian leader's remarks from Cairo, highlighted the fact that Nasser attributed the ceasefire initiative to the change of the balance of power in the Middle East.[67] In the wake of Egyptian acceptance of the ceasefire proposal, Israel also felt called upon to halt hostilities. On 7 August 1970, for the first time since the "war of attrition" began in spring 1969, combat ceased along the Suez Canal.

The ceasefire obliged the sides to refrain from changing the military status quo within zones extending fifty kilometers to the east and west of the Suez Canal. Both sides were forbidden to introduce or construct any new military installations in these zones. Within the ceasefire zones, military activity was limited to the maintenance of existing installations at their current sites and to rotation and supply of the forces then in place.[68]

In spite of the various ceasefire prohibitions, the Russians and Egyptians took advantage of the halt in hostilities to move SAM (surface-to-air missile) installations up to the Canal. The movement forward of the SAM's appeared to be a premeditated action rather than a last-minute termination of ongoing work. According to U.S. Government sources, the circulation of men and equipment associated with installing the new SAM's greatly exceeded the level of activity characteristic of the weeks preceding the ceasefire.[69]

Though the United States did not wish to make the suspected SAM movements a subject of dispute for fear of breaking down the ceasefire, after insistent Israeli complaints and after additional evidence was studied, on 1 September 1970 American officials finally admitted that Egypt had violated the ceasefire. According to Israeli sources, within one month of the halt on hostilities some ninety missile sites had been established in the standstill zone.[70] By the end of October, some five hundred to six hundred SAM launchers had been established along the Canal, about two hundred of which were located within nineteen miles of the ceasefire line. The forward elements of the new system permitted coverage of an area extending twelve miles into the Israeli-occupied Sinai Peninsula.[71] The Israelis viewed this turn of events as particularly dangerous because it allowed the Egyptians to concentrate troops with virtual impunity on the Suez west bank for a possible Canal crossing.

The Soviet and Egyptian violation of the ceasefire was apparently a calculated move to definitively eliminate Israel's air supremacy over the Canal. (Israeli air superiority had again been embarrassingly manifested by the shooting down of the Soviet-piloted MIG-21's only one week before.) Considering the U.S. enthusiasm for the ceasefire and its reluctance to guarantee the Israeli offensive threat, the Soviets presumably gambled that only Israel would take serious umbrage at the movement forward of the SAM's. After the long "war of attrition" and the heavy aircraft losses of June and July, the Israelis, in the Russian view, probably would not wish to initiate offensive combat activities and run the risk of incurring additional substantial losses, particularly if American backing were questionable.

In the probable Soviet view, the termination of Israeli air superiority along the Canal would best guarantee the maintenance of the ceasefire and, by increasing the insecurity of Israel's hold on the east bank of the Canal, would provide incentives for an Israeli pullback. As Brezhnev stated a few weeks later: "Those who have been trying to impose their will 'from a position of strength' on the Arab countries and who have conducted aggressive actions, now have the possibility to think better of it and to abandon that hopeless and adventurous line...."[72]

During the months that followed the ceasefire, additional Soviet personnel and military equipment were dispatched to Egypt. It is conceivable that these additions of men and weapons may have been offered as a further incentive for Egyptian acceptance of the ceasefire.

In mid-September 1970 attention shifted to Jordan, where pro-Western King Hussein had decided to move against armed Palestinian terrorist groups. While the Soviets for many years had not publicly taken a political stand in relation to the Palestinian organizations, favorable references to the groups began to appear in the Soviet press from the beginning of 1969.[73] The Palestinians were declared to be a "progressive" element seeking the liberation of the occupied lands.

When Hussein moved against the Palestinians, American decision-makers were conscious of the possibility of Soviet intervention. In a show of determination perhaps partially motivated by chagrin at Russian violations of the Suez ceasefire, the American leadership ostentatiously reinforced the Sixth Fleet in the Mediterranean and placed American troops in Germany and the United States on alert. In addition, close liaison was established with the Israelis, who had mobilized their forces on the Syrian border (since Syria backed the Palestinian organizations and was also a client of the Soviet Union[74]).

Though the Russians on September 18 informed the United States that the Soviet Union was seeking to keep other countries from intervening in Jordan, on 20 September 1970 some three hundred Syrian tanks moved into Hussein's kingdom. Because Soviet military advisers were present in the Syrian armed forces, Washington believed that the Soviets had advance knowledge of the Syrian move, if they had not, indeed, encouraged it.[75]

While during the crisis the Soviets maintained that they had made representations to Damascus to avoid intervention, subsequent Soviet statements raised doubts regarding the strength of Moscow's alleged protestations. Soviet Party chief Brezhnev, speaking in Baku on October 2, pointed out that, not only had the Soviet Union sought to curb "armed intervention by the imperialist powers," but "we have tried to contribute in every possible way toward . . . stopping the extermination of the units of the Palestine resistance movement."[76] Brezhnev's statement raised questions as to whether Soviet efforts were limited to blandishments to King Hussein or had assumed a more active form, such as encouraging the Syrians into action.

At any rate, Soviet military advisers in the Syrian forces had not crossed the border into Jordan, the Syrian air force had not intervened (presumably for fear of drawing the Israelis into the fray), and Syrian ground forces soon withdrew from Jordan after some 130 of their tanks were destroyed.[77] American and Israeli joint action presumably deterred the Russians and Syrians from taking any more serious action in favor of the Palestinian organizations. In the eyes of the Soviets, the defeat of the Palestinian guerrillas in Jordan represented a serious setback to the "progressive" cause. In Brezhnev's words, the results of the Jordanian struggle were "truly tragic."[78]

The defeat of the Palestinians, like every setback of the "progressive" cause in the Middle East, prompted Moscow to strengthen the Russian commitment to its Arab clients. Support for Moscow's friends in the Middle East would have to be graphically reasserted because the "imperialists," gloating over their success, might now assume that the Soviet Union was no longer a reliable guarantor of its clients' interests. Brezhnev, therefore, raged at the United States and Israel in the wake of the Jordanian crisis: "Nowadays it has become very dangerous to trifle in such a cynical way with the destinies of independent states and peoples. By doing this, it is possible not only to burn your fingers, but also to lose your whole arm."[79]

The Soviet desire to reaffirm support of the "progressive" states was demonstrated almost immediately following the death of Egyptian leader Nasser on 28 September 1970. As the new Egyptian president, Anwar Sadat, indicated two months later, the Soviet Union agreed after Nasser's death to increase support for Egypt.[80] In the months that followed, additional Soviet aircraft and other weapons were sent to Egypt, Syria, and Iraq,[81] and greater numbers of Soviet pilots and air-defense personnel made their appearance in Egypt.[82]

As a counter to the Soviet arms build-up, and reflecting the better relations prevailing between Washington and Tel Aviv after the Jordanian crisis, the United States agreed to resume shipments of Phantom and Skyhawk aircraft and tanks to Israel.[83] Therefore, at the beginning of 1971, Washington and Moscow were again at loggerheads in the Middle East.

Soviet policy toward the Middle East in the period from the Six-Day War until Nasser's death in 1970 demonstrated a pattern of continually rising involvement. Attempting to demonstrate that Moscow was a firm and reliable protector of the "progressive" Arab states, the Soviet Union after the Six-Day War immediately undertook to replace Egyptian military equipment losses. Replenishment of Syrian and Iraqi arms inventories soon followed. At either Soviet or Egyptian behest, Russian military advisers were then introduced into operational units of the

Egyptian armed forces. These military-unit advisers supplemented small numbers of Soviet weapons instructors and other military consultants who had served in Egyptian training facilities and military academies in previous years. Soviet advisers were also later introduced into military units of other "progressive" Arab states.

The introduction of Russian military advisers into operational Egyptian units was the most far-reaching involvement of Soviet armed forces personnel outside the communist camp in the post-World War II period. While the need for Egyptian command training was readily apparent, it must be recalled that Cairo's armed forces stood in direct and immediate confrontation with the military forces of Israel, a country which enjoyed friendly relations with the United States. Acceptance of the risk of possible involvement in a conflict with Israel, with its consequent dangers of American participation, indicated that Moscow viewed its stake in the Arab world as high and worth defending.

The Russians probably felt that a repetition of the Six-Day War debacle could cause the Soviet Union to lose all credibility as a protector of those in the Arab world and elsewhere who were seeking to fight "imperialism." The Arab-Israeli confrontation therefore had more than a regional significance. As the U.S.S.R. Supreme Soviet pointed out: "What takes place in this area [the Middle East], at the junction of the African and Asian continents, has a direct relation to the fates of the peoples of all the countries of Asia and Africa and to the fate of general peace and security of peoples."[84] Because the Soviets felt that Israel should not be allowed to dictate a peace to the "progressive" Arab states, Soviet arms had to be sent to the Arabs, and the recipient armed forces had to be trained and reorganized in the most effective manner possible.

The Soviet leadership probably felt that involvement of increased numbers of Russian personnel in military training activities in Egypt would not provoke the Americans into action, particularly since the latter were already heavily engaged in Vietnam. Moreover, American official attitudes toward the post-Six-Day War Israeli conquests was more than a little ambiguous. Nonetheless, the Soviets were not anxious to have the Egyptians involve themselves in hostilities. A premature war, before the Egyptian armed forces were adequately trained and equipped, could lead to military disaster, a fall of the "progressive" Egyptian regime, and a consequent discreditation of Soviet efforts on the Arabs' behalf.

Middle East politics had a dynamism of their own, however, and Egyptian leader Nasser felt called upon to take decisive action against Israel. This action would begin the process of recovering the occupied territories and would reassert Egypt's leading position in the Arab world. Against a background of Soviet cautions and possible objections, Nasser began the "war of attrition" against Israel.

The "war of attrition" turned out to be a largely one-sided affair, however, as Israel exploited its air superiority to inflict heavy losses on the Egyptians. Undoubtedly more griping to Cairo and Moscow, however, were the publicity-generating air and ground incursions that Israel launched periodically into the Egyptian interior. The continued rage of the Arab public against Israel, coupled with Moscow's desire to restrain Nasser from any self-defeating act of desperation against Israel, apparently convinced the Russians that their interests would be served by providing limited sustenance to Nasser's military campaign.

Soviet published commentary on the Egyptian military efforts became more favorable, and during the visit of Anwar Sadat to Moscow in December 1969 the Soviets apparently agreed to commit additional air-defense equipment to Egypt. The Israelis, in turn, further escalating their military pressure against Nasser, in January 1970 embarked on deep-penetration air raids on targets in the heavily populated Nile Valley. The Israelis thereby expanded their goals from simply reducing the effectiveness along the Canal of the Egyptian "war of attrition" to coercing the Egyptians to accept a permanent ceasefire or peace settlement.

Against this background, Nasser secretly flew to Moscow and obtained Soviet consent for the dispatch to Egypt of Soviet air-defense personnel. Moscow's commitment of troops in a direct combat role in a non-Communist country was unprecedented. It once again revealed the special importance of the "progressive" Arab cause in Moscow's eyes. It also demonstrated that the Soviet Union could strongly resist any attempt by Western-oriented powers to use military superiority to determine the course of political events in its clients' bailiwick. Before undertaking this step, which must have seemed momentous, Moscow tested the reaction of Washington to the dispatch of Soviet equipment and personnel. When no violent objection was forthcoming, probably largely because the United States also opposed the deep-penetration raids, the Soviets committed their air-defense troops. Later, a number of Soviet pilots followed.

The installation of the new Soviet air-defense system and a concurrent American decision to suspend aircraft sales to Israel caused Tel Aviv to abandon its deep-penetration raids. After the suspension of deep penetration, combat activity intensified along the Suez Canal. Soviet-manned missile sites and aircraft moved forward, engaged the Israelis, and caused the air losses of the latter to rise sharply.

The Soviets at this point, seeking to minimize the risks of further confrontation, and having accomplished to a large measure what they set out to do—to neutralize Israel's military superiority—convinced

Nasser that a ceasefire would now be appropriate. Under the cover of the ceasefire, the Soviets completed construction of the new air-defense system. Israel's free hand was removed, not only over Egypt's cities, but also along the zone of immediate confrontation. Because Cairo could build up forces along the Canal's west bank without interference, Israel's defensive positions in Sinai—not Egypt's, as before—were now insecure. The weight of political-military initiative had been shifted by the Soviets from Israel's hands to Egypt's. Cairo had not regained the occupied territories, but its negotiating assets were much improved. The Soviets in the course of a few months had been able to reverse the political situation.

The Soviet limited "victory" in Egypt was balanced by the setback to the "progressive" Palestinian forces inflicted by King Hussein in Jordan. While the Palestinians were being devoured, Moscow contented itself with issuing warnings to Israel and the United States to remain at bay, while probably encouraging an ineffectual Syrian intervention. After the Syrians were mauled and the Palestinians largely annihilated, Moscow was then faced by a situation in which no gains could be achieved and only risks could be incurred. The Soviets then had the unpleasant task of restraining the Syrians from further action.

Having seen the benefits of strong Russian political-military support in the Egyptian case and then having witnessed the fruits of failure in Jordan, the Soviets were strongly drawn toward providing further assistance and reasserting solidarity with the "progressive" Arabs. The death of Egyptian President Nasser, accompanied by the consequent uncertainties for Egypt's future, also militated in favor of increasing direct Soviet assistance to the Arabs. Unfortunately for the Soviets, the United States, in the wake of the Jordanian civil war and the Suez Canal ceasefire violations, was becoming increasingly wary of Soviet intentions and was moving in the direction of greater support of Israel.

II Nasser's successor, Anwar Sadat, was less willing than his predecessor to balance Moscow's shortcomings against its virtues. The new president's leadership was being challenged by Nasser's associate Aly Sabry, a politician who was considered "Moscow's man" in Cairo.[85] Sadat's ill feelings toward Sabry and his increasing reliance on the support of anti-Communist forces within Egypt undoubtedly raised new concerns in Moscow. Soviet anxiety was also spurred by Sadat's increasingly frequent statements that 1971 would be the "year of decision" in Arab-Israeli relations—the year in which Arab military action would compel Israeli withdrawal from the occupied territories.

The beginning of 1971 saw the frustration of two major Middle

Eastern peace initiatives. The Rogers Plan for a partial Israeli pullback along the Suez Canal was again revived with an expression of Israeli interest in December 1970. After a flurry of Egyptian, Soviet, and American contacts, President Sadat expressed interest in the pullback idea. Israel welcomed Sadat's initiative but stressed that the matter would have to be settled in direct Israeli-Egyptian talks rather than through Four Power talks, as Egypt and the Soviet Union preferred.[86]

In spite of disagreement on the format of the talks, the Rogers Plan might well have met with some degree of success had the U.N.-appointed mediator Dr. Gunnar Jarring not introduced complications. Jarring, seeking to achieve a total solution to the problem, on 8 February 1971 submitted a memorandum to the Egyptian and Israeli governments in which he proposed *inter alia* that Israel withdraw from all the occupied territories and that Egypt sign a peace agreement with the Jewish state. Jarring's attempt to seek a total resolution of the Middle Eastern problem evoked maximal demands from both Egypt and Israel in reply to the Jarring memorandum.

Egypt placed qualifications on Israel's right to free navigation through the Suez Canal and the Straits of Tiran, demanded demilitarization and introduction of a Four Power peacekeeping force in the Israeli Negev region, and insisted on an undefined "just" settlement of the Palestinian problem. In turn, Israel flatly stated that it would not withdraw to the pre-1967 borders.[87] Jarring's proposals, by rekindling the Egyptian-Israeli antagonism regarding ultimate demands, interfered with the implementation of intermediate first steps.

Sadat, faced by the impasse on the diplomatic front, turned to the Soviet Union for increased military assistance to prepare for battle against Israel. In March 1971, the Egyptian president journeyed to Moscow and told the Soviet leaders that 1971 was the "year of decision" and that "things could not wait."[88] On this occasion, the Egyptian leader apparently requested advanced Soviet MIG-23(25) interceptors to combat the American Phantom fighter-bombers that had been acquired by Israel. The Russians allegedly told Sadat that it would take five years to train Egyptian pilots on the MIG-23(25). The Soviets stated that they would only supply the advanced interceptor with Soviet pilots and under the condition that they would remain under Russian control. Sadat reluctantly agreed to this proposal, but the delivery of MIG-23(25)'s was considerably delayed.[89]

In order to reaffirm their commitment to Egypt, the Soviets did, however, agree to dispatch a very large number of additional MIG-21 interceptors to Egypt.[90] The Russians also agreed to double the density of Egypt's surface-to-air missile system and to maintain Russian air-defense crews in Egypt. The prolongation of the stay of Russian air-defense personnel was reportedly intended to cover the gap while additional Egyptian air-defense crews were being trained to operate the new SAM's.[91] Soviet air-defense crews were, however, withdrawn from the Suez Canal area into central Egypt.[92]

In spite of the Soviet agreement to provide additional weapons to Cairo, the Russians were apparently discomfited by Sadat's calls for armed action, that is, independent action without Moscow's blessing. The Kremlin also was undoubtedly disturbed by the uncertain direction of the Egyptian leader's foreign- and domestic-policy leanings. Already in January 1971 Soviet Chairman Podgorny, visiting Egypt, had declared that the "imperialists and their hirelings" could be repulsed only when "the people . . . choose a correct plan of action, maintain vigilance against enemies and seek support among true, reliable friends and allies."[93] Podgorny's remarks seemed intended to signal to President Sadat that he should not be tempted to take a course involving too much "independence" or autonomous action. Moscow's support, Podgorny indicated, was essential for ultimate success.

Moscow extended this logic by again indicating that it thought that Israeli obduracy with regard to a political settlement was calculated "to smash the Arab national liberation movement and overthrow the progressive regimes in the UAR (Egypt) and other Arab countries . . . ,"[94] that is, presumably to tempt the Arabs into a disastrous military operation or to cause a turning away of the "progressive" regimes from reliance on the Soviet Union.

The cautious trend of Soviet thinking in mid-1971 was interestingly reflected in a long discussion held by a group of Syrian Communists (led by Khaled Bakdash) in Moscow in May 1971. According to the notes taken by the Syrian Communists (which were published one year later), Soviet political figures and theoreticians made the following observations: (a) the Soviet Union was not in favor of renewed Arab-Israeli war, "except in the case of extreme necessity"; (b) war without adequate preparation would lead to the liquidation of the "progressive" regimes; (c) war could also lead to a confrontation between the Soviet Union and the United States; (d) Soviet opposition was not to a military solution per se but was motivated only because the Soviet Union was "realistic"; (e) opposition to an Arab-Israeli war did not prevent the Soviet Union from improving Arab military capabilities; (f) the situation of "no war, no peace" benefited the Israelis; and, therefore, (g) the position of the Soviet Union was based on struggle for a "just political solution." The Soviet position in favor of a "just" (pro-Arab) political settlement, according to the Russians, strengthened the "progressive" Arab regimes and deprived Israel of its vital foreign support. The Soviets added, moreover, that "in the estimate of our experts" the

Egyptian and Syrian armies were then currently incapable of militarily defeating the Israelis.[95]

The Soviets wished to keep the Arabs oriented toward a political solution and were clearly disturbed by Sadat's intention to undertake war in 1971. On the other hand, the Russians did not want to risk losing the loyalty of the "progressive" Arab states.

Moscow's unease regarding Egypt's course was undoubtedly heightened by the removal of the pro-Soviet Aly Sabry as Egyptian vice-president on 2 May 1971. On May 17, following the resignation of six cabinet ministers, the Egyptian newspaper *Al Ahram* announced that 110 people associated with Sabry had been arrested for seeking to overthrow the Sadat government.[96] While Sadat later declared that the Soviets had engineered the alleged Sabry coup attempt,[97] it is unlikely that the Egyptian leader had solid evidence of Russian participation or that the Soviets had done anything more than passively endorse Sabry's ambitions. This interpretation is confirmed by Soviet Chairman Podgorny's immediate trip to Cairo (25 May 1971) to smooth over affairs with Sadat. If the Egyptian president had been convinced of Moscow's role in the Sabry "coup," it is unlikely that Sadat would have amicably received Podgorny.

The Soviets were obviously quite anxious that the Sabry coup not become a pretext for a break in Soviet-Egyptian relations. Podgorny, therefore, hastened to Cairo with two items presumably calculated to appeal to Sadat. On one hand, the Soviet chairman promised Sadat that within four days of his return to Moscow MIG-23(25) aircraft would be dispatched to Egypt.[98] Presumably other weapons were also offered. In addition, Podgorny requested that Egypt sign a Treaty of Friendship and Cooperation. In Podgorny's words, the Treaty, signed 27 May 1971, "strengthen[ed] and cement[ed] what [had] matured in Soviet-Egyptian relations in recent years."[99] The Treaty, therefore, was to be a graphic demonstration of Egyptian-Soviet solidarity, a model for the "progressive" world.[100] The Treaty, of course, also conveniently papered over the tensions between Sadat and the Soviet Union over the Sabry affair. It also lessened the possibility that the Sabry incident could be used to stir up anti-Soviet sentiments in Egypt and elsewhere.

The military clauses of the Treaty committed the Soviet Union to train Egyptian troops in the use of Soviet arms and equipment "delivered to the UAR (Egypt) for the purpose of strengthening its capabilities in the cause of liquidating the consequences of aggression . . ." (Article 8). While Soviet leaders previously had made references to the provision of "material" help to Egypt to "liquidate the consequences of aggression," this was the first time that the Soviet Union had entered into an official public undertaking specifically tying delivery of Russian weapons to reconquest of the occupied territories.

As partial compensation for this very important Soviet commitment, the Russians obtained an implicit pledge from the Egyptians to engage in consultations with the Soviet Union before any independent armed action was undertaken. According to Article 7 of the Treaty: "In the event of the appearance of situations creating, in the opinion of both sides, a threat to peace or a breakdown of peace, they (both parties) will immediately enter into contact with each other for the purpose of coordinating their positions in the interests of eliminating the threat which arose or of reestablishing peace."[101] Whatever goodwill had been generated between Cairo and Moscow as the result of the offer of more weapons and the signature of the new Treaty, however, was quickly dissipated.

On 19 July 1971 pro-Communist elements in the Sudan seized power from General Dzhafar Numeiry, an anti-Communist "progressive" nationalist. Both Libya's leader, Colonel Moamer Qaddafy, and Egypt's Sadat had no wish to have a Communist regime on their borders, particularly since the Sudan takeover could serve as a model for their own countries. As a result, the two leaders undertook joint efforts to overthrow the Sudanese Communists.

First, top pro-Communist Sudanese military leaders who had been living in exile in England were arrested in Libya when their BOAC aircraft made an unexplained, unscheduled stopover at Benghazi enroute to the Sudan. Next, the Egyptian air force transported a Sudanese paratroop brigade that had been stationed in Egypt back to Khartoum. As a result of the arrival of the paratroop brigade, and with Egyptian advice, a successful countercoup was staged against the pro-Communist forces on July 22–23.[102]

In the wake of the countercoup, restored Sudanese leader Numeiry began arresting and executing the members and leadership of the Sudanese Communist Party. After an initial, matter-of-fact statement in the Soviet press that "radical changes" would continue in the Sudan but that "Communists will also be punished,"[103] the Russians shifted into a shrill propaganda and diplomatic effort against Numeiry. While it undoubtedly grieved the Soviets to attack the "progressive" nationalists, it would be difficult for Moscow to sacrifice the Sudanese Communists without protest. The Sudanese terror might serve as a model for other anti-Soviet elements in the Middle East, and Moscow's acquiescence in the physical liquidation of the Sudanese Communists could be misinterpreted by Arab and other Marxist-Leninists.

Keynoting the anti-Sudanese offensive, *Pravda*, in a highly authoritative article signed "Observer," noted that "imperialist agents" were blaming the Soviet Union for the July 19 coup. "Observer" denied these stories and said that "divisions between the Soviet Union and the Arab world help imperialism." Sudanese leaders were warned that "there should be no illusions" that the Communists could be persecuted without damaging close relations with the Soviet Union.[104]

In the midst of a violent campaign of vituperation against the Sudanese leadership, an unusual TASS communiqué was issued that summarized Soviet efforts on behalf of the now largely defunct Communist Party. The communiqué indicated that Chairman Podgorny on July 25 had sent an appeal to Sudanese leader Numeiry not to inflict severe punishment on the Communists. In addition, the Soviet Ambassador in Khartoum on July 26 had made a declaration to Numeiry in which the Sudanese leadership was accused of committing "unfriendly acts" against Soviet representatives in the Sudan, damaging Soviet property, and undertaking "threats and acts of violence" against Russian employees in Khartoum.[105]

The accusations and implied threats leveled at the Sudanese leadership, of course, were not intended to by-pass Egyptian ears. After all, Sadat's activities had laid the groundwork for Numeiry's anti-Communist countercoup. Central Committee Secretary B. N. Ponomarev, visiting Egypt during the course of the Sudanese events, cautioned in the final communiqué of his visit that "attempts to spread anti-Communism aim to inflict a split into the ranks of Arab revolutionary fighters against imperialism, Zionism, and Israeli aggression. . . . These attempts are also directed toward breaking down the solidarity and cooperation between the Arab peoples and their friends."[106]

The Egyptians were thus duly warned that Soviet patience had limits and that Soviet support in the Arab-Israeli dispute must be reciprocated by consideration for Russian interests. Moscow underscored its irritation by temporarily slowing down weapons deliveries to Egypt.[107] Sadat later indicated that, between July and September 1971, "relations with the Soviet Union [were] almost cut off [because of] Sudan."[108]

In October 1971 the Egyptian leader visited Moscow, and, in his words, the "misunderstanding" regarding Sudan was "dissolved." In the course of the meeting an unspecified agreement was reached. "In accordance with this [overall] agreement," Sadat later said, "a certain agreement would be implemented between us before the end of 1971. The Soviet leaders themselves set [the date?]."[109] The unspecified "agreement" may have involved the delivery of additional Soviet-operated advanced weapons such as the MIG-23 (25) interceptor and more probably other items such as surface-to-surface missiles.[110] Whatever the precise content of the "agreement," it is highly probable, considering Sadat's statement that the Sudanese tensions had been dissolved, that it was intimately related to Sadat's declared intention to embark on military action in 1971.

Moscow thus attempted, in the wake of the Sudan and Sabry affairs, to smooth over relations with the "progressive" Arabs by stressing the principal common element that brought the Soviet Union and the Arabs together—the Arab-Israeli dispute. In order to achieve this reuniting, Moscow apparently made some very important concessions to Sadat that, in the Egyptian's mind, made possible a resort to war in 1971 against Israel. Moscow's gesture to Sadat indicated the depth of Soviet desire to make the ill feelings of the Sudan and Sabry episodes a thing of the past. In Moscow's view, protection of the Arab Communists and pro-Communists may have been an important temporary desire, but it did not compare in significance with permanent Soviet interest in maintaining the loyalty of "progressive" Arab nationalists. The latter, unlike the Communists, enjoyed a mass following—the essential property of power in Soviet eyes.

According to Sadat, however, the Soviet-Egyptian October reconciliation agreement had still not been implemented by mid-December 1971. Sadat thereupon, on December 11 or 12, requested a meeting in Moscow before the end of the year. The Soviet leadership did not reply to Sadat's message until December 27 and declined to receive the Egyptian leader until February 1972. According to Sadat, even if the "agreement" had been put into practice "in the middle or end of December, I would not be able to implement what I had told my people"[111] (presumably war could not have been launched). Thus, it appears that in October 1971 the Soviets had promised Sadat some type of delivery or action of sufficient magnitude to effect Egypt's decision in favor of war. By December, however, the Soviets had apparently reneged on their commitment.

Two major factors may have affected Moscow's decision. Most importantly, during November, Indian and Pakistani hostilities grew in connection with the rebellion in Bangladesh. On December 3, full-scale war broke out between the two countries. With the United States and China taking a position in support of Pakistan, the Soviet Union, implementing a recently signed Treaty of Friendship and Cooperation, felt strongly called upon to give India full political and military backing. In anticipation of an American military gesture the Soviets dispatched a naval task force to the Indian Ocean.[112] In addition, some Soviet military equipment located in Egypt was reportedly picked up and transferred to India.[113] With Soviet and American forces standing in confrontation in the Indian Ocean, Moscow probably was extremely reluctant to contemplate an additional clash in the Middle East.[114]

Secondly, the United States was once again asserting military support for Israel. On December 2, President Nixon met with Israeli Prime Minister Golda Meir, and an agreement was reached concerning further American supplies of jet aircraft to Israel.[115] The impact of the American commitment, coinciding as it did with the Indo-Pakistani crisis, undoubtedly strengthened Moscow's inhibitions against spurring an Arab-Israeli war.

In the beginning of 1972, Sadat announced that he was "delaying the zero hour (for combat with Israel) until I meet with the Russians. . . ."[116] At the February Moscow meeting, the Soviets apparently prevailed on the Egyptian leader not to make any untoward move before the upcoming May 1972 Nixon-Brezhnev summit meeting.[117] Because of the new Russian foreign-policy drive to seek improved relations with the large Western powers, the avoidance, at least temporarily, of any incidents that might cast the Soviet Union in an unfavorable light became an important interest for Moscow. At the same time, the Soviets did not want to jeopardize their ties with the "progressive" Arabs. Thus, in exchange for Sadat's undertaking to postpone his attack temporarily, the Soviets apparently agreed to renew or make a new commitment to provide Egypt with an improved capability to threaten Israel strategically, possibly through provision of surface-to-surface missiles. This commitment was reflected in reports emanating from Egypt that the Soviet Union had agreed to help Cairo correct the deficiencies of its own faulty domestically produced medium-range ground-to-ground missiles.[118]

In order to spur previously agreed Soviet weapons deliveries and to seek to avert any Soviet-American summit agreements prejudicial to Egyptian interests, Sadat again journeyed to Moscow in April 1972. The Egyptian leader told the Russians that they should (a) not agree to Middle Eastern arms limitations before "Israeli aggression was eliminated," (b) not permit preservation of the situation of "no peace and no war," and (c) not enter into negotiations on Arab borders.[119]

In addition, Sadat urged the Russians to make good on their earlier commitments. According to Sadat, he and Brezhnev "agreed that the diplomatic, peaceful solution always demanded by the Soviets [could] not be achieved without a military move." Sadat claimed that he cited as a precedent in point a major offensive launched by the North Vietnamese on 1 January 1972, which had forced the Americans to give serious attention to the then stalled Paris Vietnam peace conference.

Sadat purportedly reminded Brezhnev that President Nixon would visit Moscow in spite of the North Vietnamese offensive, even though the American president knew that Hanoi's actions had been facilitated by Soviet arms. Sadat allegedly suggested to the Soviet leader that after President Nixon's Moscow visit, it would become apparent that the U.S.

position on the Middle East had not changed. Consequently, Sadat told Brezhnev that "the Soviets would have to begin within five months— from May, that is, immediately following Nixon's visit, to November . . . to supply Egypt with the strength it lacked . . . so that this strength would be a point of departure toward negotiating or making a military move."[120]

The Soviet-Egyptian communiqué at the end of Sadat's April visit endorsed the propriety of Egyptian use of nonpolitical means to recover Arab lands and stated that further steps were being taken to strengthen Soviet-Egyptian defense cooperation. When Sadat returned to Cairo he declared that Egypt had "a guarantee that within a reasonable period we will have the power to liberate our land."[121]

Soviet Minister of Defense Grechko visited Egypt in mid-May, apparently in connection with Soviet weapons commitments. During the Grechko visit, an agreement was reportedly reached concerning the continued Soviet naval presence in Egyptian ports.[122] Egyptian War Minister Sadeq described his visit as "important" and "successful."[123]

In spite of the apparent mood of public understanding in Soviet-Egyptian relations, an undercurrent of tension was building up between Moscow and Cairo. These tensions were generated partially as a result of Sadat's feelings that Moscow was improving its relations with Washington at Egypt's expense and partially because of the Egyptian sense that delivery of long-promised weapons was being unacceptably delayed. The developing Soviet-Egyptian tension had been reflected in Cairo's decision in mid-February 1972 to expel the chief Soviet military advisor from Egypt. The Soviet officer had reportedly openly criticized Egyptian military ability and prowess.[124]

By June Sadat's patience with the Russians had worn thin. After receiving a Soviet explanation of the Nixon-Brezhnev talks,[125] on June 1, the Egyptian president sent Brezhnev a seven-point questionnaire on the future of Soviet-Egyptian relations.[126] One of the seven questions inquired when the Soviets would supply the offensive military weapons which the Egyptians had repeatedly requested and which the Russians over and over had said were on the way. Only on July 7 did Soviet Ambassador Vinogradov bring the Soviet reply. Instead of answering Sadat's questions, the Soviet answer apparently only reiterated ritualistic formulations on the good relations prevailing between Egypt and the Soviet Union.[127]

Sadat, who was infuriated by the Russian response, allegedly told Vinogradov that (a) all Soviet advisors in the Egyptian armed forces must leave within ten days, (b) all Soviet military installations in Egypt must be handed over to Egyptian control, (c) all Soviet-controlled military equipment must be sold to Egypt or removed from the country, and (d) all future Soviet-Egyptian negotiations would have to be conducted in Cairo. Upon hearing Sadat's demands Vinogradov departed immediately for Moscow.[128]

In the wake of Sadat's statements, Syrian President Assad, possibly at the urging of Moscow, visited Cairo and asked the Egyptian leader how he could embark on such a serious action when Syria had just signed a $700 million arms deal with the Soviet Union. Sadat told Assad that he should not worry about the public repercussions of the Egyptian action and should do what was best for Syria.[129]

The Soviets next requested that the Egyptians send a high-level delegation to Moscow to explain Sadat's decision. In response to this request, the Egyptian president dispatched Premier Aziz Sidky.[130] When Sidky returned from Moscow on July 14 without receiving a commitment for the offensive weapons which Sadat desired, the Egyptian president informed the Central Committee of the Arab Socialist Union (ASU), the official Egyptian political party, on 17 July 1972 that (a) the Egyptian armed forces had taken over all the duties and functions formerly performed by Soviet experts and advisers, (b) all military installations and equipment emplaced in Egypt after the Six-Day War would become the exclusive property of Egypt and would be placed under the control of the Egyptian armed forces, and (c) an Egyptian-Soviet meeting for consultations on the coming stage of relations should be carried out under the framework of the Soviet-Egyptian Treaty of Friendship and Cooperation.[131]

The Egyptian newspaper *Al Ahram* later indicated that Sadat's decision to expel Soviet military personnel applied only to Soviet advisors serving in Egyptian military units, and not to Soviet personnel holding positions in Egyptian military academies and other institutions where weapons training was conducted.[132] Sadat also later indicated that Russian use of Egyptian Mediterranean ports would be continued.[133] Presumably, this statement indicated that shore-based Russian naval personnel need not be removed from Egypt.

Sadat told the ASU Central Committee that his decision to reduce the Russian presence in Egypt had been motivated by three factors: (a) the Soviet limitation on the kinds of arms it was supplying to Egypt, (b) Soviet "support" for the situation of "no war, no peace" in the Middle East, and (c) Soviet readiness to concede Arab territory in a Middle East peace settlement.[134]

Sadat's basic grievance, of course, was the Russian failure to provide weapons that he considered necessary for the launching of an offensive action against Israel. (Russian niggardliness may have been magnified, however, by Sadat in order to forestall domestic criticism of his leadership.) According to Western sources, Sadat was primarily interested in

TU-22 medium bombers armed with *Kitchen* stand-off missiles, which could be launched from outside Israel's fighter range, *Scud* 150–450-mile-range surface-to-surface missiles, and *Sandal* SS-4 1,100-mile-range surface-to-surface missiles,[135] in addition to his well-publicized desire for MIG-23(25) interceptors.

The Russians, in announcing termination of the presence of advisers in Egypt, stated that Soviet military personnel had "fulfilled their function" in Egypt and that Moscow and Cairo had agreed that "military personnel sent to Egypt for a limited time" would be withdrawn.[136] While Sadat apparently limited his demands for withdrawal to Soviet advisers serving in Egyptian military units (some five thousand of a total of some fifteen thousand[137]), the Russians out of pique withdrew virtually all their personnel. At the end of the withdrawal, only one or two hundred Soviet military personnel remained.[138] Most Soviet-controlled equipment, such as the five or six Russian-piloted MIG-25 advanced interceptors, the sixty Russian-piloted MIG-21 and SU-11 interceptors, and the TU-16 reconnaissance aircraft that had been used to surveil the American Sixth Fleet, were withdrawn from Egypt. While some SAM sites (presumably the most advanced types) were dismantled, earlier-model SAM-2 and SAM-3 units, as well as some mobile SAM-6 units, were left in Egypt.[139]

In the wake of the Russian departure, Sadat put out feelers to France and England with propositions that these countries supply weapons to Egypt.[140] These attempts to obtain arms from the West, however, came to nought.

While Sadat was pursuing his contacts in the West, the Egyptian military was strongly agitating for an attack on Israel.[141] Sadat, presumably hoping that the Russians had reversed their position regarding arms supplies, again sent Premier Aziz Sidky to Moscow (16–18 October 1972). After Sidky reported on his reception in the Soviet Union, some members of the ASU Central Committee suggested that Egypt break relations with the Soviet Union.[142] This sentiment apparently reflected the continued Soviet resistance to Egyptian demands for advanced offensive weapons. The Russians did apparently agree, however, to resume supplying spare parts for the Egyptian air force and, perhaps, other elements of the Egyptian military and to return some mobile SAM-6 antiaircraft missiles that had been withdrawn in July.[143] In addition, Soviet Ambassador Virogradov returned to Cairo after a two-month absence.[144]

In the meantime, while Soviet-Egyptian relations were very slowly improving in the wake of the expulsion of Soviet advisers, the Russians were demonstratively stepping up their efforts in support of Syria. The increase of Soviet activity in Syria followed the February 1972 visit of

Politburo member Kirill Mazurov to Damascus and the subsequent negotiation of a reported $700 million arms deal shortly before the Egyptian expulsion decision. Part of the new arms deal was the Russian commitment to supply Syria with SAM-3 missiles.[145]

Following intensive Israeli retaliatory air raids on terrorist bases in Syria and Lebanon in the wake of the murder of Israeli Olympic athletes in Munich, the Soviet Union, in September, October, and November 1972, organized a highly publicized airlift of air-defense components to Syria.[146] The rapid introduction of advanced Russian air-defense equipment also raised the required presence of Soviet training and advisory military personnel in Syria. Previously, some three thousand Soviets were stationed in Syria as advisers to Syrian military units. Now, the quantity of Russian personnel would be raised by several thousand.[147]

The Russians were presumably especially eager to expand their military ties with Damascus to minimize political damage occasioned by the Egyptian expulsion and to guarantee access to Syria's Mediterranean ports.[148] Another fruit of the stepped-up Soviet support for Syria was the gain of bases for the Soviet TU-16 reconnaissance operations against the American Sixth Fleet, which were transferred from Egypt to Syria.[149]

While the Soviets were increasing their military support for Damascus, cooperation between Cairo and Syria was also being stepped up. In the wake of the November 13 visit of Egyptian War Minister Ahmed Ismail to Damascus, Egyptian interceptors began flying rear air cover for the Syrians, thereby allowing the Syrian air force to engage in offensive air operations against the Israelis.[150] The immediate result of the new Syrian activism was the loss of six Syrian MIG-21 aircraft in an aerial action that the Israeli air force apparently instigated.[151] Again, as in the past, however, the Israeli action was severe enough to enrage the Arabs but not serious enough to cause them to doubt their own combat capabilities. Syrian and Egyptian newspapers and radio stations began raising an outcry in favor of increased coordination of military efforts between the Arab "brothers."[152]

Sadat, even before the Syrian border tensions, had apparently contemplated the initiation of hostilities against Israel in autumn 1972.[153] According to his own account, he had made a commitment to several parties, however, to avoid action before the American presidential elections.[154] It is possible to speculate that one of his promises was given to the Soviets, who wished to keep the détente-oriented Nixon administration in office. Presumably, such a commitment could have been made in connection with the October Sidky visit to Moscow and the Russian pledge to resume military spare-parts shipments.

The trend toward increased unity of efforts between the Syrians and Egyptians probably pleased the Russians. In a situation of heightened hostility against Israel, the Egyptians, for lack of an alternative source of weapons supply, would be drawn back into the pro-Soviet fold. The Russians, certainly after the October 1971 "agreement" with Sadat, had never overtly opposed Arab armed action against Israel. The argument between Sadat and the Russians which led to the July 1972 expulsion of Soviet advisers was concerned less with Russian opposition to armed action than with the type and pace of Soviet weapons deliveries.

Indeed, even in the darkest days of Soviet-Egyptian relations, after the expulsion of Russian advisers from Egypt, Soviet newspaper and magazine articles favorably quoted from the April 1972 Soviet-Egyptian communiqué that the Arab states "have every justification to use other [nonpolitical] means for the recovery of Arab lands seized by Israel"; and from the July 1972 Soviet-Syrian communiqué pledging Soviet military support "for the quickest liquidation of the consequences of Israeli aggression."[155]

For good relations to return between Moscow and Cairo it remained, therefore, only for Sadat to lessen the extent of his designs against Israel and to reach a compromise with the Russians regarding the weapons he wished to receive. Indications that an acceptable compromise had been reached appeared in late 1972 and early 1973.

On 21 December 1972 Sadat reportedly ordered the Egyptian armed forces to prepare for battle within six months. In addition, the 1968 agreement permitting the Soviet navy to use Egyptian ports was also extended.[156] On 1 January 1973 Libyan leader Qaddafy removed Libyan volunteers from the Egyptian Canal front because of an apparent disagreement with Sadat concerning the expediency of a limited war, as opposed to a total war, against Israel.[157] The Egyptian leader, evidencing a new, less ambitious war orientation, apparently favored more limited goals than Qaddafy.

Sadat's new limited-war goals were to be such that risks for the Soviets would appear to be only minimally present. According to the Egyptian leader, two principles would be repeatedly mentioned to the Russians: (a) no Soviet troops were required in Egypt, and (b) Egypt did not intend to provoke a confrontation between the superpowers.[158]

On 8 February 1973 Communist Party General Secretary Brezhnev received Sadat's national security adviser, Hafez Ismail, in Moscow. The Ismail visit apparently marked the definitive end of the period of tension between Moscow and Cairo. According to the Soviet press, the Brezhnev-Ismail talks were conducted in a "warm, friendly atmosphere," a standard formulation indicative that major disagreements had been absent. The talks reportedly touched on measures for "the further strengthening of Soviet-Egyptian relations." Both sides, in an important political move, agreed that a partial Israeli pullback from the occupied territories (as envisaged by the Rogers Plan) was unacceptable.[159]

The Soviet endorsement of the Egyptian rejection of an intermediate settlement formula virtually committed the Soviets to assist an Egyptian military effort against the Israelis. However, the Egyptians, probably under Soviet urging, had still not closed the door to nonmilitary moves toward settlement. Egyptian Foreign Minister al-Zayyat was quoted by the Soviet press after the Ismail visit to the effect that "we are not saying that we are declaring war. We only declare our decisiveness to defend ourselves. Meanwhile, efforts in the political and diplomatic areas are being undertaken simultaneously with efforts in the military area."[160]

Regardless of the still open-ended nature of the Egyptian approach to the occupied-territories problem, it was soon clear that the Soviets had committed themselves to satisfying Sadat's revised request for weapons and possibly other assistance in the event of war. On 27 February 1973 Brezhnev and Soviet Defense Minister Grechko met with Egyptian War Minister Ahmed Ismail Aly in Moscow. Their conversation was described as "warm and friendly," touching on "questions presenting mutual interest."[161] By the beginning of April, Sadat was able to declare: "The Russians are providing us now with everything that's possible for them to supply. And I am now quite satisfied."[162] Presumably based on the weapons commitments received from the Russians, Sadat now felt ready to say that "the time has come for a shock. . . . Everyone has fallen asleep over the Middle East crisis."[163] Sadat had decided to renew war.[164]

Sadat's decision to move toward a military "shock" was not initially greeted with enthusiasm by the Soviets. National security adviser Hafez Ismail was again dispatched to Moscow in July 1973, presumably to explain the Egyptian sentiment in favor of launching hostilities. Unlike the February conversations, Ismail's July talks in Moscow were not classified as "warm and friendly." Instead, the Egyptian's July 13 talk with Brezhnev was now described as "frank and friendly,"[165] a formulation used when some disagreements are present.

According to Egyptian statements quoted in the Soviet press, the proclaimed purpose of Ismail's visit was to "receive information on the position which the Soviet Union occupied in the negotiations with the United States [during the Nixon-Brezhnev American Summit meeting of June 1973] on the Middle East.[166] Brezhnev, in reply to Ismail's queries, apparently told the Egyptian that the Soviet Union wished to avoid jeopardizing the American-Soviet détente, which was expected to last some twenty to thirty years.[167]

Ismail apparently was insistent on the Egyptian assessment of the desirability of launching hostilities against the Israelis. This insistence probably accounted for the "frank" atmosphere noted in the communiqué.

The Soviets were placed in a dilemma with regard to their response to Ismail. The Politburo and the Soviet government, in discussing the results of Brezhnev's trip to the United States, in accordance with the Soviet "Program of Peace" (proclaimed at the 1971 XXIV Party Congress), had declared that "the hotbed of war" in the Middle East must be liquidated by achieving a full withdrawal of Israeli forces from the occupied territories and a respect for the rights of all peoples and states in the area.[168] Brezhnev himself, in his speech upon receiving the Lenin Peace Prize, on the day before his talk with Ismail, declared that it was necessary to "extinguish the hotbed of aggression in the Near East. One cannot allow the aggressors and adventurers to continue to hold this huge area in an explosive condition."[169] While the extinguishing of "hotbeds of war and aggression" is not necessarily inconsistent, in the Soviet vernacular, with undertaking military action, Soviet protestations in favor of peace in the Middle East might well be misunderstood in the West if a Soviet client were to launch a war.

Possibly as a consequence of Ismail's visit, the phrase "hotbed of war" would not be used in Soviet diplomatic communiqués or leadership statements touching on the Middle East until the beginning of the Yom Kippur War. Moreover, and much more importantly, in his five major speeches between the Ismail visit and the beginning of the Yom Kippur War (four of which touched on foreign affairs) Brezhnev would entirely exclude mention of the Middle East from his presentations.[170] This was a highly significant departure from the consistent Soviet view of the Middle East as one of the top three problems in Soviet-Western relations (along with Vietnam and "European security").

The Soviets were placed in a difficult position by the Egyptian insistence on war. A commencement of hostilities might jeopardize détente, a major goal of Soviet foreign policy. On the other hand, resistance to the Egyptian designs could lead to a repetition of the July 1972 breakdown of Soviet-Egyptian relations. Such a disruption of relations would be extremely prejudicial to Moscow's position among radical regimes and movements in the Third World. Chinese propaganda was already portraying the Soviet-American summit meetings as part of a super-power conspiracy to freeze change. In the words of Peking, the United States and the Soviet Union "came to a secret tacit agreement . . . to avoid direct military conflict through the Moscow summit talks and other channels, using Arab national interests as chips in counter-revolutionary political deals."[171] In addition, Sadat, backed by other Arab anti-Communists, had already shown that he was ready to toy with the Western powers should the Soviets not be forthcoming. The Soviet Union, if it were to maintain its image as a partisan of "liberation struggles," therefore, would have to back Egyptian ambitions, at least passively.

On 30–31 July 1973 a meeting of the heads of Communist Parties of the Warsaw Pact nations was held in the Crimea. Brezhnev spoke to the meeting regarding Soviet foreign policy, including the Middle East. In the communiqué issued at the conclusion of the meeting, the Near East problem was described as one of the "sharpest problems" of world affairs, to be solved only by "full withdrawal of Israeli forces from the occupied Arab territories."[172] No mention was made, however, of a political solution to the problem. It was clear that the Soviets, if not endorsing the Egyptian resort to war, were also not actively opposing it.

The line of minimal or no resistance to Egyptian designs had been accentuated a few days earlier in an exchange of telegrams between Brezhnev, Podgorny, Kosygin, and Sadat on the occasion of the twenty-first anniversary of the Egyptian revolution. Contrary to usual practice, the texts of the telegrams were not printed in the Soviet press. Only a summary appeared which indicated that the Soviet leaders had wished Egypt success "in the struggle . . . for liquidation of the consequences of the Israeli aggression of 1967. In this struggle, the Soviet Union as before will act on the side of the righteous cause of friendly Egypt." Sadat was reported to have replied that "the Egyptian people, fighting against the conspiracies of imperialism, at the present time are full of firm and unbending decisiveness to return their usurped lands. . . ."[173]

The Politburo, discussing the results of the Crimean meeting of Party leaders a few days later, indicated that détente was not intended to be a one-sided foreign-policy posture. In the words of the Soviet leadership, "in contemporary international conditions as before, vigilance is necessary against the intrigues of the reactionary forces seeking to interfere with the strengthening of the positive advances in the world arena."[174] While conciliation with the West on some fronts was necessary, this by no means justified Soviet quiescence, particularly when previous Soviet gains appeared in jeopardy. The Soviet decision to balance any impression of weakness conveyed by the policy of détente with a show of strength set the stage for Sadat's final turn toward war.

During August and September 1973 reports began reaching the West that Soviet *Scud* medium-range missiles had been dispatched to Egypt.[175] The arrival of the long-awaited weapons, with their capability to threaten Israel strategically (plus whatever other assurances the Egyptian leader had received from the Russians), was all that Sadat required to consider launching war. With the safety of Egypt's population better assured than at any time in the past by virtue of the *Scud's* deterrent properties, and with the Soviets apparently acquiescing to his plans, Sadat was ready to order his troops into battle. In August 1973, according to "Soviet sources" in Cairo, Sadat gave the word to attack in October.[176]

Unlike the situation immediately following the Six-Day War and during the "war of attrition," Soviet assistance after Nasser's death in 1970 was no longer urgently required to assure the survival of the "progressive" Arab regimes. By successfully rearming and providing an effective air defense for Egypt, the Soviets, ironically, had given the Arabs the possibility for action independent of Moscow's desires.

Nasser's successor, Anwar Sadat, early demonstrated his independence from Moscow by currying favor with domestic and Arab world anti-Communists. Sadat joined his political independence with calls for decisive actions against Israel. These appeals for action against the Jewish state were particularly disturbing to Moscow because (a) the Soviets assumed that in any new war the Arabs would again be defeated by the Israelis, thus highlighting the inefficacy of Moscow's support, and (b) the Soviet Union concurrently did not wish to jeopardize the policy of détente it was about to undertake in relation to the major Western powers.

With these factors in mind, the Soviets in early 1971 warned Sadat that too much talk of independent action might cause Egypt to lose Russian support, the only guarantee for ultimate success against Israel.

Moscow's confidence was shaken, however, by the political downfall of Egyptian pro-Soviet forces led by Aly Sabry in May 1971. In order to reduce the risk of an anti-Soviet backlash, Soviet Chairman Podgorny hastened to Cairo to sign a treaty committing Moscow to supply arms for the reconquest of the occupied territories. As partial compensation for this significant Soviet concession to Egyptian ambitions, Sadat agreed to consult Moscow before any armed action was undertaken.

Soviet-Egyptian good feelings were short-lived, however, as Cairo assisted in the execution of the countercoup which led to the crushing of the Sudanese Communist Party. Moscow's anger at this move was real, but it also did not last long. Driven by fear of losing the loyalty of the "progressive" nationalists, the Russians soon after the Sudan affair made another major concession to Sadat's desire to reignite war against the Israelis.

The Russian concession, reflected in the Egyptian-Soviet "agreement" of October 1971, apparently was of grand enough proportions to convince the Egyptians that war could be safely undertaken against the Israelis. The Indo-Pakistani war and possibly other circumstances intervened, however, and the Soviets did not fulfill their October 1971 "agreement." After some hesitation, the Soviets received Sadat in Moscow in February 1972. The Russians, in exchange for a Sadat commitment to delay initiation of hostilities until after the Nixon-Brezhnev summit, renewed or offered new military undertakings in support of Sadat's ambitions.

In April 1972 Sadat, reflecting his anxieties regarding a superpower deal on the Middle East behind his back, again apprised Moscow of his concerns.

The ambiguous nature of the Soviet position in the wake of the Nixon-Brezhnev summit, however, and the dilatory Russian response to fulfillment of weapons and pledges and possibly other promises made in October 1971 and February 1972 caused Sadat to lose patience with the Russians. In a move that may have been intended more as a symbolic gesture of defiance than as a wholesale across-the-board expulsion, Sadat in July 1972 ordered home Soviet advisers in Egyptian military units. The Egyptian leader also closed Russian bases in Egypt. The Soviets replied to Sadat's move by removing virtually all Russian personnel from Egypt.

As Sadat tried to court the West and Moscow considered the consequences of the major rupture of Soviet and Egyptian ties, both sides came to the conclusion that a reuniting of efforts was preferable to a continued break. For Sadat, it became increasingly apparent that an attack on Israel was impossible without assurance of Soviet weapons and spare parts. For the Russians, the entire premises of their policy in the Third World and among "progressive" elements generally would be undermined if it seemed that the Soviet Union, in concert with the capitalist countries, was engaging in a superpower condominium directed against "progressive" change. The mutual appreciation of the confluence of Soviet-Egyptian interests led to Aziz Sidky's visit to Moscow in October 1972, the restoration of the military spare-parts flow to Egypt, and finally to Hafez Ismail's "warm and friendly" reception in Moscow in February 1973.

In the wake of the February 1973 resurrection of the Soviet-Egyptian entente, the Russians apparently acceded to some of Sadat's outstanding weapons requests. The Egyptian leader pronounced himself fully satisfied with the Russian response and declared that it was time for a "shock" in the Middle East.

The Soviets, however, apparently expressed reservations with regard to Sadat's plans during Hafez Ismail's visit to Moscow in July 1973, but these reservations were short-lived. Even more sensitive to charges of superpower condominium and weakness in the face of "imperialism" after the second Nixon-Brezhnev summit the Russians were not prepared to risk another break with the "progressive" nationalist forces. Noting the dangers of imperialist encroachments in the time of détente, the Soviets justified to themselves the need for acceding to Sadat's request for weapons and other assistance. While not endorsing Sadat's plans for attack, the Soviets said nothing that might be misunderstood as a condemnation of the Egyptian leader's plans.

Russian policy toward the Middle East during the 1971–73 period can thus be understood as a continuing series of capitulations in the face of Egyptian insistence on the renewal of war with Israel. These sequential surrenders were motivated by the fear of losing hard-earned Russian gains among "progressive" nationalists in the Arab world and elsewhere. Though recalcitrant in fulfillment of their continued pledges to the Arabs, largely because of a desire not to jeopardize other major Soviet interests in establishing a détente with the Western powers, the Soviets were eventually dragged into acceding to Arab revanchist desires. The Russian compliance with the Egyptian urge to resort to war, however dangerous the consequences might have seemed to the Soviet leadership, graphically illustrated the importance Moscow continued to attach to the "progressive" cause and the effort to undermine or contain "imperialism."

III The evolution of Soviet weapons supply to Egypt, the most important and crucial Arab belligerent, can be divided into four phases in the post-1967 period: (1) the post-Six-Day War rearmament, (2) the "war of attrition" major reinforcement, (3) the post-Sabry/Sudan "freeze" and reconciliation gesture, and (4) the pre-Yom Kippur War selected increment. An illustration of the approximate evolution of Soviet weapons supply in terms of some major military systems (jet aircraft, surface-to-surface missiles, surface-to-air missiles, artillery, and tanks) in each of the four periods is outlined in table 2.[177]

In the post-Six-Day War period Egypt's devastated air force was rebuilt through the addition of large numbers of obsolescent MIG 15/17 fighter-bombers that presumably were readily available from Soviet surplus stocks. These fighter-bombers, only useful in a ground-support role, were augmented by a substantial number of modern SU-7 ground-attack aircraft. The number of SU-7's delivered was far in excess of the quantity of similar aircraft possessed by Egypt before the Six-Day War. These ground-attack aircraft provided the Egyptians with a means sporadically to harass and fend off Israeli troops along the Suez Canal. The SU-7's and MIG 15/17's, of course, were only of limited

TABLE 2. EGYPTIAN WEAPONS HOLDINGS, 1967–73

	Post-Six-Day War (mid-1967 to mid-1969)	"War of attrition" (mid-1969 to mid-1971)	Post-Sabry/ Sudan (mid-1971 to mid-1972)	Pre-Yom Kippur War (mid-1972 to mid-1973)
Aircraft[a]				
MIG-21 interceptors	100	100→200[b]	200→220[c]	220→210
MIG-19 interceptors	45→ 0	0	0	0
MIG-15/17 fighter-bombers	60→120	120→200	200	200→100
SU-7 fighter-bombers	0→90	90→110	110→120	120→ 80
IL-28 light bombers	20→30	30→ 25	25→ 10	10→ 5
TU-16 medium bombers	0→12[d]	12→ 18	18	18→ 25
Total	225→352	352→553	553→568	568→420
Surface-to-surface missiles				
SAMLETs	some→25	25	25	25→100
FROG 3's	0→24	24	24	24
FROG 7's	0	0	some	some
SCUDs	0	0	0	0→ 30[e]
Total	some→49	49	49→49+	49+→154+
Surface-to-air missiles (number of launchers)				
SAM-2's	150→180	180→420	420→600	600→ ⎫
SAM-3's	0	0→260[f]	260[f]	260→ ⎬780
SAM-6's	0	0[f]	0→some[f]	some→ ⎭ substantial
Total	150→180	180→680	680→860+	869+→780+
Artillery				
Medium and heavy guns	several ⎫→500	500→1,540	1,540	1,540→1,690
Self-propelled guns	hundred ⎬→150	150	150	150
Total	several hundred →650	650→1,690	1,690	1,690→1,740
Antitank weapons				
Antitank guns	numerous	numerous	numerous	numerous
Snapper missiles	some	some	some	some
Sagger missiles	0	0	some	substantial

[a] Mid-1967 figures represent holdings after the intial Soviet resupply.
[b] Plus several Soviet-controlled TU-16 electronic reconnaissance aircraft, present in Egypt until July 1792.
[c] Plus four Soviet-controlled MIG-21 squadrons.
[d] Plus six MIG-21 squadrons, two to four SU-11 interceptor squadrons, and four to six MIG-23 interceptors—all Soviet-controlled.
[e] Interview data. It is believed that they arrived in Egypt in August 1973 or earlier.
[f] Some Soviet-controlled.

TABLE 2. EGYPTIAN WEAPONS HOLDINGS, 1967–73 (*continued*)

	Post-Six-Day War (mid-1967 to mid-1969)	"War of attrition" (mid-1969 to mid-1971)	Post-Sabry/ Sudan (mid-1971 to mid-1972)	Pre-Yom Kippur War (mid-1972 to mid-1973)
Tanks				
T-62 medium tanks	0	0	0→ 10	10→ 100
T-54/55 medium tanks	250→650	650→1,200	1,200→1,500	1,500→1,650
T-34 medium tanks	70→150	150→ 250	250→ 400	400→ 100
IS-III and T-10 heavy tanks	20	20→ 50	50	50→ 30
PT-76 light tanks	0→ 50	50→ 150	150→ 100	100→ 75
Total	370→870	870→1,650	1,650→2,060	2,060→1,955[g]

[g] Interview sources state that this figure is approximately 20 percent lower than it should be. With this adjustment, tanks would number about 2,350.

usefulness for any concentrated offensive effort unless they were protected from enemy attack while in the air.

The MIG-21 interceptors provided by the Soviets to the Egyptians after the Six-Day War could have provided part of the tactical air cover required. However, the Russians, after the Egyptian defeat, had elected to resupply only 60–85 percent of Egypt's prewar MIG-21 holdings. The reduced stock of first-line interceptors would compel Egypt to husband its resources on strategic air defense, thus seriously limiting possibilities of providing combat-zone air cover.

In accordance with Soviet prewar policy, the limited strategic deterrent that had been provided to Egypt was renewed, though in reduced form, by the delivery of a few medium-range bomber aircraft. As a result of the deliveries, Egypt's bomber holdings stood at twelve TU-16 medium bombers and thirty IL-28 light bombers by mid-1969. (Before the Six-Day War, Egypt possessed thirty TU-16's and forty IL-28's. During the war, all but thirteen IL-28's had been destroyed.) It should be noted that the Russians, in addition to not fully replenishing Egypt's bomber inventory, had also failed to upgrade Cairo's bomber stock. The most current Soviet medium bomber, the supersonic TU-22, was not provided to the Egyptians.

Though both the IL-28 and the TU-16 were becoming increasingly obsolescent, the TU-16's, with their twenty-thousand-pound bombloads, still represented a formidable destructive instrument. Egypt's principal problem with the TU-16, however, as before the Six-Day War, was in working out a way to penetrate the bomber's weapons load to its target. Without long-distance interceptor aircraft (needed because of the breadth of the occupied territories) to serve as escorts, the vulnerable subsonic TU-16's, because of their inability to pierce the Israeli air defense, would be largely restricted to launching stand-off missile attacks of low destructive power against Israeli targets.

Because only a few TU-16's were delivered initially, however, and each aircraft could carry only two stand-off missiles,[178] the significance of any Egyptian stand-off missile attack in the postwar period was sharply reduced, even from Cairo's not overly terrifying pre-Six-Day War capabilities. The Soviet failure to fully rebuild Egypt's bomber inventory, therefore, freed Israel from the need for excessive concern with strategic air defense. Consequently, Tel Aviv would have additional aircraft at its disposal to guarantee more easily combat-zone air superiority and to threaten Egypt's interior.

With regard to surface-to-air missiles, the number of SAM-2 launchers provided to Egypt was not significantly increased after the Six-Day War, presumably because of their low wartime effectiveness. While more advanced and more effective models of the SAM-2 would be provided later, during the "war of attrition," the Soviets apparently did not see fit initially to compromise the performance data of these more advanced systems by introducing them into combat in Egypt.

Concerning surface-to-surface missiles, the Egyptians were provided with a limited number of *Samlet* coastal-defense cruise missiles. Similar to the *Kennel* air-to-surface missile earlier deployed on TU-16's in Egypt, the *Samlet* was an eighty-kilometer-range cruise missile which carried a one-thousand- to two-thousand-pound conventional warhead.[179] The *Samlet* was presumably intended to deter Israel's small navy from seeking to envelop the coastal flanks of Egypt's Suez Canal defenses.

The Egyptians also received a small number of *Frog* 3 unguided missiles. Because they were unguided and because their warheads were relatively small (weighing some three hundred pounds),[180] the few *Frogs* provided were only marginally useful for military purposes. Presumably, they were delivered to satisfy symbolically the longstanding Egyptian request for surface-to-surface missiles and to provide an extremely limited quick-reaction battlefield interdiction capability for the Egyptians. Such a tactical interdiction capability might have been useful if the Israelis suddenly began to mass high-value equipment for a cross-Canal assault into Egypt and Egyptian aircraft were unable to operate effectively due to Israeli air superiority.

In the postwar period, Egyptian artillery stocks were rebuilt to only about one-third of their prewar level. This quantity of artillery gave the Egyptians the capability to keep the Israelis at bay but not sufficient firepower to give them confidence in launching a decisive offensive effort. Antitank weapons were also replenished in the postwar period, though no major effort was undertaken to modernize Cairo's stocks with large numbers of contemporary antitank missiles.

Egypt's tank inventory, on the other hand, was gradually built up after the Six-Day War to a level equal to approximately 70 percent of the prewar sum. An increasing portion of the tank stocks was made up of contemporary T-54/55 tanks. By mid-1969, the number of T-54/55 tanks in Egypt significantly exceeded the prewar level. The Russian decision to upgrade the Egyptian tank stock was reflected in the fact that, though the quantity of World War II-era T-34's was also slowly increased, the proportion of T-34's to T-54/55's in the Egyptian forces declined from 3:5 to 1:4. The improvement of the Egyptian tank stock may have been dictated less by military-technical concerns than by the simple factor of availability. As previously noted, T-62 medium tanks were entering the Soviet Forces in large numbers in the early and mid-1960s, and presumably more T-54/55 tanks were available for export.

The post-Six-Day War Egyptian weapons build-up thus can be seen as a Soviet effort to rebuild the Egyptian armed forces to a point where Nasser's regime would not be completely vulnerable to Israeli attack. On the other hand, Moscow did not provide a weapons supply sufficient for Cairo successfully to attack Israeli forces and to recover the occupied territories. Nasser's realization that the Soviets were not ready to provide weapons permitting quick and massive counteraction against Tel Aviv led the Egyptian leader to adopt a policy of delaying Egyptian offensive action and embarking on a long-term reconstruction of the Egyptian armed forces.

Once the renewal of the armed forces had evidenced substantial progress, however, Nasser was drawn toward finding a form of military pressure against Israel. In Nasser's view, such military pressure hopefully would not require resort to total war but, at the same time, would inflict substantial punishment on Tel Aviv's forces. The formula hit upon, the "war of attrition," would allow Nasser to bleed the Israelis slowly without having to undertake a major offensive action; that is, such a "war" would not require a major movement forward of Egyptian troops (which Cairo, with its existing weapons, still could not successfully execute).

Though the Soviets initially opposed Nasser's plans, they had already given the Egyptians sufficient weapons to launch limited hostilities. The Russians, therefore, were incapable of forestalling the Egyptian actions, even if they judged such a move politically expedient. The Soviets could, of course, have curtailed Cairo's campaign by refusing to ship replacement ammunition. The Soviet desire to appear firmly in support of the Egyptians, however, militated against any overt restraint of Nasser.

When the Israelis, in retaliation for the Egyptian "war of attrition," resorted to devastating air attacks on the Egyptian forces and interior,

Moscow stepped in to dilute Israel's weapons superiority. First, the Soviets dramatically built up the Egyptian air defense through a doubling of Cairo's stock of MIG-21 interceptors and a trebling and qualitative improvement of the Egyptian inventory of surface-to-air missiles. In addition, Soviet-piloted interceptors, air-defense crews, and SAM-2 and SAM-3 installations were dispatched to Egypt.

In a much less noticed concurrent move, however, the Russians also markedly increased Egypt's tactical offensive capabilities. SU-7 and MIG-15/17 ground-attack aircraft were increased by some 50 percent, the Egyptian artillery inventory was built up by some 200 percent, and tanks were increased by 100 percent. In addition, the strategic threat was slightly raised by adding more TU-16 bombers. In all categories of weapons, with the notable exception of long-range bombers, the Egyptians, at the close of the "war of attrition," were in a better position than they had been before the Six-Day War.

While the build-up of Egypt's tactical offensive capabilities might have been part of a long-term Egyptian-Soviet plan for restoration of Cairo's military establishment, the grandiose nature of the Soviet supply effort during the "war of attrition" appeared to represent a basically new Russian orientation toward Egyptian military designs. Rather than simply providing weapons to deter the Israelis from taking further action against Egypt, the Soviets seemed ready to endorse the possibility of, and to provide the means for, limited Egyptian action against the Israelis.

Confirmation of the new offensively oriented Soviet frame of reference was provided by the delivery of amphibious landing equipment to Egypt (possibly for cross-Canal operations) in summer 1970.[181] In addition to the landing equipment, the most modern Soviet military bridging equipment (the PMP portable bridge) was also delivered in this period. Soviet-assisted tactical planning for cross-Canal operations also apparently began in the post-1970 period.[182]

In spite of the Russian decision to give the Egyptians a trans-Suez offensive capacity, however, the dimensions of Soviet restraint should not be ignored. The Soviet restraint on weapons supplies was one of the prime causes of Sadat's decision to expel Soviet military advisers in July 1972. The Russians, in spite of the "war of attrition" build-up, had not provided the Egyptians with the MIG-25, their highest-performance interceptor (referred to by Westerners in this period as MIG-23), nor had they dispatched contemporary means of strategic attack such as the TU-22 medium bomber or the *Scud* and *Sandal* medium-range missiles. These Russian limitations, in Egyptian eyes, seriously restricted Cairo's capabilities to undertake offensive action. The struggle to remove these limitations constituted the crux of the constant wrangling that took place between the Egyptians and Soviets in the period between the "war of attrition" and the Yom Kippur War.

In Nasser's opinion, the American delivery of Phantom fighter-bombers to Israel (begun in September 1969) had disrupted the equilibrium that would have allowed him to wage the "war of attrition" successfully. As he told James Reston, the Phantom "can carry about seven tons of bombs and it is a long-range plane which can reach any part of our country. . . . Why did the United States agree to give such weapons to Israel when the Israelis were in a position of air superiority? The answer is that these weapons were given to be used against us in offensive action, against our military formations, and against our industrial buildings, and against our civil population. . . . These weapons are not to defend Israel against aggression, but to give Israel the power to force us to accept what the United States wants."[183] The Phantom, according to Nasser, made Egypt vulnerable and, hence, subjected Cairo to the dictates of Tel Aviv.

In order to remove this lever from Israel's hands, Cairo needed to ensure that it had (a) an air defense which could frustrate any Israeli attack, and (b) a means to strike deep into Israeli-held territory for the purpose of deterring Israeli attack and/or putting reciprocal pressure on Tel Aviv. As Nasser stated, "If (Israeli) air raids reach the industrial centers, this will not only be the industrial centers of Egypt, it will also be the industrial centers of Israel."[184]

As pointed out previously, an Egyptian (nonballistic missile) strategic strike capability would also have the military advantages of forcing Israel to maintain more of its combat aircraft in a strategic air-defense role, thus lessening the capability of Tel Aviv both to maintain air superority over the tactical battlefield and to project strikes into Egypt's interior. An Egyptian strategic threat was therefore important if Cairo were to undertake any major offensive action.

Cairo's request for the MIG-23(25) was connected, on the one hand, with the Egyptian desire to acquire the surest means of interception of attacking Phantoms. As Sadat remarked, the MIG-23(25) was "needed to counter the Phantoms."[185] Soviet provision of an augmented and apparently effective air-defense system to Egypt, however, presumably allayed some of Cairo's anxiety regarding the need for the MIG-23(25) as an air-defense interceptor. A second Egyptian concern, the need for the MIG-23(25) to escort Egyptian bombers over Israeli-held territory, remained to be satisfied, however.

When queried about Egyptian receipt of TU-16 bombers and Soviet-piloted MIG-25 aircraft (in late 1971), Egyptian leader Sadat made the following reply: "Israel says that if we try to get our own land back, she will strike at Egypt's heartland once again. They have already bombed our factories and schools with napalm in January 1970. Naturally, we have to be prepared to pay them back in kind. If they hit our heartland, we will hit theirs—and we have developed a capability to do so."[186] The capability to which Sadat referred could, of course, be realized only if Egyptian bombers or other weapons successfully reached their targets.

Because of the short combat radius of MIG-21 interceptors (350 miles), the Egyptians had no high-performance aircraft which could safely escort and adequately protect the TU-16 bombers over the Israeli heartland. As previously mentioned, Nasser's friend Mohamed Heikal had cited this deficiency as one of the principal motivations for adopting the "war of attrition" strategy rather than a posture involving a deep projection of Egyptian power. The MIG-23(25), however, had a combat radius of some seven hundred miles,[187] making it ideal for the escort of bombers.

The Soviets, probably realizing the potential of the MIG-23(25) for permitting a major Egyptian bombing attack and offensive action, and not wishing to compromise the security of the advanced aircraft, resorted to various delaying tactics to hold off delivery of the plane to Egypt. Reportedly, according to Sadat, the Russians claimed that the MIG-23(25) was so complicated that it would take five years to train Egyptian pilots in its operation. (Egyptian experts allegedly told Sadat that six months was a more likely time period for retraining MIG-21 pilots.) In any event, the Soviets stated that they would initially supply MIG-25's to Egypt only with Soviet pilots and only on the condition that the aircraft remain under Soviet control. Sadat, though resentful of the Russian conditions, accepted Moscow's offer because Egypt needed a "credible deterrent" to the Phantom.[188]

Four to six Soviet-piloted MIG-25's reached Egypt in late 1971 (some two years after the initial Egyptian request) and were used by the Soviets exclusively for reconnaissance flights at extremely high altitudes (eighty thousand feet) over the occupied territories and Israel proper.[189] Though the Israelis attempted to intercept the MIG-25, they were unsuccessful because of their Phantom's inability to close with the MIG-25 at its high altitudes of operation. Regardless of persistent Egyptian efforts, MIG-25's were never delivered to Egyptian control, nor were any more than the initial four to six ever provided to Egypt even under Soviet operation. The MIG-25 thus never provided a solution to Cairo's search for a means to guarantee penetration to Israeli strategic targets.

The Soviet TU-22 supersonic medium bomber, because of its 300–400-mile-per-hour speed advantage over the TU-16, would presumably have increased Egyptian strategic bombing penetration possibilities.[190] In addition, the higher speed of the TU-22 would have permitted a less vulnerable basing of the aircraft in the deepest areas of Egypt, without providing Israel with significant additional warning time. According to Western sources, the Egyptians allegedly wished to receive the TU-22 armed with the *Kitchen* stand-off missile, the most advanced and presumably longest-range Soviet air-to-surface model.[191] If an ultra-long-range stand-off weapon could be obtained, the Egyptians may have thought, bomber aerial vulnerability problems would be significantly reduced. The Russians, however, both before and during the Yom Kippur War declined to provide the TU-22 and the *Kitchen* missile to Egypt.[192]

Ballistic missiles offered an even more tempting strategic bombardment alternative for the Egyptians. Ever since the late 1950s, Egypt had sought to obtain surface-to-surface missiles. With their quick flight time, ballistic missiles offered the best answer to Egypt's penetration dilemma. Precisely because of their effectiveness and lack of warning time, however, ballistic missiles invited enemy first strikes. They also, of course, might spur Egyptian "adventurism." Perhaps for these reasons, Russia, until the eve of the Yom Kippur War, did not dispatch even a few medium-range ballistic missiles to Egypt.

In the period after the Sabry/Sudan coups and the "freeze" in Soviet-Egyptian relations that followed, the Soviets sought to recoup the loyalty of Cairo through the provision of certain added and newly supplied weapons. A few Soviet-controlled MIG-25's were finally sent to Egypt, the Soviet aircraft and SAM air-defense presence was somewhat increased, tanks were added, and new weapons such as the refined (and possibly guided) *Frog* 7 tactical rocket and *Sagger* antitank missile were delivered. More importantly, the Russians entered into the undisclosed "agreement" of October 1971, which apparently committed the Soviets to some action or delivery in connection with an Egyptian resort to hostilities.

When the Russians did not live up to the terms of their "agreement" and did not provide Egypt with the kinds of "offensive weapons" which Cairo sought (presumably weapons associated with strategic bombardment), Sadat expelled Soviet military advisors in July 1972. In the wake of the expulsion, a reconciliation took place between Cairo and Moscow, and an apparent modus vivendi regarding weapons supplies was agreed upon. In spring 1973, as mentioned, Sadat pronounced himself completely satisfied with Soviet arms deliveries.

While one can only speculate on the contents of the Soviet-Egyptian reconciliation accord, an examination of the change in Egyptian arms holdings in the period before the Yom Kippur War may provide some clues. In terms of aircraft, before the Yom Kippur War Egypt's total inventory showed a marked decline, largely because of the retirement into storage of obsolescent and worn-out aircraft.[193] However, significantly, Egypt's stock of TU-16 bombers had been increased. (Egypt's

TU-16's, by the start of the Yom Kippur War, were armed with *Kelt* stand-off missiles.[194] The 180-kilometer-range *Kelts* were presumably of far shorter range and lower payload than the previously sought *Kitchen* missile. On the other hand, they provided double the range of the *Kennel* stand-off missile possessed by Egypt before the Six-Day War. The *Kelts*, hence, considerably enhanced the possibility of successful missile launches without Israeli interception of Egyptian bombers.[195]) In addition, a few SU-20 highly advanced ground-attack aircraft were provided to Egypt and Syria in early 1973. This delivery was extremely significant because the cited aircraft was still not deployed even in the Soviet armed forces.

Turning to surface-to-surface missiles, Egypt's stock of coastal-defense *Samlet* missiles had been considerably built up. More importantly, Egypt had received some thirty *Scud* medium-range missiles. The 180-kilometer-range *Scud* could hit Israeli southern coastal cities from the northeastern corner of unoccupied Egypt near Port Said. Most significantly, though partially serviced and operated by Soviet personnel, the *Scuds* had been placed under Egyptian operational control.[196]

The addition of this rocket allowed Egyptian forces sure strategic penetration for the first time and was undoubtedly an important factor in Egyptian calculations regarding war. In the event of war, Israel would not be able to attack Egypt's heartland without risking retaliation. Interestingly enough, two years before, Sadat had referred to possible future supply of medium-range missiles to Israel as "a very serious escalation of the Middle East dispute."[197] This remark perhaps was revealing of Sadat's attitude toward the *Scud*.

Concerning surface-to-air missiles, Egypt in the period preceding the Yom Kippur War apparently received increments of mobile SAM-6 low-level antiaircraft missiles mounted on the PT-76 light tank chassis. Though some of these weapons first appeared around Aswan in 1971, most were believed to have been withdrawn in the wake of the July 1972 expulsion of Soviet advisers from Egypt. (Many of the weapons, in fact, may not have been removed from Egypt.)[198] Considering their wartime rate of use, significant numbers of missiles appear to have been added in 1973.[199]

In the year before the war, Egyptian artillery was marginally increased. In addition, infantry-operated antitank weapons such as the *Sagger* missile were apparently delivered in large numbers.[200]

Though the overall number of Egyptian tanks dropped (according to some figures) because of the retirement of obsolescent T-34's, the number of more contemporary T-54/55 and first-line Soviet T-62 tanks supplied to Egypt increased fairly significantly.

Summarizing the prewar weapons increments, then, it appears that the Soviets made major changes in two dimensions: (1) they increased the strategic threat to Israel by the addition to the Egyptian forces of the assured penetration capabilities of the *Scud* and the provision of additional TU-16's; and (2) they augmented Egypt's tactical offensive capabilities by increasing the supply of antiaircraft and antitank weaponry.

According to some sources, Soviet weapons supplies to Egypt in the years after the Six-Day War had apparently been governed by certain limitations. At the time of the 1972 expulsion of Soviet advisers, Sadat reportedly had told the Central Committee of the Arab Socialist Union that as early as 1971 he had protested against "any and all limitations in relation to the use of weapons of any type. . . . Egypt's political decision must remain exclusively in the hands of Egypt's political leadership . . . without having to ask permission for anything of this kind from anybody abroad."[201] Thus, if Sadat's account was correct, certain unspecified uses of Russian-supplied weapons were apparently banned.

What uses were banned? And were there any other Russian limitations? The only detailed answer to these questions has come from Moscow's antagonists, the Chinese. According to Peking, Russian arms sales to the Arabs had four no's attached to them: (a) no selling of offensive weapons, (b) no permission to use the weapons sold to recover the lost territories, (c) no adequate supply of ammunition and spare parts, and (d) no delivery to the buyer of certain weapons sold (that is, operation of advanced weapons would be by Soviet personnel only).[202]

While one cannot substantiate the implied Chinese accusation that the Soviets adhered to a formal set of restrictions regarding weapons sales, Sadat's repeated complaints concerning the nature and conditions of Russian arms deliveries seem to bear this out. If not formalized, certain limitations similar to those on the Chinese list seem to have been consistently maintained in practice by the Soviets.

Surveying the various limitations on the Chinese list, we find that the following curbs were removed by Moscow before and during the Yom Kippur War: (a) Egypt received an "offensive weapon" (the *Scud* missile), which provided for the first time the assured capability of subjecting Israel to a strategic bombardment—Egypt's repeated appeals for "offensive weapons" seemingly had been motivated by the desire to receive this capability; (b) Soviet weapons were used extensively to attack the Israelis and recover the occupied territories; (c) ammunition and spare parts were supplied to the Arabs by air during the war; and (d) the *Scud* missiles, though serviced by Soviet personnel, were placed under Egyptian command and control.

If Russian limitations, in fact, had been maintained in a manner similar to that of the Chinese listing, which seems probable, the Soviet Union made rather substantial qualitative concessions in response to

Sadat's insistence on war. By eliminating certain previously observed Soviet restraints, Moscow opened the way for the Egyptian leader to wage war.

Quantitatively, however, at least in terms of "offensive weapons," the Russians were still restrained. Only thirty *Scuds* were supplied, and the few MIG-25's which made their reappearance in Egypt (that is, after their July 1972 removal) did not arrive until the closing periods of the Yom Kippur War. Even then they remained under Soviet control.[203] Thus, while permitting Sadat to undertake his chosen course, Moscow did not go out of its way to facilitate realization of the Egyptian leader's goals.

The weapons inventories of the other Middle East arms clients of the Soviet Union on the eve of the Yom Kippur War consisted of the following:[204]

SYRIA
Aircraft
    200 MIG-21 interceptors
     80 MIG-17 fighter-bombers
     80 SU-7 fighter-bombers
    Some IL-28 light bombers
Surface-to-air missiles
    12 batteries of SAM-2 and SAM-3
    Substantial numbers of SAM-6
Surface-to-surface missiles[205]
    Some Frog 7 missiles
Artillery
    Substantial numbers of medium and heavy guns
    75 SU-100 self-propelled guns
Anti-tank weapons
    Substantial numbers of antitank guns and *Snapper* and *Sagger* anti-tank missiles
Tanks
    30 IS-III heavy tanks
    240 T-34 medium tanks
    900 T-54/55 medium tanks
    Some T-62 medium tanks
    100 PT-76 light tanks

IRAQ
Aircraft
    90 MIG-21 interceptors
    60 SU-7 fighter-bombers
    30 MIG-17 fighter-bombers
     8 TU-16 medium bombers

One squadron of TU-22 medium bombers (piloted and controlled by Soviets)

Surface-to-air Missiles

Some SAM-2 and SAM-3

Artillery

700 medium and heavy guns

Tanks

900 T-54/55 medium tanks

90 T-34 medium tanks

45 PT-76 light tanks

In Syria, Russian activity had risen particularly after the summer 1972 Soviet-Syrian arms accord. Soviet advisers had been introduced in larger numbers in Syrian military units, including those in the immediate proximity of Israeli forces. The participation of Russian personnel in Syrian air defense also markedly increased as more sophisticated Russian SAM's were introduced for the first time.

Syria, like Egypt, had received large inputs of weapons such as tanks, antitank missiles, and mobile SAM's, which increased its tactical offensive capabilities. While apparently not receiving the strategic capability against principal Israeli cities represented by the *Scud*, the Soviet delivery of short-range (40-kilometer) *Frog 7*'s allowed the Syrians, because of their propinquity to the Israeli heartland, to hit neighboring Israeli military airfields and villages.

Iraq, also, had received large numbers of tanks. In addition, perhaps because of its warmer relations with the Soviet Union, Iraq, unlike Egypt, had highly advanced Soviet-controlled supersonic TU-22 medium bombers based on its territory. While these aircraft may have been intended by the Russians to exercise a Persian Gulf-oriented role, their presence in Iraq could not but deter Israeli strategic strikes.

In summation, Soviet arms deliveries from the Six-Day War to the Yom Kippur War exhibited the following variations in content and emphasis. After a gradual infusion of replacement weaponry into the shattered Egyptian forces in the two years following the 1967 debacle, Soviet supplies markedly increased in the 1969–71 period of the "war of attrition." Not only was Egyptian air defense improved, but a cross-Canal tactical offensive capacity was provided.

While the Soviets, in the "war of attrition" period, partially countered the introduction of advanced American Phantom fighter-bomber aircraft into the Israeli forces by providing an excellent air-defense system, Egypt was denied an effective strategic bombardment capability to balance fully the added threat posed by the high-payload Israeli

Phantoms. The Russians, in all probability, maintained this limitation in order to restrain any independent Egyptian initiative to launch major hostilities.

In the wake of Russian Middle East setbacks occasioned by the abortive 1971 Sabry and Sudan coups, the Soviets, in order to curry Arab favor, provided added weapons to Cairo and apparently committed themselves to certain undisclosed actions and deliveries in connection with possible Egyptian resort to hostilities. Egyptian dissatisfaction with the fulfillment of the Soviet pledge led to the expulsion of Russian military advisers from Egypt in July 1972.

In early 1973, a reconciliation was reached between the Soviets and Egyptians. Cairo's supply of tactical armaments was selectively augmented, and Egypt for the first time received an "offensive weapon" (the *Scud*) which permitted military action to be carried to the homeland of Israel. Moreover, the weapon was placed under the control of Egypt, not the Soviet Union, as had been the case with the MIG-25 aircraft. Tel Aviv, in the event of a renewal of hostilities, would have the 100 percent surety that if it struck the Egyptian interior, its own urban centers could be hit. This firmed guarantee of the protection of the Egyptian heartland had long been sought by Nasser and Sadat, and presumably it eased the latter's decision in favor of hostilities.

In addition to provision for the first time of an assured limited strategic threat, the Soviet Union may have dropped certain other previously existing restraints. Arab stocks of ammunition and spare parts, which formerly may have been strictly limited, certainly were augmented during the course of hostilities, if not before. In addition, restrictions on certain uses of Soviet-supplied weapons, which, according to Sadat's statements, were maintained by the Russians, were either dropped or modified before the commencement of war.

In parallel with Egyptian developments, the forces of Russia's other clients in the Middle East were significantly built up. In short, the Russians, though probably reluctant to see hostilities between the Arabs and Israelis commence, eliminated the barriers to the Arabs' resort to war. Most significantly, this move was probably not the result of a premeditated act of volition. The Russians, fearful of losing the loyalty of the "progressive" Arabs, had succumbed to Sadat's persistent blandishments. The Arabs, not the Russians, now controlled the flow of events toward war in the Middle East.

IV By the beginning of September 1973, Sadat and his Syrian allies were moving inexorably toward hostilities with Israel. While the Russians were not blocking Arab resort to war, they also appeared not to be encouraging it. Some evidence is available, in fact, which suggests that the Russians, in the months preceding the Yom Kippur War, urged the Arabs to wait two to three more years before launching war.[206] The two- to three-year hiatus mentioned by the Soviet may have constituted the time required for training Arab pilots for the MIG-23(25) or other advanced aircraft, or, alternatively, it may have referred to the period of completion by the Egyptians of training on the Soviet-designed plan to reconquer the occupied territories. Reportedly, only the first stage of the plan—the crossing of the Canal—had so far been mastered.[207]

The Chinese, perhaps detecting the Russians' cautions to the Arabs, noted that "the Soviet revisionist clique has sent high ranking officials to the Middle East in an effort to quiet down the strong discontent of the Arab people. . . ."[208] Whatever the nature of the back-channel Soviet attempts to stem the Arab movement toward war, these efforts were neither successful nor publicly visible. The dominant note propagated by the Soviet media in the month preceding the outbreak of hostilities concerned, not the danger of war in the Middle East, but, rather, the hazards of anti-Sovietism.[209]

Moscow's concern with the inroads of anti-Soviet influence in the Arab world and elsewhere was probably heightened by the downfall of the Chilean Marxist regime of Salvador Allende in early September 1973. The Chilean events were taken extremely seriously in the Soviet Union and dominated the Soviet media through the month of September. In certain organs, such as the Trade Union Council's newspaper, *Trud*, coverage of the aftereffects of the Chilean uprising would extend well into October and would even shadow reportage on the Middle East War.

The overthrow of Allende was characterized by the Soviet leadership as the product of a conspiracy between local "reactionaries" and aggressive foreign "imperialists." In the words of the Soviet Communist Party Central Committee, the anti-Allende coup was "the culmination of the subversive activities of Chilean reaction" which was "supported by foreign imperialist forces for all of the three years of the Popular Government's tenure in power. . . ."[210]

From the point of view of the Soviet leadership, the fall of the Allende government probably served as an extremely undesirable accompaniment to its foreign-policy posture of détente with the major Western powers. Radical elements in the Middle East as well as in other areas of the Third World had already criticized détente as a betrayal of the "progressive" movement.[211] The overthrow of the Allende government would undoubtedly lead to further questions. For example, were the advantages of a more benign Soviet foreign policy worth their price?

Apparently some Communists answered no. General Secretary Brezhnev, in a highly unusual move, would acknowledge in late September that the agreements resulting from Strategic Arms Limitations Talks (SALT I) with the United States, held up in the past as a paragon of détente, had been criticized, possibly in the Soviet Union, as useless "half-measures."[212]

Soviet self-consciousness about the détente posture, heightened by the Allende coup, would prompt serious concern about the "intrigues of imperialism" and those of local "reactionaries" in and against the "progressive" Arab states. In addition, the threat of Arab deviation in the direction of Peking would also be a cause for concern.[213] Soviet disquiet at the flow of world events in the late summer of 1973 would spur a turn away from cautions toward endorsement of Arab attempts to achieve a "united front" to prepare for battle against Israel.

From the Soviet point of view, the establishment of an anti-Israeli "united front" would probably have the following advantages: (a) the possibility for the avoidance of an abysmal defeat for the "progressive" regimes would be enhanced in the event of an Arab resort to war; (b) the attention of traditional, nationalist anti-Communist, and ultra-revolutionary elements in the Arab world would be diverted from criticism of the Soviet Union to confrontation with Israel; (c) an opportunity would be provided for the Soviet Union to demonstrate its militance, even in a time of détente, by endorsing Arab actions against "expansionist" Israel; and (d) a magnet would be created to attract the traditional, oil-rich Arab kingdoms into an anti-Western orientation.

While the cause of détente might be set back by a Soviet-endorsed Arab anti-Israeli crusade, there was reason to believe that damage would not be excessive. U.S. support for Israel was, in Moscow's view, more than a little ambiguous. As the Soviet radio, drawing on a recent American vote against Tel Aviv in the United Nations, pointed out to its Arab listeners, "Israel is increasingly isolated. The United States is no longer in a position to stand unconditionally and unreservedly on the side of the aggressors."[214] Because of the supposed qualified U.S. backing of Israel, Moscow probably assumed that its risks in supporting Arab aspirations for battle were correspondingly reduced.

On 10 September 1973, in an important prelude to war, Egyptian leader Sadat met with Syria's President Assad and Jordan's King Hussein in Cairo. The announced purpose of the meeting was to coordinate the efforts of the three leaders in the "struggle against Israeli aggression." As Jordan and Syria had not maintained relations since the September 1970 *fedayeen* crisis, the Cairo meeting clearly marked an important watershed in intra-Arab relations. It can reasonably be surmised that by the end of the meeting, the three leaders had agreed on joint efforts to prepare the coming war. Moscow signaled its appreciation of the prowar bent of the Cairo meeting by pointing out that "the struggle against Israeli aggression is the one field in which the Arab countries can best use not that which divides them but that which unites them."[215]

In the wake of the Sadat-Assad-Hussein meeting, perhaps as a warning to the Arabs, the Israeli air force, on September 13, drew Syrian MIG's into combat over the Mediterranean. While it is still not clear whether the Israelis intentionally provoked the air battle, the result of the confrontation was a humiliating Syrian loss of eight to thirteen aircraft with one Israeli plane shot down.[216] According to one source, after the air clash Syrian President Assad telephoned Sadat and asserted that the time had arrived to issue final battle orders to their troops. The Egyptian president agreed.[217]

Following the September 13 aerial confrontation, reports appeared in the Middle East indicating that during the course of the battle Soviet advisers in Syria had refused to permit the firing of SAM missiles at Israeli aircraft passing near their positions. As a result of these alleged Soviet actions, some Russian advisers were reportedly expelled from Syria, and the movement of others was restricted. As in the case of many other reports in the pre-Yom Kippur War period, there are grounds for believing that the reports of Soviet-Syrian tension may, in fact, have been Arab-inspired "disinformation" to cover the growing preparations for war. For one thing, Soviet movements in Syria had always been highly limited and controlled.[218] The trend of Russian statements in mid-September seemed to belie any overt Soviet resistance to Arab war plans.

By the middle of September it was more and more apparent that Moscow had, in fact, fallen into line as at least a partial backer of the pending Arab attack. In addition to news commentary praising Syrian courage in the September 13 air battle, Soviet foreign broadcasts and newspapers began repeating false reports from the Arab press indicating that Israeli forces were massing on the Golan Heights borders with Syria. (In fact, the only major Israeli reinforcement in the Golan Heights was the September 26–29 movement of one armored brigade into the area.)[219] Radio Moscow told its listeners in the Arab world on September 17, for example, that "the Arab press reports that Israel is massing troops and equipment on the occupied Golan Heights region."[220] These accounts were repeated in other Soviet overseas transmissions.[221]

More alarmingly, the reports of Israeli troops concentrations began to be picked up by Soviet domestic organs. The official newspaper of the Soviet ministry of defense, *Krasnaya zvezda*, on September 23 quoted

Israeli Chief of Staff General David Elazar to the effect that Israel was going "over to a policy of unleashing attacks." The newspaper continued that Tel Aviv had made "large military preparations . . . on the ceasefire line with Syria and on the borders of Lebanon" and that newspapers had published photographs of "the concentration of military equipment in the border areas." In addition, Israeli aircraft were accused of continually violating Arab air space.[222]

The false accusations of an Israeli force build-up on the Syrian border were reminiscent of the pre-Six-Day War period; however, unlike in 1967, the Soviets were echoing rather than generating the misinformation.

In addition to verbal support, the Soviets were also apparently stepping up their weapons supplies. A study of the Bureau of Intelligence and Research of the Department of State apparently indicates that some one thousand tanks (25 percent of the total Soviet shipments from the Six-Day War until October 1973) were delivered to the Arab belligerents in the month preceding the Yom Kippur War.[223]

Concurrent with the appearance of more militant tones in Soviet policy and the press, Soviet General Secretary Brezhnev journeyed to Sofia on September 18, purportedly for talks with Bulgarian leader Todor Zhivkov. On September 21, the Italian Communist newspaper L'Unita published a report that the Soviet leader (on September 20) had decided to extend his stay in Bulgaria for one day (until September 21) in order to go to an undisclosed location.[224] The mystery of the L'Unita information was subsequently heightened by reports that Egyptian leader Sadat had no publicly announced appointments in Cairo during the period of Brezhnev's visit to Sofia.[225] Sadat's seeming disappearance, coupled with the absence of the Egyptian ambassador to the Soviet Union, Yahya abd-al Qadir, from Moscow,[226] raised speculation that the Egyptian leader and Brezhnev had held meetings in Bulgaria. The existence of Brezhnev-Sadat meetings cannot be definitely confirmed, however, and may well be false. For what it is worth, the Bulgarian radio reported that during Brezhnev's visit, the Soviet leader, besides attending official receptions and delivering a major policy speech, briefly visited Razgrad oblast, presented awards to several workers, and engaged in talks in the Vrana government residence in Sofia.[227]

Later in Cairo, on September 22, according to one report, Sadat called in Soviet Ambassador Vinogradov and handed him a letter to transmit to Moscow.[228] If this report is correct, Sadat's letter may have been the final Egyptian signal to the Soviets that war was imminent. While one cannot in certainty confirm that Sadat did transmit a letter to Brezhnev on September 22, several indications appeared which suggest that by mid-September the Soviets may have become aware of the imminent onset of war and were making suitable preparations.

On September 25, a small article appeared in *Krasnaya zvezda* which indicated that a five-day military exercise had just concluded in Hungary. The exercise reportedly included participation by the Hungarian army and "some units of the Southern Group of Soviet Forces."[229] This military exercise, which on the surface appeared routine, would seem more ominous two weeks later when it emerged that Hungary had become the principal staging area for the shipment of weapons and ammunition from Warsaw Pact stocks to the Arab belligerents.[230]

On September 26, Soviet Minister of Defense and Politburo member Marshal A. A. Grechko, air force commander Chief Air Marshal P. G. Kutakhov, Ground Forces Commander-in-Chief General I. G. Pavlovsky, and chief of the Political Administration of the Soviet Armed Forces General Yepishev were reported in the Carpathian Military District checking on "training." The high level of the armed forces leadership present for a simple inspection in a single, not overly significant, military district was unusual indeed. The reason for the visit may have been the fact that the Carpathian Military District borders on Hungary.[231]

One can hypothesize that in the coming weeks it was envisaged that military equipment located in the western Soviet Union might be trans-shipped through the Carpathian Military District for onward movement to Egypt and Syria from Hungary, that the troops in the Carpathian Military District were to be prepared to move into Hungary if any NATO threat emerged in the aftermath of the drawdown on Warsaw Pact Munitions and equipment, or that simply a joint Soviet-Hungarian military meeting was taking place.[232] These hypotheses are, of course, purely speculative.

Apart from military preparations, Moscow began to signal to the West that war was imminent. According to "a Soviet diplomat" (possibly Ambassador to the United States Dobrynin), the Soviet Union from June to September 1973 had already repeatedly warned the United States that the military situation in the Middle East was becoming more serious. While the Soviets claimed to have told the United States that war was "imminent," American officials alleged that Russian warnings were in fact much more vague. In the month preceding the Arab attack, however, the Soviet behind-the-scenes warnings ceased.[233] In their place, public declarations and acts conveying the seriousness of the emerging situation came to the fore.

At the U.N. General Assembly, for example, Soviet Foreign Minister Andrei Gromyko declared that in the Middle East "the flame of war risks breaking out at any time and who can predict to what consequences this will lead?"[234] In the communiqué issued at the end of

Chairman Kosygin's visit to Yugoslavia (September 24–October 1), both parties expressed "deep anxiety" over the situation in the Middle East.[235] Finally, on October 3 Soviet dependents were gathered hurriedly and flown out of Syria and Egypt by Russian aircraft.[236]

The seemingly unnecessary evaluation of Soviet dependents (no other Communist or foreign dependents were removed) and other overt acts accessible to the West[237] presumably were intended, at least in part, to provide a signal of the Arab attack to the major capitalist powers.[238] These highly unorthodox Soviet moves may have been designed both to express caution to the Arabs and to lessen the likelihood that an otherwise totally surprised West would respond to the Arab attack in a spasmodic manner. The tacit notification to the West presumably was intended to convey an impression of Russian responsibility and restraint.[239] This picture of restraint and responsibility would be deeply stained, however, a few days later as thousands of Russian-built tanks charged against Israeli positions and plunged the Middle East again into war.

In the month preceding the Yom Kippur Arab attack on Israeli forces Soviet attention shifted from urging the Arabs to postpone war to endorsement of Arab preparations for hostilities. The turnabout in Soviet attitudes may have been conditioned to a great degree by the overthrow of the Chilean Marxist government of Salvador Allende in early September. The downfall of Allende heightened Soviet anxiety that the forces of "imperialism" would use détente to seek to undermine the "progressive" movement. In order to deliver a riposte to the "imperialists" and to clarify the Soviet understanding of détente to the West, the Russians decided to acquiesce to Arab inclinations to embark on war.

The Soviet decision in favor of endorsing the Arab resort to war was probably eased by two considerations. Firstly, the United States seemed somewhat ambiguously committed to Israel. Secondly, Arab nations of all political stripes had been brought closer together in a "united front" directed against Israel. This "united front" would make the destruction of the "progressive" regimes less likely during the course of a war, would stem the dangerous growth of Arab criticism of the Soviet Union, and would preserve the unity of the Arab "progressive" forces.

In the wake of the commencement of Soviet support for the Arab resort to war, Russian newspapers and foreign broadcasts began to echo false Arab accusations that Israel was building up forces on its borders in preparation for an attack on Syria. In addition, certain military steps were taken which in all probability were connected with preparation for the possible resupply of the Arabs during the course of the coming war.

In spite of its endorsement and preparation for the Middle East war, however, the Soviets did not cut all ties to the West. In seeming contravention to the Arabs' supreme interest in secrecy, the Russians, continuing a series of veiled warnings to the West, made several public statements at the end of September which hinted at the imminence of war. More importantly, the Soviets demonstratively removed their dependents from the belligerent Arab states three days in advance of the Arab surprise attack. While not going so far as to sabotage the Arab war plans, the apparently needless Russian advance evacuation of dependents was a gesture which indicated both reservations as to the Arabs' cause and a sense that the West's reactions would have to be mollified.

CHAPTER FIVE † THE OCTOBER WAR

At 2:00 P.M. on 6 October 1973—Yom Kippur, the most holy day of Jewish worship—massive Egyptian and Syrian forces launched Operation *Badr*, a simultaneous attack on undermanned Israeli positions along the Suez Canal and in the Golan Heights. Though the Egyptians and Syrians achieved tactical surprise, their choice of the Jewish holiday as a day of attack was not completely successful.[1] Not only was the Yom Kippur assault damaging from the point of view of public relations, but Israeli mobilization was considerably eased by the concentration of reservists in places of worship and by the absence of significant civilian road traffic.

On the Suez battlefront, the initial objective of the attacking Egyptian forces was two Israeli supply roads running parallel to the Canal some twelve kilometers inland.[2] If this line was secured, the Egyptians, in accordance with their basic Soviet-designed plan, had the option to move forward and seize the Mitla, Giddi, and other passes leading into Central Sinai. (The Egyptians hoped—it was the basic goal of their attack—to seize the territory west of a north-south line running through Bir Gifgafa.) Subsequently Cairo's forces, in a third phase, could attempt to regain the remaining areas of the occupied peninsula. If difficulties were encountered in any phase of the plan, the Egyptians, whose main emphasis was on deliberate and cautious, step-by-step advances, were apparently ready to accept only very partial and limited gains. The Syrians, for their part, in a massive push would seek to expel the Israelis from the entire occupied Golan Heights.[3]

To accomplish these objectives, the Egyptians, in the first phase of the battle, relied on heavy artillery bombardment to reduce Israeli strongpoints along the Bar-Lev Line, the string of defensive works on the east bank of the Suez Canal. As Tel Aviv's scanty means of fire along the Canal were being suppressed, some eight thousand Egyptian infantrymen, many armed with *Sagger* antitank rockets, would cross the Canal in dinghies and advance to forward positions inland from the Bar-Lev Line. The mission of these troops was to seek to prevent Israeli tank reserves from moving to the front. Egyptian commando units would also be landed deep behind the Israeli lines to attempt to interdict the movement of Israeli reinforcements toward the battlefield.[4]

Once the battlefield was isolated, the Egyptians would kill or capture the Bar-Lev Line's defenders and heavily reinforce the bridgehead with tank-supported infantry divisions. Armored divisions would be held in reserve, however, presumably to stem any Israeli counterattacks on the Canal's west bank. When the bridgehead was secured, the decision would be taken regarding the next stage of the plan—the move to the Sinai passes.[5]

As concerns the Syrians, they intended to strike forward first with tank-reinforced infantry divisions, and if the opportunity for quick advance presented itself, they would then commit their reserve armored divisions to the battle.[6]

The tasks of the Egyptian and Syrian forces in the first phase of the Yom Kippur War were thus (a) to penetrate Israeli forces on the immediate line of combat confrontation, (b) to isolate these forces, and (c) to destroy them. In order to accomplish these tasks, Egyptian troops had to be protected from assault by Israeli armor and aircraft.

The initial penetration of Egyptian infantry and Syrian mechanized units proceeded smoothly, in great measure because of the tremendous advantage of artillery and tank firepower enjoyed by the Arab forces. This firepower destroyed, pinned down, or drove back Israeli forces along the initial lines of contact. Artillery firepower advantages were so great that ground-attack aircraft of the Egyptian air force were largely not committed in the first stage of the assault and thus were spared the necessity of having to confront the Israeli air force. In the beginning phases of the war, for the most part, the Egyptian air force remained in its bombproof concrete hangerettes.[7] The Syrian use of ground-attack aircraft in the war's first days was somewhat more active than that of the Egyptians, though still spare.

The only part of the Egyptian air force actively utilized in the early part of the war was the TU-16 medium bombers, which were used in stand-off missile attacks, primarily on Israeli airfields and other military objectives in the Sinai. Some twenty-five to forty of the *Kelt* stand-off missiles were launched by TU-16's. Most, however, fell victim to Israeli flak and interceptor aircraft.[8] A few of the *Kelts* apparently did penetrate, however, and scored hits on Israeli radar sites and supply depots in Sinai.[9]

It is interesting to note that neither the Egyptian air force nor the Iraqi air force—the two Arab air units with a strategic bombing capability—attempted, other than in a very few isolated sorties, to strike at targets within Israel proper. (The most advanced Soviet bombers in the Middle East, the supersonic TU-22 *Blinders*, controlled by the Soviets on Iraqi airfields, were not used at all in the war. Presumably to encourage this posture, the Israelis, unlike in 1967, did not attack Iraqi air bases.)[10] It is not clear whether Arab reluctance to engage in strategic air strikes was motivated by the desire to confine military activities, for political reasons, to the post-1967 occupied territories or by a belief that the Israeli strategic air-defense system would be difficult to penetrate.

In order to balance the Arab ground firepower advantages and to hold the attackers at bay while the Israeli forces came to full mobilization, Tel Aviv, unlike the Arab states, was compelled to rely principally on the ground-attack capabilities of its air force. From the Israeli point of view, it was essential that Arab momentum be contained, not only because of the threat to Israel proper posed by the Syrian incursion in the north but also to enable the mobilized reserves to be introduced into battle in an orderly, rather than a piecemeal and chaotic, manner.

The Arabs and their Soviet mentors, realizing the importance of ground-attack aircraft in the Israeli force design and eminently conscious of the weakness of Arab air forces, had established an integrated mobile, ground-based tactical air-defense system based on the SAM-6 missile and the ZSU-23-4 quad radar-controlled, rapid-fire antiaircraft gun. This air defense was particularly formidable within the immediate proximity of the Suez Canal and Damascus plain, where fixed-position SAM-2 and SAM-3 sites augmented the mobile weapons.

Though the Israelis were aware of the type of antiaircraft weapons possessed by the Arabs, they were taken aback by both the effectiveness of these weapons and the intensity of their employment. As one Israeli pilot described the situation as he attacked an Arab ground target, "It was like flying through hail. . . . The skies were suddenly filled with SAM's and it required every bit of concentration to avoid being hit and still execute your mission."[11]

Because of the Arabs' urgent need to keep the Israeli air force from hitting their bridgeheads, Israeli air strikes against the invading forces were met by withering fire from antiaircraft guns and SAM's. In the first afternoon of battle, some thirty Israeli A-4 Skyhawk attack aircraft and several F-4 Phantom fighter-bombers were shot down—more than 25 percent of total Israeli air losses during the entire war.[12] During the first three days of the eighteen-day confrontation the Israelis would lose more than one-half of the approximately 120 Israeli aircraft downed in the war.[13]

Israeli losses at the expense of the SAM-6 mobile missile were particularly onerous. Though the United States possessed electronic-countermeasure (ECM) equipment to foil the SAM-6,[14] these particular ECM devices were not furnished to Israel before the Yom Kippur War. As a consequence, Israel suffered heavy losses from the mobile Soviet-built missile. Of 120 aircraft lost by Israel during the Yom Kippur War, some eighty were reportedly downed by SAM-6's. Many of the forty other destroyed Israeli aircraft were shot down by ZSU 23-4 rapid-fire antiaircraft guns when Israeli planes rapidly dived to extremely low altitudes in order to evade climbing SAM-6's.[15]

The SAM-7 *Strela* shoulder- or vehicle-launched, small antiaircraft rocket was also frequently used, particularly by the Egyptians, and reportedly scored many hits. However, due to the small size of the explosive charge of the *Strela* and its poorly timed fuse, the weapon brought down virtually no Israeli planes.[16] As in the past, the Arabs were singularly ineffective in air-to-air combat, and only four Israeli planes were reportedly brought down in dogfights.

While the dense array of antiaircraft defense equipment deployed by the Arabs provided a protection for the Syrian and Egyptian forces, it also created air-control difficulties for Cairo and Damascus. Particularly over the Egyptian front, Cairo's air-defense forces apparently shot down a number of their own planes. This was a significant weakness since it inhibited the operation of friendly aircraft over the zone of immediate combat. The air-defense recognition problem was apparently less severe in Syria, where the Lebanese coastline provided well-marked landmarks, allowing Syrian pilots to channel their return into the Syrian interior accurately. The Egyptians apparently had greater difficulty in finding their reentry paths.[17]

Though Tel Aviv's aircraft did succeed, for the most part, in penetrating the Arab air defenses (out of 18,000 wartime sorties, 120 Israeli aircraft were shot down),[18] the effectiveness and intensity of Israeli strikes were reduced in the first days to a degree sufficient to allow the Syrians to break through Israeli defenses on the Golan Heights and to permit the Egyptians to maintain the security of troops already on the east bank of the Canal. Moreover, Cairo's forces were able to establish more than ten bridges and to bring hundreds of tank reinforcements across into the Sinai breach. The Egyptians, who had to cope with the difficult physical barrier of the Suez Canal, were also assisted by the ease with which Russian-supplied bridging equipment could be repaired and moved after successful Israeli air strikes.[19]

Though the Israelis expended significant air effort in seeking to halt the Egyptian push, the bulk of their air force strikes was directed against the extremely dangerous Syrian thrust only a few miles from Israel proper.[20] Israeli air attacks on the Golan Heights, while effective, did not cause the Syrians to retreat, and, in fact, on October 7, the Damascus forces committed their armored divisions to the attack. These divisions, like those of Egypt, had been held in reserve the previous day. (The Egyptians, however, did not commit their armored divisions until one week later.) It seemed, therefore, that the Syrians were seeking to follow the Soviet pattern of explosive, deep, mass-armored penetration much more closely than were the Egyptians, who were initially engaged in a more conservative and defensive-oriented broad-front holding action.

Egypt's success in maintaining its perimeter was being significantly eased by the success of Soviet-supplied infantry-operated antitank weapons such as the *Sagger* missile and the RPG-7 rocket launcher. Though the Israeli armed forces were aware of these weapons, individual tank commanders had not been adequately briefed on their effectiveness. Because of this factor of surprise, the *Saggers* were particularly psychologically disturbing to Israeli armored-force personnel. As one Israeli tank commander described the shock effect of the *Sagger*, "You are rolling along feeling invulnerable and suddenly you see a single man holding onto a stick standing 2000 yards ahead of you. You cannot believe that this single man has the power to destroy the huge tank, but in a few seconds the tank is a wreck."[21]

Egyptian troops had been highly trained in the use of the *Sagger*, and some soldiers reportedly had fired thirty thousand practice shots on a simulator in the year prior to October 1973. After this intensive training, the Egyptians were dispatched into the desert during the Yom Kippur War and told that their only task was to fire four or five *Saggers* against Israeli tanks. After this mission was accomplished, their war duties would cease.[22] Incentives such as these, some observers believe, contributed significantly to the improved performance and steadfastness of Arab troops during the war.

Due to Israeli tactical-level ignorance of the potentiality of the Russian-built antitank weapons, significant mistakes were made in the early days of the war. On October 9, for example, the Israeli 190th Armored Brigade of sixty tanks, unaccompanied by infantry, pierced the Egyptian front and headed toward Qantara on the Canal. Rather than scattering, as they had in earlier Arab-Israeli wars, the Egyptian defenders held their positions and bombarded the passing brigade with *Saggers*, RPG-7 rockets, and tank guns. After thirty-four of his sixty tanks had been destroyed, the surrounded Israeli brigade commander surrendered to the Egyptians.[23] After this incident, Israeli tank units would be loath to advance without readily available infantry assistance and good air support.[24]

By Tuesday, October 9, the Egyptians had firmly established their bridgehead in Sinai to a depth of some ten kilometers. The Syrians, who were taking the brunt of Israeli air strikes, were suffering high losses but were still maintaining some offensive initiative in the Golan Heights.

However, on October 9, a significant factor developed which would change the character of the war: Syrian SAM-6's on the Golan Heights, after heavily engaging the Israeli air force for three days, stopped firing; it was believed that the cause for this cessation of fire was the exhaustion, or near exhaustion, of missiles.[25] As the Israeli air force was increasingly concentrating attention on the SAM launchers themselves, the lack of rockets forced the withdrawal of some of the launchers to the Damascus plain. The gain of more absolute air superiority by the Israelis over the Golan Heights, as a consequence of the letup of SAM firing and the destruction of some seventy Syrian aircraft in air-to-air combat, joined with the completion of mobilization, allowed the Israelis on October 10 to liquidate the remnants of the Syrian advance in the Golan. The final Israeli Golan counterattack was not without effort, however, as dug-in Syrian infantry resisted fiercely with RPG-7 and *Shmel* antitank weapons. As a result of the five-day incursion, the Syrians suffered the loss of several hundred of the one thousand tanks that had originally crossed the Israeli lines and finally were beaten back.[26]

Because of the exhaustion of Syrian SAM's and the depletion of Damascus' tank stocks, coupled with heavy ammunition expenditures by the Egyptians, the Soviet Union agreed (possibly pursuant to a prior commitment) to resupply the Arab belligerents. On October 7, the first Soviet ships carrying supplies for the Arab wartime effort departed the port of Odessa.[27] On October 10, air-transported equipment began arriving in Egypt and Syria. By October 12, the airlift was in full swing with a total of some sixty to ninety Soviet flights per day coming into Egyptian and Syrian airfields. After the beginning of the Soviet airlift neither Syria nor Egypt would again manifest a shortage of ammunition or supplies.[28] (The United States semiclandestinely began supplying spare parts and some combat consumables to Israel on or about October 10 via Israeli aircraft. This resupply was necessitated by Israeli shortfalls of 105 mm tank ammunition, 175 mm artillery rounds, air-to-air and air-to-surface missiles, and other items. The U.S. resupply was publicly announced and reached full dimensions on October 14, when it was apparent that the Russians would not restrain supplies. After October 14, the United States supplied not only consumables but also aircraft and other weapons.[29])

While Tel Aviv's air force bombed Syrian and Egyptian runways on which the Soviet supply planes landed and occasionally flew by the side of Russian planes as they made their approaches, the Israelis did not directly attack any Soviet aircraft or ships. The same situation prevailed for American ships and planes making deliveries to Israel.[30]

The commencement of the Russian air- and sealift to the Arabs was, of course, an event of tremendous political and military significance. Without any resupply, qualified observers believed, the Egyptians had the stocks to continue fighting for only some five days after the commencement of hostilities. With a resupply of certain key items, Egyptian fighting capabilities were prolonged some two weeks beyond this five-day period.[31] The Syrians were in a similar, but even weaker, position. The Soviet air- and sealift, therefore, was instrumental in permitting the prolongation of the war. Significantly, inauguration of the airlift marked the first time that the Soviet Union had ever engaged in a massive, continuous resupply of a non-Communist client during the actual course of full hostilities.

By the conclusion of the Soviet air- and sealift in mid-November, approximately one hundred thousand tons of military equipment had been delivered to the Arabs. Of this sum, some eighty-five thousand tons of equipment were delivered by sea on some 30 freighters, and the remainder was shipped by air on some one thousand flights of AN-22 and AN-12 transport aircraft.[32] The United States, in comparison, delivered some fifty thousand tons of equipment to Israel, of which some twenty-two thousand six hundred tons were shipped by air on one hundred fifty flights of C-5A and four hundred twenty missions of C-141 aircraft.[33]

By the conclusion of the Soviet air- and sealifts in mid-November, the Arabs were believed to possess about 10 percent less arms than they possessed at the beginning of the war.[34] (Certain weapons stocks such as tanks were qualitatively upgraded however. Syria, for example, received a reported eight hundred fifty replacement tanks, of which some seven hundred were first-line Soviet T-62's, presumably supplied because of their ready availability.[35]) Israel, on the other hand, was believed to be somewhat above its prewar weapons level after the American resupply effort because of its success in repairing damaged equipment.[36]

Slightly prior to the beginning of the Soviet airlift of equipment and ammunition to the Arabs, the Israelis had made a decision to forgo acute pressure on the Egyptians temporarily and to concentrate instead on defeat of the Syrians. Since the Israeli leadership thought that the Egyptians would be difficult to dislodge, it was decided first to attempt to break the Syrians totally, to destroy their arms, and to achieve complete control of the situation in the north.[37] Once dominance in the north was realized, a more favorable political situation could be achieved and more troops could be sent to the south.

According to former Defense Minister Dayan, speaking on October 9, "We want(ed) to make a supreme, productive, and effective effort to get Syria out of the war. . . . I believe and hope that we can bring Syria to a situation where it will in fact cease firing and will not have effective firepower. . . . At the same time, the war should cost Syria so dearly that it will regret what it did."[38] To break the Syrians, Tel Aviv chose two methods: (a) Israeli troops would shift from a cautious approach of inching forward on a broad front in the Golan Heights to a method in which forces would be concentrated, and a breakthrough on a narrow front would be attempted toward Damascus;[39] and (b) the Syrian interior would be subjected to a strategic bombing in an attempt to cut communications, energy supplies, and generally to inflict economic punishment.

The decision in favor of the strategic bombing of Syria was taken by Tel Aviv because an Israeli study had shown that, because of the concentrated location of fuel and electrical energy sources in Syria, a program of deep bombing would be successful in bringing Damascus' economy to a halt. It was reportedly decided not to bomb Egypt strategically, on the other hand, because fuel and electricity supplies were more dispersed. In addition, the Egyptian interior was well covered by SAM sites installed during the "war of attrition." Because of the late arrival of SAM's in Syria under different circumstances, most had been emplaced on the Damascus plain, thereby leaving strategic objectives in Syria open to air strikes.[40]

The justification publicly cited by Israel for the beginning of deep bombing of Syria was the firing of *Frog* rockets by Damascus' forces. On October 6, Syrian forces had fired three *Frog* missiles at Israel. On October 8, seven *Frogs* were fired. On October 9, six *Frogs* were launched. Several of these missiles, carrying five-hundred-pound warheads, had hit Israel's settlements and inflicted significant property damage.[41] As Israeli Defense Minister Moshe Dayan pointed out, the Syrian firing of *Frogs* constituted the first combat use of surface-to-surface missiles in the Middle East. Also, as Dayan suggested, generally in the Middle East conflict, with the exception of "mistakes" such as the Israeli 1970 strike on the Abu Zaabal metallurgical works, "urban centers had not been hit by either side."[42] While it is probable that the Syrians were aiming the unguided *Frogs* at the Ramat David airfield in northern Israel, and not at the populated points ultimately struck,[43] the Syrian bombardment, by hitting settlements, did serve as a point of moral justification for Israel's decision to commence strategic bombing.

During the course of the strategic bombardment of Syria, two oil refineries at Homs were hit; fuel tank farms and loading facilities at Adra, Tartous, and Latakia were bombed; the Mediterranean terminal for Iraqi crude oil at Banias was destroyed; and electric-power generating stations at Homs and Damascus were shattered.[44] In addition, the Israeli navy participated in the bombardment of the petroleum facilities at Latakia and Tartous.[45] The damage inflicted to Syria's energy infrastructure was massive and serious. Though it is difficult to assess whether the strategic bombardment had any effect on the course of combat or on Syria's will to wage war, presumably the strikes were at least significant in signaling to Syria's partner Cairo that such damage could also be visited on Egypt's economy and cities. This signal would be an important factor in the ensuing days.

In addition to economic targets, the headquarters of the Syrian air force and the ministry of defense in downtown Damascus were attacked by the Israeli air force. Because of partially inaccurate weapons delivery, sections of the city's diplomatic quarter were hit, including the Soviet cultural center. As a result, foreign civilian casualties were incurred. The Israelis recognized that, due to political difficulties, strikes on Syria's capital could not be repeated. However, presumably the intent of Tel Aviv had been to communicate to Syria that surrender must be forthcoming. In the words of Moshe Dayan, "it would be difficult to make Damascus a permanent target. It was decided to do it now as part of the overall, supreme effort to get Syria out of the war. The only limitation is to avoid hitting the civilian population; apart from that, nothing is sacred."[46]

In addition to the aerial bombing of Syria, Israel's navy, armed with the domestically-produced *Gabriel* missile, was playing havoc with the Syrian shoreline. The operations against Syria followed early moves against radar and other installations on the northern Egyptian shore, which, combined with Israeli bombing of Port Said, raised speculation in Egypt that an Israeli amphibious invasion was in preparation.[47] The fear of an amphibious attack may have been one of the factors causing the Egyptian high command to delay commitment of its armored forces to the Sinai bridgehead.

On the Syrian coast, in addition to bombarding oil refineries, the Israeli navy subjected various shore points to intensive fire. The incessant activity of Tel Aviv's navy caused the Syrians to move two brigades from the Golan battle zone to cover against an Israeli amphibious landing.[48]

In addition to shore bombardment, the Israeli navy engaged in battle with Syrian and Egyptian Russian-built *Komar* and *Ossa* fast patrol boats armed with *Styx* missiles. The Israelis enjoyed great success employing electronic and other countermeasures against the *Styx*. While one account states that no *Styx* missiles scored hits on Israeli boats,[49] another source claims that three Israeli craft were sunk during the war.[50] On the other hand, the Israeli *Gabriel* inflicted serious damage on Egyptian and Syrian stocks of Russian-supplied patrol boats (some thirteen Egyptian and Syrian boats were believed sunk). In the course of the naval battles at the mouth of Syria's harbors, some inaccurate Israeli missile launches did occur, and several foreign commercial ships were hit. In the port of Tartous, on October 12, for example, the Soviet freighter *Il'ya Mechnikov* was accidentally sunk by *Gabriel* missiles that had been fired at Syrian missile boats.[51]

Along with the strategic bombing and naval harassment of Syria, Israeli forces, now fully mobilized and in control of most of the Golan Heights, searched for and exploited a weak point in the Syrian force deployment. From October 11 through 13, Israel mounted a rapid attack that took its forces to the town of Sassa, halfway down the road to Damascus from the post-Six-Day War ceasefire line.

While Israel's advance was at first quickly paced, frustration was soon encountered when Syria's forces regrouped around a fallback line of prepared defensive positions running through Sassa. Syrian resistance was further stiffened by the addition of Moroccan, Iraqi, Kuwaiti, and Jordanian infantry and armored forces dispatched to assist Syria. As one Israeli official commented, on October 13 "we met an avalanche of people and tanks."[52] Though many of these tanks, including one entire Iraqi armored brigade, were destroyed, the Israelis felt that further gains in Syria would come only at a very high price.[53]

Syrian defense capabilities had also been bolstered by the rapid infusion of Russian arms, including consumable items, such as ammunition and rockets, as well as replacement weapons, such as tanks. Israeli soldiers on the Sassa front indicated that they were subjected to the most intense continuous artillery shelling they had witnessed in wartime service. Blanket artillery fire was being delivered by the Syrians for some twenty-one hours per day on this front, and there was apparently little attempt to spot targets.[54] The apparently massive availability to the Syrians of artillery ammunition, especially after the shortfall of antiaircraft missiles a few days earlier, was indicative of the extent to which the Soviet air- and sealift had satisfied Syrian needs.

In addition to the flow of supplies, the Russians were providing help in other dimensions. Soviet military advisers, for example, remained with Syrian ground forces and air-defense units in the zone of combat, though not in immediate front-line positions.[55]   Coupled with this, Soviet advisers were present in Syrian command posts at every echelon, from the battalion up, including supreme headquarters.[56]

Because of the shortage of tank crews in Syria, Soviet personnel drove tanks unloaded from Russian ships from Latakia and Tartous to Damascus. Further, air-defense missile units under exclusive Russian operation and control were established at Latakia and Damascus, presumably to help protect the Soviet sea- and airlift. At sea, a Soviet *Kotlin*-class destroyer was placed off Latakia Harbor to provide antisubmarine protection for Soviet ships entering with war supplies.[57]

While Israeli pressure was mounting on the doorsteps of Damascus, the Egyptians, who had spent October 10–12 enlarging their bridgehead and suppressing the last pockets of Israeli resistance on the Bar-

Lev Line, felt that it was time to provide assistance to their beleaguered allies. On October 13, Egyptian armored divisions were brought across the Canal for the first time in the war, and, on October 14 and 15, Cairo's forces launched an attack toward the Sinai passes.

The Egyptians, keeping with the conservative orientation of their operation, had not moved a great number of their SAM-6 missiles across the Canal and to the forward areas of their combat operations.[58] As a consequence, when the Egyptian attack was launched, the advancing tanks were very soon out of the effective zone of SAM cover. In addition, the added firepower of Cairo's infantry antitank weapons could not be fully utilized in an attack situation of rapid advance and maneuver. As a result, the combined efforts of Israeli aircraft and the accurate gunnery of Israeli tank crews inflicted a decisive defeat on the Egyptians. By October 15, the attacking forces, with a loss of some two hundred tanks and large numbers of casualties, were repulsed into the Sinai bridgehead.[59]

Having awaited just this opportunity to weaken and disorganize the Egyptians, and having reached a stalemate on the Syrian front, the Israelis decided to shift the focus of their efforts to the south to penetrate Egyptian lines and then invade the Egyptian-held west bank.[60] On October 16, Israeli forces under the command of General Ariel Sharon drove forward at the point of junction of the Egyptian Second and Third Armies. Exploiting a gap between the two forces, Sharon's armored forces fought a vicious battle to seize and hold a Canal crossing point. After many delays and difficulties, Sharon was able to introduce a small group of troops and tanks on the west bank of the Canal.

Though Israeli troops at the east bank crossing point were still engaged in fierce battle to maintain the crossing, the forces that had moved to the west bank met little resistance since the bulk of the Egyptian forces, including the armored divisions, were now in Sinai. Either because of communications difficulties inhibiting full understanding of the seriousness of the situation or because of a political decision to maintain the hold on Sinai at all costs, the Egyptian leadership did not withdraw the armored divisions or other major units from Sinai back to the east bank.[61] As a result, Sharon's troops began to inflict increasing damage.

First and most importantly, Israeli troops on the east bank were able to destroy four Egyptian SAM sites.[62] The gaps opened up in the SAM defenses allowed Israeli aircraft to provide better protection of the crossing and close air support to the forces on the west bank of the Canal.

As the Israeli grip on the Canal crossing was firmed, Tel Aviv committed more armored forces to the east bank, and the Israeli forces wheeled north and south to cut off access of the Egyptian Second and

Third Armies on the west bank of the Canal to their rear bases of support and logistics. Because of the apparent Egyptian desire not to withdraw ground forces from the west bank, the principal resistance to the Israeli attack was provided by the Egyptian air force. In this first major commitment of Cairo's aircraft during the war, SU-7 ground-attack aircraft attacked the Israelis in their trans-Canal salient, while MIG-21's supplied top cover. As a supplement to Egypt's strategic air defense, while Egyptian interceptors were committed to the tactical zone, some twenty North Korean pilots flew passive air-defense missions in the interior of Egypt.[63] In the air battles that ensued, Tel Aviv's air force downed some two hundred Egyptian jets with a loss of only three Israeli jets.[64]

By the final stages of the trans-Canal air battle, Egypt had lost so many pilots that training planes with student pilots were committed to the attack on the Israelis.[65] By this time, both Egypt and Syria were desperately in need of flying personnel. While the Soviet provision of materiel was helpful to the Arabs, it was not as urgently required as pilots now were. However, in spite of the acute Arab need, the Soviets did not dispatch any pilots to engage in an active combat role.[66]

Concurrent with the beginning of the Israeli west bank incursion, Egyptian President Sadat warned Tel Aviv not to contemplate thrusts into the depths of Egypt. In a speech to the Egyptian People's Assembly on October 16, Sadat, after rejecting a ceasefire in place, declared: "Our Egyptian rockets, of the *Zafir* type, which can cross Sinai, are now on their pads ready to be launched by the single order to press a button. They would reach the farthest depths of Israel." Sadat continued that a command to launch the rockets could have been given at the beginning of the war, "but we realized the responsibility of using some types of weapons and we refrained from using them. But we must remember what I once said: an eye for an eye, a tooth for a tooth, and depth for depth."[67]

Sadat's reference to the *Zafir*, an Egyptian rocket developed in the early 1960s but never deployed because of guidance-system difficulties, was believed to be a "cover" alluding to Soviet *Scud* missiles, probably delivered before the war and operationally deployed sometime before October 12.[68] The 150-mile-range *Scuds* were believed to be under Egyptian command but operated at least partially by Russian personnel.[69] Sadat, by invoking the *Scud* threat, apparently wished to deter Israel from retargeting its air force from the Syrian interior to the Egyptian heartland. This warning would acquire new urgency as Israeli forces rapidly spread over the east bank of the Suez Canal and the Israeli air force demonstrated its renewed air superiority.

After the firm establishment of the Suez crossing, Israeli forces had continued their advance southward toward the city of Suez and northward toward the Cairo-Ismailia road. The rapid movement of Israeli tanks was spurred by Tel Aviv's air force, which now began applying newly arrived American guided weapons such as *Maverick* "smart" bombs with devastating effectiveness against Egyptian armor. The Israeli ground and air strikes also were destroying great numbers of SAM installations on the west bank. By the time of ceasefire on October 22, some one-third of Egypt's SAM launchers had been destroyed or captured.[70]

With the Egyptian Third Army now cut off and the Second Army soon to be in a similar position, and with Israel rapidly restoring its absolute air superiority as the result of the destruction of SAM sites and the bulk of Cairo's air force, it now became imperative for Egypt to obtain a ceasefire. As a consequence, Egyptian President Sadat, after consultations with Soviet leader Kosygin from October 16 through 19, agreed to a proposal for a ceasefire in place. The ceasefire was implemented with some difficulty first on October 22 and then again on October 24.

Just before the ceasefire went into effect, however, Sadat, in a gesture of defiance against Israel, demonstrated that his missile warning of a few days before was not intended as a bluff. On October 22, several Soviet-operated, Egyptian-controlled *Scuds* were fired at Israeli troops in the west bank salient.[71] The firing of the missiles was confirmed by the Cairo newspaper *Akhbar el Yom*, which indicated that a "Zafir rocket" was launched from deep inside Egypt and hit Israeli forces "in a position believed by the Israeli command to be out of the range of rockets."[72] Former Israeli Defense Minister Moshe Dayan also later publicly confirmed that long-range rockets of the *Scud* type had been fired against Israeli troops.[73]

The use of the *Scuds*, it should be recalled, had been threatened on October 16 after the Syrian setbacks in the north and the failure of the Egyptian thrust toward the Sinai passes. Sadat apparently wished to signal to Israel that Egypt had a strategic guarantee and should not be toyed with. The actual launching of the *Scuds* on October 22 was presumably intended to be a graphic demonstration that strategic rockets were indeed present in Egypt, that they were functioning, and that the next time they could be used against the Israeli heartland.

The firing of the *Scuds*, though virtually unnoticed in the Western press, was an event of extreme significance. The rockets were, after all, the key Soviet contribution to the assured strategic deterrent long desired by Sadat. Indeed, the controversy over the Soviet failure to provide offensive weapons like the *Scud* had been the root of the bitter dispute which culminated in the 1972 expulsion of Russian military advisers from Egypt.

Because the *Scuds* did represent the unique example of a Soviet provision to Egypt of a strategic weapon with assured penetrability and because Moscow had long deplayed delivery of such weapons, one might suppose that the Soviets had insisted on certain usage restrictions or consultation procedures before the *Scuds* were employed. This hypothesis is strengthened by the lack of deployment, threat, or use of the rockets in the early successful stages of the war. Furthermore, even if no formal procedures or restrictions existed, one would assume that the participation of Soviet personnel in the operation of the missiles would provide a channel of information allowing higher Soviet authorities to interpose objections against firing of the missiles.

While it is not certain whether Moscow was consulted on the Egyptian launching of the *Scuds* on October 22, the Soviet personnel present apparently cooperated with the Egyptians in executing the launches. It is probably reasonable to assume that, if not the highest Soviet leadership, at least some relatively authoritative Soviet echelon sanctioned the launching of the *Scuds*. This assumption is even more credible given the fact that there was a six-day interlude between Sadat's threat of *Scud* employment and the actual launches.

The firing of the *Scuds* was the first instance in which Soviet personnel had participated in offensive, as distinguished from air-defense, activity against the Israelis and, as such, may have marked an important escalation in the degree of direct Soviet military involvement in the Middle East. Whether this shift to direct offensive participation had been approved by the highest political and military authorities in Moscow remains a moot, though extremely important, point.

The losses suffered by the belligerents during the Yom Kippur War by the time that a definitive ceasefire had been established on the Egyptian and Syrian fronts at the end of October were momentous; in terms of equipment, they exceeded the magnitude of many of World War II's largest battles. During the course of the war, Egypt lost two hundred thirty-two combat aircraft and Syria lost one hundred ninety-six, while Israel lost one hundred six to one hundred twenty planes. In terms of tanks, Egypt lost six hundred thirty-one, Syria lost five hundred forty, Iraq lost eighty-one, and Jordan lost twenty-two, while Israel lost 420.[74] As regards casualties, two thousand four hundred twelve Israelis were killed.[75] Arab casualties are not known but are believed to total in the area of fifteen thousand killed and wounded.[76] As the result of Soviet and American resupply efforts, however, by the end of 1973 all belligerents had recouped virtually all their wartime losses, with the exception of human lives.

The Arab conduct of the Yom Kippur War has been described by some observers as a typical Soviet-style military operation. This analysis is largely incorrect.[77] In violation of Soviet military doctrine, which advocates deep penetration and projection of firepower through the entire depth of the opponent's military formations as well as his homeland, Arab military efforts for the most part concentrated on the area of the immediate tactical battlefield. Only a few isolated attempts were made to strike at Israel proper, and no efforts were undertaken to interdict in any substantial way the movement of Israel's mobilized reservists to the front.

It is probable that the Arab neglect of deep strikes was engendered more by air inferiority than by the limited political-military aims of Operation *Badr*. While one might abjure strikes on strategic targets to protect one's own homeland, similar restraints would have no sense with regard to interdiction attacks on reservists moving to the front, especially when one's own troops are already mobilized and deployed. The incentives for the Arabs to strike at the forward movement of Israel's mobilizing reservists was particularly high since arrival of these troops at the front would not only significantly decrease the Arabs' manpower advantages but would also place the Israeli reservists' rear-based heavy equipment such as tanks into the fray. It was, therefore, clearly in the Arabs' interest to attack these men and equipment at their rear depots or in transit to the front. Yet this was never done, presumably because the Arabs appreciated that their air forces would be annihilated in air-to-air combat with the Israelis. (Arab air weakness was the result of not only the qualitative inferiority of aircraft supplied by the Soviet Union but also weaknesses in the training program organized by the Soviets.)

As an alternative to strategic or deep-interdiction air strikes, the Arabs opted largely to leave their air forces in reserve while they reduced Israeli defenses with artillery firepower and kept the Israeli air force at bay with surface-to-air tactical air-defense systems. Syria and Egypt presumably hoped that Tel Aviv's air force would suffer enough attrition over the tactical battlefield to make a less formidable opponent later in the war or, even better, to make it so ineffective against Arab ground forces that they would have no need to engage it at all.

The necessity to forgo use of their air forces and to rely almost exclusively on surface-to-air tactical air defense, even if mobile, reduced the possibility of any decisive deep Arab breakthrough on the ground as envisaged by Russian military doctrine. While Israeli air superiority would be reduced over the immediate battlefield, the interdiction of the movement of Israeli ground forces on and in the rear of the battlefield would probably be only incompletely accomplished by artillery. Israel, therefore, could readily shift its forces to meet any Arab thrust. This fact, combined with the unimpeded flow of supplies and reinforcements between Israel proper and the two fronts and between the individual fronts, if necessary, condemned the Arabs to either settle for very limited gains or to conduct a war of attrition.

The effect of Arab force shortcomings in promoting stalemate was further heightened by the deficiencies of Arab personnel in operating mobile means of ground fire, such as the tank. Because of these weaknesses, the Arabs relied heavily on defensively organized, infantry-operated antitank weapons, which were deployed in a manner that did not lend itself to rapid advance and maneuver.

Because no immediately decisive results were or could be achieved by Egypt and Syria in the wake of their initial attacks, both Arab belligerents had to emphasize firepower rather than movement in order to defend their own forces and to bring military pressure on the Israelis. Ammunition consumption was thus very high, and both Arab parties quickly required replenishment. As a result, the Soviet Union, apparently committed to at least averting a defeat for the Arabs, began an intensive air and sea resupply effort to Egypt and Syria.

Simultaneously, Tel Aviv, sensing the weakened position of the Syrians, whose offensive had been blunted by Israeli reinforcements and air power, decided to concentrate its efforts on breaking Damascus' resistance. By combining tactical and strategic blows against Syria, the Israelis hoped to avert a possible stalemate, to involve the Syrians in a war of movement, and to put the Damascus regime *hors de combat*. A Syrian collapse would not only politically balance any setback received in Sinai at the hands of the stronger Egyptians but would also free forces currently deployed in the north to be diverted to the Sinai front.

The Israeli effort bogged down, however, after significant damage had been inflicted on the Syrian energy infrastructure and a successful tactical advance had been made toward Damascus. Stopped at the town of Sassa by extremely heavy Syrian fire (allowed by the Soviet resupply effort plus preplanned fallback lines) and by reinforcements provided by other Arab nations, Tel Aviv decided to forgo its aspirations for a Syrian breakdown and to settle instead for a standstill in the north in the positions that it had already achieved.

On the Sinai front the Egyptians, who spent the first week of the war in a defensive orientation while consolidating their bridgehead, moved to the offensive to provide help to the Syrians. To the Egyptians' regret, however, their force structure was ill-suited to offensive action against the fully mobilized Israelis. Attempting a massive armored strike, the Egyptians outdistanced the protection of their antiaircraft and infantry antitank protection and suffered heavy losses at the hands of Israeli tanks and aircraft.

The war might well have resulted in a stand-off at this point had the

Israelis not found a gap in Egyptian lines. Utilizing this gap, the Israelis were able to penetrate into Egypt proper, destroy portions of the Egyptian tactical air defense, and open the way for the exercise of Israeli air superiority over the Canal region. In spite of Cairo's commitment of its air force to stopping the Israeli incursion, Tel Aviv was able to maintain control of the skies and to inflict severe damage on both Egyptian air and ground forces. The subsequent encirclement of the Egyptian armies in Sinai and the apparent impossibility of recouping the situation on either the Sinai or Syrian fronts motivated the Arab leaders to accept a ceasefire.

Before bowing to what could be interpreted by the Israelis as an humiliation, however, Sadat demonstratively indicated, by firing strategic-range *Scud* missiles at the Israeli salient, that not only Egypt but also Israel was now a hostage. While the firing of the Egyptian-controlled, Russian-operated *Scuds* was a defensive gesture of warning from Sadat's point of view, Russian participation in the launches marked a departure from earlier practice, in which Soviet personnel had restricted themselves to air-defense-related duties. While it is not clear whether the Soviet political and military leadership endorsed the *Scud* firing, it is probable, given the longstanding reluctance of the Soviets to supply the Egyptians with the weapon, that some level of official Russian approval was required before the launches could take place.

In summary, the military significance of the Yom Kippur War was as follows. By virtue of surprise, the Arabs, with overwhelming advantages of deployed ground forces, achieved initial limited tactical success. The Arabs were unable to translate this tactical success into strategic success largely because of the weakness of the performance of their air forces. Because of this weakness, the Israeli air force was able to slow the Arab advance and mobilized Israeli reservists and their equipment were able to be deployed to the battlefields without interference.

After the initial successes, the shortcomings of the Arab air forces, combined with the poor performances of Arab tank forces in mobile combat, led to defeat in the two major Arab armored thrusts attempted —the October 6–10 Syrian offensive in the Golan Heights and the October 14–15 Egyptian push on Sinai. In the wake of each of these Arab defeats, in which Israeli aircraft and tanks destroyed large amounts of enemy military equipment, Tel Aviv was able to exploit Arab vulnerabilities and to achieve military successes, which prompted the Arabs to end the war. The degree of Israel's military successes, however, was not of sufficient magnitude to break the Arabs' political will and place them at Israel's mercy. We shall now turn to the political context of the October War.

On October 5, the day preceding the Arab attack on Israeli forces, the afternoon newspaper *Izvestiya*, the official organ of the Soviet Council of Ministers, carried a small item reporting the intrusion of three Israeli fighter aircraft into Lebanon. The article added that "information continues to arrive about concentrations of Israeli forces along the Lebanese borders and ceasefire lines with Syria."[78]

On October 6, *Pravda*, the morning organ of the CPSU Central Committee, *Krasnaya zvezda*, the Soviet Ministry of Defense's morning newspaper, and *Izvestiya* expanded on the charges of Israeli troop concentrations. In the words of *Pravda*'s Cairo correspondent: "Tension is increasing on the ceasefire line between Syria and Israel. According to the Egyptian press, Tel Aviv is preparing a mass attack. Israeli tank units and heavy artillery have been brought up to the Syrian ceasefire line. Israeli aircraft are also patrolling the entire length of the Lebanese border."[79] The Ministry of Defense newspaper *Krasnaya zvezda*, under the heading "Preparations of Israel," carried TASS (Soviet official news agency) reports from Damascus, Beirut, London, and New York implying that Israel was on the verge of launching a military attack on Syria.[80]

Izvestiya's Beirut correspondent, K. Kapitonov, amplified these charges in the October 6 early-afternoon edition of the newspaper and signaled to the Soviet public for the first time that Arab forces might be concentrating. Kapitonov quoted Israeli Defense Minister Moshe Dayan as recently noting "with alarm" that "supposedly the Arab countries were bringing their forces up to the ceasefire line on the Golan Heights." The Soviet correspondent continued that "it has been that way many times. Before attacking, the leaders of Tel Aviv trumpeted to the whole world that danger threatens Israel."[81] Against this background, the October 6 Arab attack on Israeli forces would be portrayed as its opposite—an Israeli attack on the Arabs.[82]

On the day following the Egyptian–Syrian invasion, *Pravda* carried TASS transmissions from Cairo and Damascus describing the supposed Israeli assault on Egypt and Syria. According to *Pravda*, "at 1330, Israel, utilizing the forces of several Air Force units, attacked Egyptian units near Zafaran and As-Sokhny in the area of the Gulf of Suez. Simultaneously, several Israeli naval cutters approached the western bank of the Gulf. The Egyptian military command announced that armed units of the opponent had undertaken an attempt to seize a part of Egyptian territory on the west bank of the Suez Canal. They were met by units of the Egyptian ground forces which, after artillery preparation, conducted a successful counterattack."

On the Syrian front, allegedly, "at 1400 local time Israeli forces attacked the forward positions of the Syrian Army along the whole ceasefire line. Syrian forces . . . answered the opponent's fire with the aim of suppressing his means of attack."[83]

In the first Soviet commentary on the war, a *Pravda* news analyst echoed the false claims of an Israeli attack on the Arabs. According to the *Pravda* commentator: "Yesterday after careful preparation and mobilization of reservists, Israeli forces launched an attack on Egypt and Syria, the possibility of which the foreign press has announced for several days. . . . Thus, the hawks from Tel Aviv have accomplished a new act of aggression, throwing a challenge to all the peaceloving forces and creating a situation in the Near East which is frought with the most serious consequences." By way of exception, however, the analyst pointed out: "As is known, the Soviet Union and the fraternal countries of socialism, consistently speaking in support of the just struggle of the Arab peoples against aggression, departed from the necessity of a political settlement of the conflict. . . ."[84]

On October 7, the Soviet government issued an official declaration on the war which to some Western observers seemed reserved.[85] The statement, cast in measured tones, put the blame for the war on "the absence of a political settlement" in the Middle East. While the fiction of an Israeli build-up of forces and an attack on the Arabs was maintained, the declaration signaled Arab initiation of the war by alluding to the past efforts of the Arabs to achieve a "firm peace" that had foundered on "the obstructionist position of Tel Aviv."

More menacing, however, was the Soviet endorsement without qualification of the "legitimate demands of the Arab states for the liberation of all the Arab territories occupied by Israel in 1967." This endorsement of Arab war aims was not coupled with any call for or reference to a ceasefire or termination of hostilities. Instead, only an open-ended threat and suggestion of surrender was directed at Tel Aviv: "If the government of Israel . . . remains deaf to the voice of reason and, as before, will continue an aggressive policy of holding the occupied Arab lands . . . this can cost the people of Israel dearly. Responsibility for the consequences of such an unreasonable course will be borne in full by the rulers of the state of Israel."[86]

At the same time that Arab war aims were being endorsed on October 7, the first Soviet ships carrying military supplies to the Arabs departed from Black Sea ports.[87] In addition—contrary to reports that later appeared in the Western press—Soviet airborne troops were also brought to alert in the first days of the war.[88]

On October 7, American President Nixon and Soviet Communist Party General Secretary Brezhnev exchanged views through diplomatic channels with regard to the war. The Soviet leader reportedly indicated that the Soviet Union shared the American desire to limit the Middle East conflict. U.S. officials expressed satisfaction that there was a consensus between Moscow and Washington not to allow the Middle East conflict to seriously damage Soviet-American relations.[89]

In spite of the apparently hopeful Nixon-Brezhnev exchange, the Soviet representatives at the U.N. Security Council meeting on October 8 were unwilling to accept either the U.S. proposal for a ceasefire at the pre-October 6 lines or a British-French proposal for a ceasefire in place.[90] This contradiction between Soviet proclamations of restraint vis-à-vis the United States and the Russian failure to endorse a quick ceasefire was apparently explained by the fact that, while the Soviets had initially expected a quick Arab defeat and termination of hostilities, the situation had developed in a different manner. Because of their early successes, the Arabs, or at least the Egyptians, were unwilling to accept a ceasefire. As Secretary of State Kissinger pointed out, the initial inability to obtain a halt in hostilities was apparently due to "a misassessment of the military situation by some of the participants."[91]

According to Egyptian President Sadat, Soviet Ambassador Vinogradov called on him the night of October 6 and indicated that Syria had requested that the Soviet Union act as an intermediary to arrange a ceasefire. Sadat rejected association with the reported ceasefire request and, on October 7, sent a telegram to Syrian President Assad inquiring about the proposal. In reply, Assad denied that any ceasefire proposition had been made. When Vinogradov called again on October 7 and repeated the alleged Syrian ceasefire request, Sadat, citing Assad's reply, turned down the initiative in terms which the Egyptian president described as "violent."[92]

Whether or not the Syrian desire for an early ceasefire was genuine, it appeared that the Egyptians, buoyed by their initial military advances, would not agree to stop fighting.[93] As a consequence, the Soviets, who at least had passively endorsed the Arab resort to war, could not easily object, especially since the Arabs were enjoying success. Due to their defensiveness with regard to the subject of détente and their strongly felt need to demonstrate solidarity with the "progressive" movement in the Arab world, the Soviets were prepared to pay the price of a temporary setback in warm relations with Washington in order not to appear to betray Arab interests. The Soviets, therefore, made a decision to set aside their ceasefire initiative for the meantime and to undertake necessary verbal and physical moves to assist the Arab cause.

Within two days (October 8 and 9), statements attributed to four major members of the Politburo (Brezhnev, Kosygin, Suslov, and Grechko) would be made endorsing the Arab war effort.[94] While all would applaud the Arab aims, only Brezhnev would speak about a Soviet role in obtaining or guaranteeing a future peace. Rather than indicating Brezhnev's pacific sentiments, however, the statement may have been more a reflection of the general secretary's broader prerogatives among the Politburo leaders.

The Soviet shift from efforts toward a ceasefire to support for a continued Arab struggle would soon be apparent in communications with the United States. The previously noted Soviet-American consensus to limit the conflict would now be undermined. As Secretary of State Kissinger later noted: "Throughout the first week [of the war] we attempted to bring about a moderation in the level of outside supplies that was introduced into the area. And we attempted to work with the Soviet Union on a ceasefire resolution which would bring an end to the conflict. This first attempt failed."[95]

On October 10, confronted by the shortfalls of Arab ammunition and weapons, the Soviet Union, in accordance with the decision to accede to the Arabs' desire to prolong the war, began the large-scale airlift of supplies to supplement its previously inaugurated sealift. Neither the initiation nor the conduct of the air- or sealift were ever specifically reported in the Soviet press.

Most of the Soviet airlift flights originated in Kiev, in the Soviet Union, or Budapest, Hungary. Many of the Kiev flights, however, made stopovers in Budapest before proceeding to the Middle East.[96] The concentration of air flights from and through Budapest indicated that the Hungarian capital was the principal staging point for flights to Syria and Egypt.

At Budapest, ammunition and weapons were gathered which apparently had been withdrawn from the substantial reserve equipment components of Soviet and Eastern European Warsaw Pact-committed forces.[97] The seeming efficiency with which the concentration of supplies and the airlift were handled suggested that, if the operation had not been specifically organized well in advance, it at least was a contingency which had been well planned for.[98]

Because of the withdrawal of large amounts of equipment and ammunition from Warsaw Pact forces, one would presume that if measures had been taken to put American troops in Western Europe on alert at an early date, this might have exercised a retarding effect on Russian supplies to the Middle East. It should be recognized, however, that substantial drawdowns of equipment from American forces in Western Europe were also taking place as part of the effort to supply the Israelis.

For direct flights from Kiev, the Soviet airlift passed over Turkey, a member of the NATO alliance.[99] From Budapest, the Russian aircraft transited Yugoslavia. The Yugoslav transit created an unusual situation since American aircraft flying supplies to Israel from Ramstein air base in West Germany also had to cross over Yugoslavia, as well as neutral Austria.[100] Because of the probable countervailing diplomatic pressures applied to nations along the airlift transit routes, there was no interference with overflights on the part of the Central and Southern

European neutrals (Austria and Yugoslavia) or the southern-tier NATO allies (Greece and Turkey).

While many Western European NATO allies denied the United States overflight and landing rights for Israel-bound aircraft (due to fears of an Arab oil embargo),[101] the Soviets likewise were not able to overfly Romania. While it is uncertain whether Bucharest was even asked for overflight permission, Romanian officials claim that they denied such privileges to the Russians.[102]

Presumably, because of nervousness regarding Soviet intentions, both Romania and Yugoslavia conducted military-readiness exercises during the Middle East War period.[103]

The weapons that the Soviets shipped to the Arabs during the war were financed in two ways. Some of the shipments apparently included items which were subsumed under earlier signed Soviet-Egyptian and Soviet-Syrian agreements. These items were usually financed on the basis of barter, and their agreed delivery time was simply accelerated. Other items, valued at some one billion dollars, were sold for cash. It is believed, however, that the Soviets did not demand immediate transfer of the cash in advance of delivery. The money for the Soviet weapons purchases was apparently pledged by the oil-rich Arab states on behalf of Egypt and Syria. Because the money was not immediately provided by the oil countries, the Soviets were able to use the Egyptian and Syrian debts as diplomatic tools after the war.[104]

Following the commencement of the Soviet airlift, some American officials still remained optimistic concerning the Soviet role. Secretary of State Kissinger, on October 12, two days after the beginning of the Soviet airlift, declared that in comparison with the 1967 Six-Day War period, the Russians were "less provocative, less incendiary, and less geared to military threats."[105] By October 15, however, the grandiose dimensions of the Russian resupply effort became clear, and the United States elected to send large sums of replacement ammunition and weapons to Israel.[106]

In addition to the airlift, the Soviets in the first week of the war began to press other Arab countries to support Egypt and Syria. Encouragement of participation by other Arab states in the war, in Soviet eyes, would presumably fortify the belligerents, increase adherence to the "progressive" front in the Middle East, and heighten Moscow's identification with that grouping. In addition, as claimed by the Soviets in private conversation, it would lessen the necessity for the Soviet Union to provide direct assistance to Egypt and Syria.[107]

Moscow's message to Algeria's President Boumedienne, which was probably typical of those sent to other Arab leaders, read as follows: "Comrade President, I believe that you agree that the struggle waged at present against the Israeli aggressor for the liberation of Arab territories occupied since 1967 and the safeguarding of the legitimate rights of the people of Palestine affects the vital interests of all Arab countries. In our view, there must be fraternal Arab solidarity today more than ever. Syria and Egypt must not remain alone in the struggle against a treacherous enemy."[108] This and messages sent to other Arab leaders encouraging their help confirmed that Moscow had decided to allow the war to be prolonged and in fact possibly marginally expanded in order to reaffirm its identification with the "progressive" movement.

The deteriorating Syrian position and the Israeli strategic bombing of Syria (which began on October 9) were first treated in a very low-key manner and were only barely mentioned in the Soviet press.[109] A portent of worse things to come, however, was provided by Soviet U.N. representative Malik, who walked out of a meeting of the Security Council following an Israeli apology for the destruction of the Soviet cultural center in Damascus and the death of a Soviet citizen there. Malik, before departing, declared: "The Soviet delegation does not wish to hear excuses and regrets from the representative of murderers and international gangsters."[110]

The reason for the impending violence of the Soviet approach would result from a second Arab rejection of a Soviet-sponsored ceasefire proposal. On October 10, Secretary of State Kissinger through Moscow and London proposed to Egypt a ceasefire in place.[111] This proposal represented a change from the American October 8 position, which favored a ceasefire on the prewar lines. With Egypt still holding the Sinai bridgehead and Syria only just removed from the Golan Heights, the Kissinger suggestion probably seemed to Moscow to offer an opportunity both to reassert détente and to end the war on terms favorable to the Arab point of view.

Coinciding with the proposal, Radio Moscow in its broadcasts to the Arabs for the first time expressed concern regarding the consequences and effects of the fighting. According to the Soviet outlet: "The bloodshed resulting from this armed conflict in the Middle East can leave a serious effect on the whole international situation. The military actions which broke out lately have caused death, tragedies, and destruction." For self-protection, however, this observation was quickly followed by a phrase indicating that "peace and justice" were only possible with "the complete liberation of all the occupied Arab lands."[112]

In spite of the Soviet and American endorsements of the ceasefire in place, however, Egyptian leader Sadat rejected the proposal.[113] Therefore, as the Soviets built up their airlift to its highest level, they concurrently felt it necessary, after again seeming to undercut Egyptian wishes, to reaffirm their support for Arab war aims. On October 12, *Pravda* published an article under the authoritative authorship of "Observer" entitled "Put an End to Israeli Aggression."[114] In the article, "Observer" summarized the various "wrongs" committed by Israel since 1967. These negative acts involved two principal dimensions: (a) Israel sought to use force and intimidation to compel the Arab countries "to capitulate before the aggressor" and acquiesce to the loss of all or large parts of the occupied territories, and (b) Israel wished "to force Egypt and Syria to turn away from the progressive path of development, from social transformations in the interests of the workers, and from cooperation with the socialist states, in a word, to bury in oblivion the political course which was worked out under . . . Nasser." In other words, Israel's continued hold on the occupied territories, in Soviet eyes, tended to undermine the Arabs' confidence in their "progressive" anti-Western social structure and foreign policy.

"Observer" reiterated Soviet support for the Arab demands, expressed satisfaction at the performance of the Egyptian and Syrian armies (the first quasi-official expression of such satisfaction), and noted that other Arab countries were aiding the belligerents. The authoritative commentary concluded that "the responsibility" for the "serious consequences" of the crisis rested on Israel and the "reactionary imperialist forces" which supported it. Again, no mention was made of the desirability of terminating hostilities.

Concurrent with the issuance of the "Observer" commentary signaling continued Soviet support for the Arab war effort, the Soviet freighter *Ilya Mechnikov* was accidentally sunk by Israeli missile boats in the harbor of Tartous, Syria. In the wake of the sinking, a violent TASS declaration was issued which set in motion a propaganda barrage against Israeli deep bombing of Syria and Egypt,[115] condemnations of which had been withheld for three days (since October 9, when the deep bombing commenced), presumably to ease the path to ceasefire. The Egyptian rejection of the ceasefire in place, combined with Moscow's wish to back the Arabs fully, prompted the Soviets to turn their venom against the Israeli air attacks.

The TASS declaration stated that the Israelis were inflicting "great numbers of civilian casualties including women and children" and had embarked on a policy of bombing civilian targets and "ships and peaceful establishments of states not participating in the war" (referring to the *Ilya Mechnikov*[116] and the Damascus Soviet cultural center). In contrast, the Arabs were said to be conducting "combat activities exclusively against the armed forces of the opponent and [have] exhibited a feeling of humanity in relation to the residents of Israeli cities. . . ."

The TASS declaration warned: "If the ruling circles of Israel assume that their activities in regard to peaceful cities and civilian objects of

Syria and Egypt will remain unpunished, then they are deeply mistaken. Aggression cannot remain unpunished and the aggressor should bear severe responsibility for his actions. . . . The Soviet Union cannot remain indifferent to the criminal acts of the Israeli military, as a result of which there are victims among Soviet citizens in Syria and Egypt, and it demands a quick cessation of bombardment of the peaceful cities of Syria and Egypt. . . . Continuation of the criminal actions of Israel will lead to serious consequences for Israel itself." The Soviet declaration therefore implied that unless Israel ceased bombing Arab civilian targets, and particularly cities, it would receive retaliation in kind, possibly administered in part by the Soviet Union. Sadat's threat and use of the Soviet-operated *Scud* missiles in the coming two weeks might well have been linked with this threat.

Following the TASS declaration, tales of Israeli atrocities, most of which were manufactured, began to appear in the Soviet media. *Krasnaya zvezda*, the Ministry of Defense newspaper, declared that "the sadists from Tel Aviv are dropping thousands of bombs and shells especially on homes, hospitals and schools, annihilating the peaceful population."[117] Radio Moscow's Domestic Service declared: "The air pirates' bombs were aimed at crowded cafes, buses filled with passengers, and lines at bus stops. We have learned today of yet another trick carried out by Tel Aviv's valiant aces. At some inhabited settlements, they dropped objects which had the appearance of ordinary household articles: transistor radios, canned goods, watches, fountain pens and pencils. Out of those who attempted to pick up these objects, mainly children, 47 were killed on the spot and 139 were seriously wounded. . . ."[118] The Trade Union Council's organ, *Trud*, stated that "Israeli pilots are dropping explosive dolls on Syrian cities."[119] Many similar atrocity stories appeared repeatedly in other Soviet organs.

In addition, the Soviet press began to print stories indicating that American "volunteers" were departing for Israel—the usual manner of suggesting that Soviet "volunteers" might soon be dispatched to the Arab countries. *Pravda*, on October 13, reprinted a story from the Spanish newspaper *Ya* which declared that 150 American pilots who had served in Vietnam had passed through Spain enroute to Israel under the guise of tourists.[120] On October 14, *Pravda* published a TASS story from Paris indicating that Arab ambassadors there had stated that Damascus had been bombed by aircraft piloted by Americans.[121] On October 15, *Pravda* printed a TASS London story which indicated that a group of "volunteers," composed of "Americans of Jewish nationality," departed from New York to Israel.[122] In addition, the Moscow TASS wire on October 15 reported that there were 30,000 American "volunteers" waiting for transport from the United States to

Israel, including "Vietnam War veterans who have signed contracts with the Israeli Government."[123]

Alluding more directly to Russian volunteers, Soviet citizen Victor Louis, regarded generally as an unofficial spokesman of Moscow, indicated that the Arabs were recruiting "volunteers" in the Soviet Union, purportedly to help open the Suez Canal.[124] (On the other hand, *Pravda*, on October 15, published an account of the State Department's denial that Americans were directly involved in the war.) Simultaneously with the publicity on American and Russian "volunteers," several thousand Soviet military personnel were, in fact, dispatched to Egypt and Syria to augment Soviet advisers and support personnel present before the war.[125]

As Moscow's position hardened behind the Arabs, both hopefulness and concern regarding the future success of the Egyptian and Syrian cause were aired. A Soviet military officer, writing in *Krasnaya zvezda* on October 13, pointed to the fact that Egypt had captured the Bar-Lev Line and the town of Qantara. Possibly making reference to the deep Sinai goal of the forthcoming October 14–15 Egyptian attack, the officer pointed out that "this city (Qantara) has great significance as it is united by highway with the city of El Arish . . . near which is located the supply base of the Israeli Army." Outweighing the optimism, however, were cautions that "now in Tel Aviv they openly threaten that Israeli forces will not stop at the 1967 ceasefire lines." For the first time, the officer gave Soviet military readers a fairly accurate summary of the size of the Israeli armed forces (430 combat aircraft, 1,500 tanks, and so forth), which to those not knowledgeable of levels of Soviet aid to the Arabs (most Soviet officers) would seem quite large. The analysis concluded on the guardedly optimistic note that the Arabs had a fine air-defense system and were "well-prepared."[126]

In addition to possible uneasiness regarding the future course of Arab military fortunes, the Soviets were apparently growing increasingly sensitive about the damage being inflicted on the Soviet détente posture. In remarks delivered at an October 15 dinner for Danish Prime Minister Anker Jorgensen (published after a two-day delay, possibly indicating some leadership controversy), Chairman Kosygin stated that "it is impossible not to see that the opponents of détente try to use any pretext to turn back to the atmosphere of 'cold war' and bring forth lack of confidence in the policy of peaceful coexistence. . . . The matter has reached the point where the solidarity of the Soviet union with the victims of aggression, the Arab countries, is presented as a source of tension. . . ." Kosygin signaled Soviet priorities, however, by pointing out that while the Soviet Union would contribute to the "reduction of international tension," it would not do this "at the expense of its own principles, which we do not change and which were confirmed at the XXIV Congress of the Communist Party of the Soviet Union. This concerns the principle of the firm rebuff of imperialist aggression."[127]

Kosygin's remarks apparently reflected the ambivalent message of support and restraint being given to the Arabs. From October 14 through October 15, Algerian leader Houri Boumedienne made an unexpected visit to Moscow to solicit more arms for the Arab belligerents and to inquire about Russian political intentions.[128] According to one source, the Russians told the Algerian leader that their support for the Arab cause was total, even if the Arabs had to go beyond the pre-1967 boundaries.[129] Soviet "total" support, however, was apparently conditioned by reservations regarding further pursuit of war. Reflecting probable disagreements between the two sides, the final communiqué described the Algerian-Soviet conversations as both "friendly" and "frank"[130]—the formula usually used to denote the presence of some disagreement.

With *Pravda* acknowledging that the "Damascus area" of Syria had come under bombardment from Israeli long-range artillery,[131] and with Soviet concerns raised with regard to détente, Chairman Kosygin traveled to Cairo on October 16 (and stayed until October 19) in order to convince Egyptian leader Sadat of the advisability of ceasefire. Coupled with a belief that détente would be jeopardized by a continuation of the war, the Soviet leadership may have developed a military logic which suggested that, after the halt of the Israeli attack in Syria, conditions were ripe for a ceasefire. Moscow may have believed that the Syrian blocking of the Israeli blitzkrieg marked the end of Israeli military, and hence political, advantages.[132]

Radio Moscow, in a broadcast to Europe on October 16, analyzed the military situation in the following terms: "The Israeli aggressor now is confronted with a situation which he wished to avoid at all costs. Israel is now forced to wage a long war on several fronts which will exhaust its strength. . . . Israel's political and military leaders hoped that by a blitzkrieg [against Syria] they would be able to bridge the contradiction between the relatively long duration of a modern war and Israel's own inability to withstand long-lasting burdens in its struggle against superior enemies. This explains the plan to first defeat one enemy, Syria, and then to turn against Egypt with all its might; this explains the concentrated use of armored and motorized units in spearhead attack; hence Israel's attempts to establish its air superiority in the Syrian-Israeli theater of operations and to dominate the air in the directions of attack in order to secure freedom of maneuvering. Their blitz decisions were taken not only to paralyze Syria but also to prevent its allies from entering into combat immediately and actively. . . . The

Israeli blitzkrieg above all was based on the utilization of temporary advantages which have been lost irretrievably due to the failure of its blitzkrieg strategy against Syria."[133]

The end of Israel's "temporary advantages," therefore, would place Tel Aviv in a weakened position vis-à-vis the basically stronger Arab states should a ceasefire take effect. In such a ceasefire situation, the Arabs would have the credible political leverage (given the demonstrated failure of Israel's blitzkrieg to achieve decisive results, particularly after Syria's forces were again rebuilt) to threaten Israel with a prolonged "war of attrition" should political concessions not be forthcoming. On the other hand, if a ceasefire were not achieved, the Israelis could shift forces from still-battered Syria to Sinai and seek to establish new "temporary advantages" for a possible blitzkrieg against Egypt. Demonstrating that the Soviets were noting this possibility, *Pravda* on October 16 reported that Israeli air raids in Syria had decreased and that Israeli forces were being diverted to the Egyptian front.[134]

Kosygin's trip to Cairo, according to Secretary of State Kissinger, was for the purpose of reconciling Arab demands for an immediate commitment to a return to the 1967 borders (voiced again in the October 16 Sadat speech[135]) with Israeli insistence on secure borders and a negotiated settlement.[136] Kosygin's attempt to bridge the gap between Egyptian and Israeli desiderata may not have been equally welcomed by all members of the Soviet leadership. Politburo member and Trade Union Council chief A. N. Shelepin, for example, speaking in Bulgaria on October 16, condemned Israel in the strongest terms and stated that Tel Aviv was backed not only by "reactionary imperialist forces" but also by "international Zionism," a term which had fallen somewhat into disuse after the 1970 "anti-Zionist" campaign. Shelepin was unequivocal in stating that the Arabs' struggle was a "natural right" and that there must be "a full and unconditional withdrawal of Israeli forces from all occupied territories."[137]

Shelepin's speech, particularly in reference to the Middle East, apparently overstepped the bounds of acceptable militance. (For one thing, his advocacy of full and unconditional withdrawal tended to undercut any ceasefire initiative.) The speech was printed in its entirety only in the Trade Union Council's own newspaper, *Trud*. The Central Committee's organ *Pravda* ignored Shelepin's remarks concerning the Middle East and referred only to his statements on Chile and trade-union matters.[138] The Council of Ministers' newspaper *Izvestiya* only stated that Shelepin "delivered a large speech" and did not describe any of his comments.[139] The Ministry of Defense's *Krasnaya zvezda* printed a lengthy TASS dispatch describing the speech which, though not specifically spelling out Shelepin's stand on the Middle East, was revealing of the anti-détente tone of his remarks: "Realistically evaluating the situation in the world and expressing just satisfaction with the relaxation (détente) achieved, the orator [Shelepin] continued, we at the same time depart from the fact that this is only a beginning. The nature and character of imperialism remains as before, as the recent events in the Near East and Chile again and again warn us."[140]

Almost as if to counter Shelepin's seemingly splitting activity, on the following day Politburo member Podgorny took the unusual step (for a senior Politburo member) of reaffirming General Secretary Brezhnev's primacy in the ruling body. At a ceremony on October 17, in which the Gold Star Medal was presented to Politburo member Marshal Grechko on his seventieth birthday, Podgorny expressed appreciation for the Minister of Defense's contribution to the "close, united collective [the Politburo] headed by Leonid Il'yich Brezhnev."[141] While Brezhnev's primacy was being reasserted in Moscow, Kosygin continued his labors in Cairo. Presumably, as the Israelis enlarged their west bank salient, Sadat became more easy to convince that a ceasefire was necessary.

On October 19, when Kosygin left Cairo bound for Damascus enroute to Moscow, Egyptian agreement on a ceasefire formula had apparently been reached. According to the Yugoslav press agency TANJUG, the following conditions were agreed to by Sadat and Kosygin:

(a) A ceasefire would be arranged with the help of the United States and the Soviet Union while Israel withdrew to 1967 boundaries with "some small corrections."
(b) The borders between the warring sides would be guaranteed by "international forces" mainly from the United States and the Soviet Union and members of the Security Council.
(c) The agreement on a ceasefire would be verified and controlled by "international peace forces," including forces from the United States and the Soviet Union.
(d) The Soviet Union and the United States would guarantee the inviolability of these frontiers by their physical presence either separately or with others.[142]

While one cannot be certain that the Yugoslav version is accurate, the presence of the Yugoslav foreign minister in Cairo at the time of the Kosygin-Sadat talks lends credence to the TANJUG report.[143] At any rate, when Kosygin returned to Moscow on October 19, the Soviet leadership communicated the Kosygin-Sadat formula to Secretary of State Kissinger. In Kissinger's words, "We began exploring a new formula for ending the war that evening, though it was still unacceptable to us."[144]

Presumably, if the Yugoslav account is correct, the Sadat-Kosygin formula was unacceptable to the United States because the proposal's insistence on an Israeli withdrawal to the pre-1967 lines seemed to reflect a superpower *diktat* which was inconsistent with Tel Aviv's desire to achieve a pullback through negotiations with the Arabs. Moreover, the formula would place American and Soviet forces in direct confrontation should implementation of the pullback not proceed as planned.[145]

While Washington was considering the Kosygin-Sadat formula and Israeli troops continued to expand their bridgehead on the west bank of the Suez Canal, General Secretary Brezhnev "sent an urgent request to President Nixon that [Kissinger] be sent to Moscow to conduct the negotiations in order to speed an end to hostilities that might be difficult to contain were they to continue."[146] Kissinger departed for Moscow on October 20 and spent two days of "intense negotiations" in the Soviet capital. In the days immediately preceding the negotiations, the Soviet press spelled out in more detail the political-military factors which indicated that the current situation was not unfavorable from the Russian point of view and which counseled the advisability of acceptance of a ceasefire rather than increased efforts to assist the Arabs. According to many of these accounts, because of Arab gains already achieved in the war, Israel's political-military advantages derived from victory in the 1967 Six-Day War had definitely been lost.

Colonel A. Leont'yev, in a *Krasnaya zvezda* article entitled "When the Mirage Dissipates," quoted a statement by General Secretary Brezhnev at the XXIV Party Congress which predicted that Israel's 1967 gains would be short-lived: "The advantages, received by the conquerors as a result of the criminal attack, in the final analysis are illusory. They will disappear as a mirage dissipates in the sands of Sinai." According to Leont'yev, Brezhnev's prediction had been realized in the October 1973 war because (a) the "myth of Israeli invincibility" had been shattered, and (b) the correlation of forces in the Middle East had changed. The latter factor was evidenced, according to Leont'yev, by the fact that the Egyptians and Syrians had shown themselves to be militarily powerful and skillful and because combat had been actively joined by many more Arab countries than in the past.[147]

Izvestiya's V. Kudryavtsev pointed out that the Arabs' psychological and socioeconomic transformations, coupled with the world energy shortage, had immeasurably strengthened the Arab cause. According to Kudryavtsev, these factors passed by the consciousness of Israel, which "believes that its possibilities are on the 1967 level." The *Izvestiya* commentator, in a rare direct Soviet anti-Semitic reference, explained that Israel's "misperception" was natural given the fact that Tel Aviv's policy was dictated by "monopolies [which] are a foreign continuation of those big American companies which Jewish capital controls."[148] *Pravda*'s Pavel Demchenko, like Leont'yev, felt that the "most important outcome" of the war was that "at the most difficult moment, the majority of Arab countries rose to defend the common just cause."[149]

While the changes to the detriment of Israel in the Middle East were being noted, Soviet observers focused on another aspect of Tel Aviv's "weakness"—its links with the United States. In *Izvestiya*'s news magazine, *Nedelya*, the above-cited Kudryavtsev stated that American support for Israel (presumably diplomatic) did "not compare with 1967." The commentator asserted that "between 1967 and 1973, there lies the period of aggression in South East Asia (the Vietnam War). . . . There is not the same international situation, not the same balance of forces, and not the same political atmosphere."[150]

In a most interesting article which appeared in *Literaturnaya gazeta* on October 17, Mikhail Sagetelyan made the most thorough case demonstrating that American support for Israel was indeed weak. It is quite possible, of course, that Sagetelyan's article may have been intentionally directed against "hawks" such as Shelepin who tended to identify Israel and the United States as simply two sides of the same "imperialist" coin. This hypothesis is strengthened by the fact that the writer, in concluding his account, asserted in an unusual polemical manner that "only politically immature people can deny the significance of this argument in assessing the situation in the Near East."[151]

Sagatelyan's argument was that, because of growing Arab unity, the Arab oil states could threaten both Western Europe and the United States "not only with an oil blockade but also with the withdrawal of their multi-billion dollar accounts from Western banks." These weapons would play an "important, if not decisive, role" because in 1973 "oil hunger in the capitalist world is much more real" than in 1967. In addition to economic factors, Sagatelyan continued, "it should be borne in mind that the United States has only recently emerged from the Vietnam conflict, having barely managed to keep the country from irreversible social upheavals. The lessons of Vietnam, when Washington . . . allowed its Saigon clients to generally influence U.S. foreign policy have not been in vain. . . . *Sober observers* [emphasis mine] draw attention to the fact that appeals for restraint are now being made not only by a whole series of the largest U.S. newspapers but also by high-ranking U.S. officials. In a number of recent public statements, they have stressed by every possible means the fact that a beneficial influence is being exerted on the U.S. situation within the country and beyond its borders by the fact that, for the first time since World War II, the United States is not taking part in any military conflict." To back this argument, Sagatelyan produced four illustrative recent American remarks: (a) the United States has only "a five day oil reserve" (Senator Mike Mansfield); (b) the United States does not intend to play "some ostentatious game in which the United States would intervene and take some unilateral step which would then fail" (President Richard Nixon); (c) Zionists control Congress. "In our country the Zionists are very wealthy, very powerful, and politically very cunning." Israeli expansionism is regrettable (Senator J. William Fulbright); and (d) the United States is striving for a ceasefire in place, and arms supplies to Israel are tied to acceptance of this proposal (Secretary of State Henry Kissinger). According to Sagetelyan, therefore, the United States was not wholeheartedly juxtaposed against Soviet interests in the Middle East.

It thus seems apparent that, by the time of Kissinger's arrival in Moscow, the dominant body of opinion in the Politburo favored a ceasefire, not only because of the dangerous decline of Arab fortunes and the negative effect of continued war on the Soviet "peace" image but also because Israel indeed had been deprived of its "advantages" within the Middle East and in the international arena. Furthermore, the fact that Israel was operating increasingly in isolation from the principal "imperialist" powers lessened the perceived necessity that the Soviet Union had to help deliver a "decisive rebuff" to Tel Aviv.

Against this background, Brezhnev and Kissinger reached an agreement on a ceasefire which, on October 21, was submitted as a jointly sponsored resolution to the U.N. Security Council. The resolution, number 338, was approved unanimously by the Council, with the exception of China, which abstained after calling for condemnation of Israel.

Resolution 338 had the following provisions:

(a) A ceasefire should take place within twelve hours of adoption of the resolution in the positions currently occupied.
(b) The parties concerned should "immediately start . . . implementation" of Security Council Resolution 242. (Resolution 242 called for the return of unspecified occupied lands, recognition of secure borders for all states, and so forth.)
(c) Immediately and concurrently with the ceasefire, negotiations should start "between the parties concerned under appropriate auspices aimed at establishing a just and durable peace in the Middle East.[152]

The Security Council Resolution reflected the following play of interests. In view of Israel's rapid forward moves on the west bank of Suez, the implementation of a ceasefire in place had clearly now become a matter of urgent Egyptian, as well as Soviet, interest. It also reflected the position which the United States had espoused since October 10.

Inclusion of reference to Resolution 242 was presumably a concession to Egyptian demands that the Israelis withdraw from the occupied territories. In deference to Tel Aviv, however, the call was to "start . . . implementation," not "to implement." The third point regarding the beginning of talks was inserted to satisfy Israeli demands for direct negotiations but was phrased in a manner which obscured whether the talks would have to be face-to-face talks on a state-to-state level as Tel Aviv desired. As Secretary Kissinger pointed out, however, this was "the first international commitment to negotiations between the parties in the Middle East conflict."[153]

Because of Egypt's rapidly deteriorating military situation, the United States may have been able to exact an agreement more completely satisfactory from Tel Aviv's point of view. Secretary Kissinger, however, restrained American demands because of his desire not to see the war prolonged (with its potential for a superpower clash) as well as his wish not to alienate the Arabs diplomatically. As the secretary of state declared, the two principles guiding American diplomacy during the war were (a) the necessity to end the war as soon as possible and (b) the requirement to end hostilities in a manner which would enable us to make "a major contribution to removing the conditions that have produced four wars between Arabs and Israelis"[154] that is, the United States should be in a position to act as an honest broker between both sides in the Middle East.

The Soviet press, which only briefly reported on Kissinger's presence in Moscow (and ceased all interpretative analysis of the Middle East during his stay), also gave only simple factual coverage to the joint American-Soviet ceasefire resolution. *Pravda* did, however, report on Kissinger's reply to Foreign Minister Gromyko's congratulatory telegram regarding the former's nomination as secretary of state. According to *Pravda*, Kissinger expressed "hope for continuation of mutual efforts to strengthen constructive relations between the United States and the U.S.S.R."[155]

Good feelings, however, were short-lived. In spite of the acceptance of the ceasefire by both Israel and Egypt, one or both parties violated the pact and fighting continued. Curiously, initial Soviet news reports were somewhat ambiguous regarding the party responsible for the ceasefire collapse. According to both *Pravda* and *Izvestiya*, "Israel used the night of October 22–23 to re-group its forces and move some of its units into the [areas of] disposition of the Egyptian forces. . . . The Israeli Air Force strafed Egyptian units. . . . These actions of Israel block fulfillment of the Security Council ceasefire resolution and force the Egyptian armed forces to deliver counter-strikes on Israeli forces in the positions occupied . . . after the ceasefire."[156]

Regardless of who initiated the fighting, however, it was soon clear that Israel was continuing its gains of previous days at Egyptian expense. Because of the desire to avert a humiliating defeat for the Egyptians and because Tel Aviv seemed to be directly flaunting the superpower agreement in a search for new "advantages," Moscow took a very serious view of the Israeli advance. On October 23, the Soviet government issued a declaration (only the second Soviet government declaration of the war) which stated that Israel's adherence to the Resolution 338 ceasefire had been "a crude lie" under whose cover "the Israeli military treacherously attacked the positions of the Egyptian forces as well as peaceful populated points of . . . Egypt. These actions of . . . Israel are an arrogant trampling on a decision of the Security Council and a challenge to the people of the whole world." The Soviet government "demanded" that Israel cease fire and withdraw to the October 22 lines. If Tel Aviv refused, "the Soviet Government warns the Government of Israel of the most serious consequences which continuation of its aggressive activities against the Arab Republic of Egypt and the Syrian Arab Republic will bring."[157]

Though not as threatening in the specific manner of the TASS declaration published on October 14, the fact that the new statement was issued as a Soviet government declaration indicated that Moscow wished to give added weight to its words. It should be noted that the statement's reference to Israeli attacks on "peaceful populated points," coming as it did the day after the Egyptian-Soviet rocket firing at Israeli troops on the west bank, may have constituted an implied threat to fire the *Scud* rockets in Egypt at Israeli cities.[158]

In response to the ceasefire violations, the Security Council again met on October 23 and adopted Resolution 339, which reiterated the call for a ceasefire and a return to the October 22 positions. The new resolution also called for the dispatch of U.N. observers to monitor the ceasefire. Concurrently, Syria announced acceptance of the October 22 ceasefire but made acceptance conditional on Israeli withdrawal from the territories occupied after 1967.[159]

In spite of the new ceasefire resolution, fighting continued on the west bank, and Israeli forces tightened the encirclement of the beleaguered Egyptian Third Army in the southern section of the Sinai bridgehead. In order to halt the Israelis, on October 24 Egyptian President Sadat appealed to General Secretary Brezhnev and President Nixon to send forces to police the ceasefire.[160] The Sadat initiative, while endorsed and possibly orchestrated by the Soviets, was received extremely negatively in Washington. The United States wanted the ceasefire to be enforced, but it also wished to avoid joint Great Power *diktats* and possible superpower confrontation.

At the United Nations on October 24, Egyptian Foreign Minister al-Zayyat informed the Security Council (in a phrase highlighted in bold-face type in *Pravda*) that "the President of Egypt appealed to the Soviet Union and the United States of America to send contingents of forces of these countries to the Near East to guarantee the ceasefire line."[161] At the same time, however, the Soviet press indicated that American U.N. representative Scali had stated that "it is still not time for participation of the Great Powers and the sending of their forces to the ceasefire line."[162]

In response to the Egyptian appeal, Soviet U.N. representative Malik declared that "Israel's violation is a carefully thought out and calculated provocation to obstruct the ceasefire and to seize territory." According to Malik, the new situation was a "serious threat to the cause of peace, and not only in the Near East." Indicating that the purpose of Soviet pressure was to induce the United States to restrain Israel, Malik declared that the United States, as coauthor of the Security Council ceasefire resolution, had taken upon itself "the responsibility to guarantee the fulfillment of this resolution by Israel" and that, therefore, "the United States should call Israel to order."

Malik added that the Security Council should adopt strict sanctions against Israel and call on U.N. member states to break diplomatic relations with Tel Aviv. Then, unlike Scali, in the first direct Russian threat of intervention in the war, the Soviet representative asserted: "I am fully authorized to declare that in light of the fact that Israel continues aggression, the proposal of Egypt to send contingents of USSR and U.S. forces to the area of conflict is fully justified and in accordance with the U.N. Charter."[163]

Malik's October 24 intervention threat, though the most pointed Soviet threat yet introduced, appeared to be qualified in two dimensions. For one thing, he mentioned parallel Soviet and American action, not a unilateral Soviet move. Secondly, he spoke of "contingents" of forces, implying a small dispatch of troops rather than a massive, open-ended involvement.

Further indications that the intervention and other threats may have encountered reservations in Moscow and therefore were carefully measured were provided by Soviet reportage of Egyptian Foreign Minister al-Zayyat's commentary at the United Nations on Israeli actions. According to the TASS story from New York, al-Zayyat had declared that "Egyptian forces were subjected to attack by rocket weapons." This report, which was untrue,[164] was reprinted in *Izvestiya*, *Krasnaya zvezda*, *Trud*, and the Moscow TASS wire.[165] Conspicuously, however, in reprinting the very TASS story, *Pravda* omitted this one line.[166]

It is, of course, possible that the TASS account was intended to serve as a possible pretext for further use of Soviet-operated *Scud* rockets against Israeli forces or even cities. If this is true, apparently someone associated with the Central Committee secretariat or staff (*Pravda's* overseers) may have objected to such an approach. Given a possible division of opinion in Moscow on the appropriate length to which the Soviet Union should go to chastise Israel, it was quite likely that the Soviet leadership was carefully graduating its threats.

Concurrent with Malik's endorsement of Sadat's Soviet-American force proposal at the United Nations, Soviet Ambassador Dobrynin in Washington at approximately 8:00 P.M., October 24, delivered a note to the president from General Secretary Brezhnev (by one account, a telephone message at 7:05 P.M.) which, like Malik's comments, approved Sadat's joint-force proposal.[167] Then, some two hours and forty-five minutes later (by another account at 9:25 P.M.), Dobrynin delivered yet another note from Brezhnev to Mr. Nixon (reportedly by telephone to Secretary Kissinger) which set the stage for the American force alert which followed. This second Brezhnev note made the Soviet threat to undertake unilateral actions unambiguous. The note did not specify the nature of the unilateral actions however.

Brezhnev's second note contained four paragraphs and began with the salutation "Mr. President" instead of the usual "My Dear Mr. President." The note's first paragraph indicated that Israel continued to ignore the jointly sponsored U.N. ceasefire resolution and that this represented a challenge to the Soviet Union and the United States. The second paragraph asserted the need to "implement" the ceasefire resolutions and "invited" the United States to join the Soviet Union "to compel observance of the ceasefire without delay." The third paragraph stated: "I will say it straight, that if you find it impossible to act with us in this matter, we should be faced with the necessity urgently to consider the question of taking appropriate steps unilaterally. Israel cannot be permitted to get away with the violations." In the final paragraph, however, the Communist Party chief told Nixon: "I value our relationship."[168]

Brezhnev's note, combined with other disturbing Soviet actions, caused much alarm in Washington. It was felt that the Soviets might be on the point of unilaterally intervening on a large scale in the Middle East. As a consequence, Secretary of State Kissinger, Secretary of Defense Schlesinger, Director of the Central Intelligence Agency Colby, and Chairman of the Joint Chiefs of Staff Moorer met in an "abbreviated" version of the National Security Council to consider the appropriate response to Soviet actions. It was decided at about 11:40 P.M., October 24, that the readiness of American forces should be raised to Defense Condition Three, a heightened-alert status for all American forces stationed around the world, including those handling strategic nuclear weapons.[169]

This dramatic gesture by the American government raised questions both in the United States and abroad as to whether the large-scale alert was justified by Soviet actions or was motivated instead by domestic political considerations. As Secretary of State Kissinger categorically dismissed the latter as a factor in the decision on the alert, it is perhaps worthwhile to consider the possible Soviet actions which led the Nixon administration to declare the alert.

On October 17 or October 18, according to Secretary of Defense Schlesinger, American officials had detected that Soviet airborne forces had been put on alert.[170] As airborne units had apparently already been alerted at the beginning of the Yom Kippur War, the October 17/18 alert may have been a move to heightened readiness over the level imposed by the earlier alert. On the other hand, it may have marked the restoration of the original alert if, for some reason, it had been canceled. (According to columnist Joseph Alsop, three of seven alerted Soviet airborne divisions were, in fact, placed at a high state of readiness at airfields waiting to take off.[171] This information cannot be confirmed however.)

In addition to the alerted Soviet airborne forces, American observers had been disturbed by the slowdown of Soviet supply flights to the Middle East on October 22 and the cessation of flights on October 23.[172] It was thought possible that the aircraft had been withdrawn to the Soviet Union to prepare to transport the alerted airborne troops to the Middle East. One commentator asserts that in the late evening of October 24–25 (according to another account, the morning of October 24), before the alert was decided, American intelligence satellites observed the take-off of what may have been the largest Soviet airlift of the crisis.[173] It was not apparent until the aircraft landed in the Middle East on October 25 that the planes carried arms and not troops.[174] While it cannot be discounted that the Soviets, at some earlier point, had thought of dispatching airborne forces, it is also possible that the withdrawal of the transport aircraft to the Soviet Union simply coincided with the adoption of the U.N. ceasefire and the planned termination of the Russian airlift. Soviet intentions with regard to the airlift are thus a moot point.

Besides the airborne troops and air transports, certain other factors preoccupied Washington. The Soviets, in the course of the Yom Kippur War, had built up their Mediterranean naval flotilla from its usual level of sixty ships to some eighty-four vessels, thereby far exceeding the total of American ships in the Mediterranean.[175] In addition, presumably to further deter Western action, they had "declared" (announced the imminent transfer of) many more ships through the Bosporus than they actually dispatched.[176]

In spite of the Russian increase, however, the commander of the U.S. Sixth Fleet, Vice-Admiral Daniel Murphy, pointed out that the United States retained an edge in firepower over the Soviets since some 40 percent of the Soviet fleet (totaling 84 vessels) was composed of support ships while only 20 percent of the Sixth Fleet (total 60 vessels), was composed of support ships.[177]

Moreover, it is important to note that Soviet ship design was based on a concept valid primarily for nuclear battle. Little provision, for example, was made for replenishment of missile ordnance on ships beyond the first loading.[178] Also, the Russian ships had no tactical air cover. The Soviet fleet deployed in the Mediterranean, therefore, was useful only as an instrument of deterrence or in a first-strike nuclear-war role.

According to Admiral Worth Bagley, commander-in-chief, U.S. Naval Forces, Europe, the Soviet fleet in the Mediterranean during the war "looked as though they were taking some care not to cause an incident," and, in fact, the Russians were "restrained and considerate."[179] While Soviet bombers operated over the Mediterranean during the war, they made no attempt to "shadow" the Sixth Fleet.[180] The Russians, for the most part, positioned their augmented naval forces in the general area south of Cyprus and Crete where the American Sixth Fleet was operating. According to Admiral Bagley, though the Russians were circumspect, "they deployed their ships and submarines so that our forces were targeted for instant attack from multiple points."[181]

The Russian deployments suggested that while the Soviets did not wish to provoke the Americans, they also wanted to deter the Sixth Fleet from any action on shore. As Admiral Bagley noted, during the war the U.S. Sixth Fleet had about three hundred aircraft and three thousand marines on station in the Mediterranean,[182] a formidable capability, at least in terms of aircraft, should the United States have elected to intervene in combat on the shore.

The Russians, on the other hand, had no tactical air capability in the Mediterranean and only a limited capacity to deploy naval infantry. The latter threat, however, undoubtedly entered into American calculations regarding the alert.

Before the war the Russians had approximately four *Alligator*-class, LST-type, amphibious landing vessels stationed in the Mediterranean. During the war, these vessels were augmented by some four additional *Alligators*. All of the *Alligators* called at Arab ports during the course of the war and were believed to have delivered tanks to the Arab belligerents. By the time of the American alert, however, two of the eight *Alligators* had already departed the Mediterranean to return to the Black Sea, and the Soviet navy had "declared" that two more would imminently depart. (One additional *Alligator*, however, was joining the Mediterranean fleet from its West African station.)

Just before the American alert, several Soviet naval vessels, probably including some *Alligators*, moved to within twenty miles of the Egyptian coastline. While this naval movement suggested a possible intervention, later analysis implied that the Russians may have been covering a Sixth Fleet force re-deployment. Even if the Russians had desired to disembark naval infantry, their capability was largely symbolic. The six *Alligators* remaining in the Mediterranean could accommodate at maximum only three hundred naval infantrymen each. This means that even if each *Alligator* was fully loaded with naval infantrymen, which by no means was certain, only eighteen hundred troops were available for landing. In all probability, in fact, only a few hundred Soviet naval infantrymen were present.[183] These troops would, of course, have been sufficient for a politically symbolic Soviet ground-force presence in Egypt, however.

Another factor which was probably considered in declaring the American alert was the October 22 Egyptian-Soviet firing of *Scud* missiles at Israeli forces. While the *Scuds* that had been fired were armed with conventional warheads, American decisionmakers may have felt that the Russians might turn next to nuclear weapons. American sources had detected the transfer of nuclear material through the Bosporus on Soviet ships before the alert. Several of the ships had called at Egyptian ports, thereby raising speculation that the nuclear material consisted of atomic warheads for the *Scuds*.[184] Adding to the mystery was the fact that Soviet ships had also departed Egyptian ports with nuclear material on board.[185]

Although U.S. analysts were reported to have detected "some missile support equipment inside Egypt normally associated with the handling of nuclear warheads," Senators Symington and Stennis of the Armed Services Committee, after examining the relevant evidence, stated that they doubted the presence of nuclear warheads in Egypt.[186] Secretary of State Kissinger also stated that "we have no confirmed evidence" that the nuclear warheads were installed. Kissinger added that a dispatch of nuclear warheads would be "a grave matter" and "a fundamental shift in traditional practices."[187] While some speculation was raised that nuclear material may have been transferred between Soviet ships in an Egyptian harbor, it is perhaps more logical to assume that the passage of nuclear material through the Bosporus was either a case of Soviet-provoked "disinformation" or a demonstrative gesture of deterrence.[188]

In summary, then, it can be seen that five major factors probably contributed to the proclamation of the American defense alert: (a) the Brezhnev notes and the Malik declaration at the United Nations proposing intervention in the Middle East, (b) the alerted status of Soviet airborne troops, (c) the pullback of Russian transport aircraft, (d) the build-up of the Soviet navy, particularly the move of Soviet naval units to within twenty miles of the Egyptian coast, and (e) the firing of *Scud* missiles at Israeli troops, coupled with the transport of nuclear material through the Bosporus.

As outlined, however, all indications of a possible Russian intervention were quite ambiguous. For this reason, Secretary of State Kissinger pointed out that the Russians had not taken any "irrevocable action" and that the American alert was largely a "precautionary" measure.[189] Secretary of Defense Schlesinger also added, "We were far away from a military confrontation. We were taking actions to preclude a military confrontation."[190]

Secretary of State Kissinger explained his desire to forestall Russian intervention in the Middle East, largely in terms of avoiding a superpower confrontation. In Kissinger's words: "It is inconceivable that the forces of the great powers should be introduced in the numbers that would be necessary to overpower both of the participants. It is inconceivable that we should transplant the Great Power rivalry into the Middle East or, alternatively, that we should impose a military condominium by the United States and the Soviet Union. The United States is even more opposed to the unilateral introduction by any great power —especially by any nuclear power—of military forces into the Middle East, in whatever guise those forces should be introduced."[191]

It is probable, in spite of Kissinger's fear of a Great Power confrontation, that the Russians were focusing their ire more at the Israelis than at the United States. While Brezhnev's tone toward the American president hardened in his note warning of intervention, he still referred to the value he placed on his relationship with Mr. Nixon. Likewise, Malik had spoken only of joint intervention. It would appear that the second Brezhnev note suggesting a possible unilateral Soviet move was meant to only heighten the pressure on the United States to restrain Israel. As Egyptian Deputy Premier Hatem later pointed out, the Soviet threat to send troops to the Middle East was "an escalation to force the United States to pressure Israel to observe the ceasefire."[192]

In spite of the vast American alert and the subsequent posturing in Washington concerning the effect which the alert allegedly had on preventing Soviet intervention, the United States in fact did exactly what the Soviet Union wished when the Russian leadership floated the intervention threats. According to former Israeli Minister of Defense Moshe Dayan, "The Americans passed on to us evidence that Soviet airborne forces were prepared to intevene directly to save the Egyptian Second and Third Armies. Unless Israel accepted a ceasefire, the United States would not stand in the way of the Soviet Union."[193] Needless to say, the Israelis fully adhered to the ceasefire. Thus, as in 1956 and 1967, the United States again proved that Soviet intervention threats were a highly effective element of Russian crisis diplomacy. (Rather than declaring a meaningless alert and putting pressure on Israel, a better response to the Russian threats might have been a diplomatic statement that the United States was also concerned with implementing a ceasefire and that we would seek to convince Israel of the necessity of such a move. However, the United States could not consider employing its influence under the threat or reality of Soviet intervention.)

Soviet official reaction to the American alert was delayed until October 27. In the interim, however, General Secretary Brezhnev delivered a speech to the World Congress of Peace-loving Forces in Moscow which indicated the direction of the Soviet response.[194] In Brezhnev's words: "The Soviet Union is ready to cooperate with all interested countries in the cause of normalizing the situation in the Near East. But such cooperation, of course, cannot [be used as a basis to justify] the actions undertaken in recent days by certain circles of the NATO countries [to create] an artificial fanning of passions through some kind of fantastic conjectures about the intentions of the Soviet Union in the Near East." Brezhnev, therefore, implied that accusations of an imminent Soviet intervention were false. In view of the fact that the United States had pressured Israel into adhering to the ceasefire, there was no necessity for the intervention threat to be prolonged or defended.

Alluding to Sadat's request for American and Soviet troops to guarantee the ceasefire, the Soviet leader declared: "President of Egypt Sadat has appealed to the Soviet Union and the United States with a request for them to send their representatives to the area of military activities. . . . We expressed a readiness to satisfy the request of Egypt and have already sent our representatives. (Prolonged applause.) We hope that the U.S. Government will act in the same way." Brezhnev thus portrayed the Soviet dispatch of some seventy observers to the newly established U.N. truce-supervising organization as the fulfillment of the Sadat request which had aroused so much sound and fury only a few hours before. (The U.N. Emergency Force which was established, alongside the truce-supervision group, specifically excluded permanent representatives of the Security Council. Soviet accession to this proviso on October 25 marked the end of tension regarding large-scale Soviet military intervention in the conflict.)

The intended thrust of Brezhnev's message on the Middle East events apparently was to demonstrate that the Soviet Union had been a re-

sponsible force in the crisis, thereby boosting its credentials as a pro-
ponent of détente, and, at the same time, to point out quite moderately
that there were elements in the West who still opposed Soviet policies.
On the détente side, Brezhnev indicated that "the Soviet Union [before
the Yom Kippur War] warned and emphasized many times that the
situation in the Near East was explosive" and that during the war,
"from the moment of renewal of military activities . . . the Soviet
Union, maintaining close contact with the friendly Arab states, undertook all political measures dependent on it to assist ending the war. . . ."
On the side of the need for "vigilance" against "imperialism," Brezhnev
asserted in a most mild tone that Israel relied on "sponsorship from
abroad," and that "we [Soviets] see the struggle taking place in the
countries of the West between the partisans and opponents of the reduction of international tension, and we see a certain inconsistency in the
positions of one or another state on various questions."

Further accenting the message of moderation and détente which the
Soviet leadership now wished to project, the Soviet press published a
highly distorted version of Secretary of State Kissinger's October 26
press conference, which seemed to suggest that the secretary was delivering praise for détente rather than warning the Soviet Union against
military intervention in the Middle East. For example, the alert of
American forces was not even mentioned in the report. Kissinger was
quoted as saying that "we do not consider ourselves . . . in a state of
confrontation with the Soviet Union" and that "on the basis of conversations with L. I. Brezhnev and constant diplomatic contacts, I have all
the basis to suppose that a common course in our efforts to achieve a
firm peace in the Near East can be reached."[195]

Taking account, however, of the intense criticism of the American
alert in the United States and Western Europe, a decision was taken to
shift the Soviet course slightly and, rather than ignoring the American
measures, to promote renewed détente by discrediting the alert as baseless. On October 27, TASS issued a declaration noting the American
alert. The declaration maintained that "officials, trying to justify this
step, referred to some actions of the Soviet Union which supposedly
give grounds for anxiety. TASS is empowered to declare that such
explanations are absurd. . . . This step of the United States, which in no
way eases the reduction of international tension, clearly was undertaken
in an attempt to intimidate the Soviet Union. However, it is appropriate
to say to the initiators that they chose the wrong address for the given
goal."[196]

Continuing the attempt to deride the alert, President Nixon's press
conference on October 26 was covered in a more unfavorable light than
was the Soviets' wont. *Pravda's* report stated that the American alert,

"according to the evaluation of the international public, in no way eases the reduction of international tensions to which, in the words of R. Nixon, the United States is striving." In addition to claiming that President Nixon had no basis on which to support the alert, *Pravda*, in a rare sally against the president, pointed out that "sharp questions" regarding the Watergate affair had been raised at the press conference. In addition, the newspaper reported on acute Western European dissatisfaction with the alert.[197]

Perhaps the most biting denunciation of the American alert was delivered by *Pravda*'s commentator Yuriy Zhukov on Soviet television. Zhukov ridiculed the American alert as baseless and stated that the Soviet Union, in its current position of strength, did not respond to threats. In Zhukov's words: "In justification [for the alert] a really absurd allegation was made asserting that the Soviet Union, imagine, the Soviet Union, had taken some kind of action which allegedly gave cause for alarm. What, in fact, prompted this, to put it mildly, really clumsy act by Washington, in placing American forces on an alert? As today's TASS statement notes, this step was taken with the clear object of intimidating the Soviet Union. However, they chose the wrong address, they tried to intimidate the wrong people, as the saying goes. In the past, when our power was immeasurably weaker, there were many who tried to intimidate us. But everyone remembers well that such attempts have invariably ended in the collapse of those who initiated them. What is one to say of the present attempt? It was a time wasting, ungratifying little scheme, one for the scrap heap as they say. I am sure that those to whom this applies will draw the necessary conclusions from the failure of their scheme."[198]

While the American alert may have been more effective in restraining Soviet actions than Zhukov's bluster implies, his basic conclusion was correct. The United States, by placing pressure on Israel, had accomplished Soviet objectives, and not vice versa. While one can make a very credible case that stopping the Israelis was also in U.S. interests, one should note that it was not an American initiative which halted Tel Aviv. If Dayan's account is true—the United States declared that it would not stand in the way of a Russian intervention—this move detracted from the credibility of any future U.S. security guarantee as the basis for an ultimate Israeli pullback to pre-1967 boundaries. Instead, Israeli officials would probably insist on massive quantities of arms as a "security guarantee" in exchange for any future withdrawal.[199]

In addition to relations with the United States, Israel, and the Arab belligerents, the Soviet Union was preoccupied during the war by the propaganda barrage released by its rivals in Peking.[200] Indicative of the depth of Soviet antagonism was the issuance in the midst of the war of a three-page polemical article viciously attacking the Tenth Congress of the Chinese Communist Party.[201] As the Congress was held some two months before (August 24–28), it is probable that Chinese propaganda attacks on the Soviets in connection with the war prompted the Soviet decision to publish the denunciation.

The anti-Chinese article noted that the X Chinese Congress had labeled the Soviet Union as the "main enemy" and had associated the late Chinese Politburo members Lin Piao and Chen Po-ta as "super spies" and "special agents" of the Soviet Union. The article condemned China for raising a "war psychosis" vis-à-vis the Soviet Union and denounced Peking for unleashing "a mad campaign of slander on Soviet-Arab friendship, seeking to achieve its undermining and thus objectively assisting the aggressive aspirations of the Israeli aggressors and their imperialist sponsors."

The "campaign of slander" to which the Soviets referred involved voluminous Chinese accusations that the Soviet Union had colluded with United States to stifle the Arab war effort. These accusations became particularly pronounced after the "imposition" of the U.S.-Soviet joint ceasefire resolution.[202] The Communist Party newspaper *Renmin Ribao* summarized Chinese accusations against the Soviet Union in the following rhetorical challenge and question: "The Soviet revisionist renegade clique, while colluding with the other superpower, poses as the 'protector' of the Arab countries. A fine 'protector' indeed! If you [the Soviet Union] really support the Arab people in their just struggle, why did you hurriedly evacuate your military experts [sic] and their family dependents on the eve of the war? Why have you continued to ship manpower [Jewish emigrants] to Israel since the war started? After the armed forces and people of Egypt and Syria had hit back and scored successes, you sent them some arms in your own interests, but when the other superpower brought pressure to bear on you and made threats, you immediately coupled coercion with deception to tell people to 'cease fire in place.' Everything Soviet revisionism has been doing to sabotage the struggle of the people of the Arab countries has made people further realize the sinister, double-crossing tactics of social imperialism."[203]

After the appearance of several articles in the Soviet press during and after the war dismissing the individual Chinese charges and accusing Peking of "talking a good fight," the Soviets, some one month after conclusion of the war, hit back with a basic critique of Chinese conduct during the Yom Kippur War.[204] The objections raised by the Soviets were revealing of both the restraints under which the Soviets felt themselves during the war and the depth of the leadership's concern with détente.

The Soviet article questioned the Chinese evaluation of the war as a "good thing and not a bad" and asked how "the blood of Arab women and children . . . , the ashes and ruins of burned Arab cities and villages can bring good to the peoples." The Chinese goal in the war, according to the Soviet critique, was "to drag the Soviet Union and United States into it, . . . and if possible, [to create] a direct military confrontation between them." The Chinese were further accused of seeking "in every way to expand the scale of the military conflagration and to increase the number of direct participants in it." In addition, the Chinese had delayed the work of the Security Council's ceasefire deliberations. "Because of this Peking tactic . . . the Arabs suffered large losses."

In sum, the Soviets accused the Chinese of encouraging the breakdown of the limits of the Yom Kippur War. While the Soviets were by no means guiltless in this regard, their verbal attack on Peking indicates that they were at least aware of the significance of war limitations and the necessity to avoid conflict with the United States. Viewed in this context, the American alert may have been seen as more threatening than Moscow publicly allowed.

In addition to the discussion of the Chinese role, several other analytical statements appeared in the immediate wake of the ceasefire which sought to sum up the political and military lessons of the Yom Kippur War. Politburo member A. P. Kirilenko, discussing the political lessons of the war in the keynote address on the fifty-sixth anniversary of the October Revolution, indicated that the outbreak of the Yom Kippur War "incontestably proves the correctness of what we have insisted on all these years and what we support now—firm peace can be achieved . . . only on the basis of liberation of all the territories occupied by Israel and guarantee of the just rights of the Arab peoples of Palestine. This is the heart and essence of the problem." In the Politburo's view, therefore, the fact that the Arabs had resorted to war proved the reality and significance of the "contradiction" between Israel's continued hold on the occupied territories and the Arabs' desire for return of these lands. As Kirilenko observed: "The events showed the firm decisiveness of the Arabs to end the occupation of their territory. This decisiveness found reflection in the growing consolidation of the Arab world and in the significantly higher fighting spirit of the Arab armies."

Once granted the depth of Arab feelings, full support of Arab territorial claims, in the eyes of the Politburo, was an expedient Soviet political position. On the basis of this support, the negative effects of détente in alienating Moscow's revolutionary clients could be offset, and ties with the "progressive" movement in the Middle East and elsewhere could be solidified. In Kirilenko's words: "Let me emphasize that in this case, as always, when the matter concerns the strengthening of the bases for a just peace, freedom, and national independence, the country of the Soviets was and will be with the peoples who defend the sacred right of being masters in their own home . . . from imperialist encroachments."[205]

The Soviet sense that the masses of Arab people and leaders of "progressive" groups favored full Israeli withdrawal from the post-1967 occupied territories would lead to Soviet difficulty after the war in espousing moves for partial, step-by-step solution of the problem as advocated by U.S. Secretary of State Kissinger. While the step-by-step approach was not necessarily opposed to Soviet interests since it did result in increasing benefits for the "progressive" Arabs against Israel, the fact that the United States took the leading role in mediating the partial settlement (largely at the insistence of the Egyptians) erased most of the potential advantages that could have derived from full Soviet backing of such a solution.

As a result, the Soviet Union would adopt a reserved position with regard to the step-by-step approach and would instead emphasize expressions of solidarity with those Arab forces demanding an immediate total Israeli withdrawal. (This posture would also more fully satisfy those members of the Politburo who thought that any détente measures should be coupled with decisive backing of "anti-imperialist" forces.) According to Soviet calculations, these more extreme forces would probably come increasingly to the fore as the step-by-step solution inevitably foundered on Israeli "expansionist" resistance.

With regard to the Soviet role in bringing the Yom Kippur War to a close, Kirilenko noted that "the Soviet Union, acting in contact and agreement with the friendly Arab states, undertook active participation in diplomatic actions directed toward the most rapid cessation of the war and settlement of the conflict." By distinguishing between "cessation of the war" and "settlement of the conflict," Kirilenko demonstrated that, like the Americans, the Politburo placed high priority in seeking to end the war in a manner which would promote settlement of the Arab-Israeli territorial dispute in a manner favorable to its own perceived interests. As Kirilenko asserted, in a perhaps premature show of optimism, from the Soviet point of view, "one can see that more favorable conditions now exist for a firm and just settlement of the crisis than at any time before."

One can speculate that the Soviets had been aiming for, and thought that they had achieved, a termination of war in which significant Arab gains were preserved and the Israelis were denied a sense of full victory. This outcome might cause Tel Aviv to adopt a more flexible posture on territorial concessions and to cease exploiting military "advantages" over the Soviet-backed Arabs. This denouement, Moscow probably thought, would result in a heightened appreciation of the Soviet Union's assistance among the "progressive" Arabs. Moscow's expectations, at least temporarily, however, went awry due to Egyptian President Sadat's anti-Soviet inclinations and his belief, also at least in the short run, that the United States was the most likely instrument both to regain the occupied lands for Egypt and to infuse capital into the lagging Egyptian economy.

On the military side, Soviet commentators attached principal significance to the following dimensions of the Yom Kippur War: (a) the psychological victory derived by the Arabs during the first ten days of the war as the result of reoccupation of conquered territory and the destruction of large amounts of Israeli equipment,[206] (b) the effectiveness of antiaircraft systems in reducing Israeli air advantages,[207] (c) the Israeli success in utilizing tanks to break through to the Arab rear,[208] (d) the importance of Arab military-equipment advantages,[209] (e) the success of the Arabs in "forcing" the Israelis to become involved in large and costly battles which Tel Aviv could not carry on over an extended period of time,[210] and (f) the weaknesses of positional warfare as opposed to war of maneuver.[211] In sum, the tenets of Soviet military doctrine emphasizing the importance of the beginning period of war (even in time of conventional weapons usage) and deep offensive penetration were felt to be confirmed. Because it was Israel that achieved the deep penetration, Arab military "victory" was deemed to be primarily "psychological."

Soviet responses to the Yom Kippur War can therefore be summarized in the following manner. The Soviet leadership, though anxious about the consequences of allowing the war to be prolonged, apparently decided to give the Arab states significant leeway to decide the conditions of waging the conflict and bringing it to a close. No Soviet attempt would be made to contradict the Arabs publicly or urge them to terminate the war before they were ready. In view of the Soviet position as an active arms supplier of the belligerents, this placed Moscow in the uncomfortable and unaccustomed position of having its fate at least indirectly manipulated by others. The adoption of this highly abnormal stance was presumably motivated by Moscow's acute fear of losing the loyalty of the "progressive" Arabs and thereby undercutting the foundations of the compromise between coexistence and confrontation which made détente a palatable policy option for the Soviet leadership.

The early Arab success in the Yom Kippur War appeared to surprise the Soviets, who initially had signaled to the United States a desire for an early end to hostilities. When the Egyptians were able to hold on to their early gains and rejected the initial Soviet ceasefire proposal, Moscow began sending supplies by sea to the Arabs, encouraged other Arab countries to participate in the struggle, and endorsed Arab war aims. Shortfalls of Arab supplies soon led to the beginning of an airlift, which brought a heavy active Soviet involvement and presence into the war zone.

Egyptian rejection of the October 10 Kissinger proposal calling for a "ceasefire in place" prompted the Soviets to again vigorously affirm their support of the Arabs' aims and to build up the volume of their airlift. Israeli deep air strikes, which had been virtually ignored for several days, were now severely condemned, and intimations were made that Soviet "volunteers" or retaliation would be forthcoming if the attacks continued.

Finally, after some ten days of war, when the Soviets began to assess the consequences of the military stalemate in Syria coupled with the damage being inflicted to the Soviet détente image, the Politburo decided that an opportune time had arrived to more seriously urge the Egyptians to accept a ceasefire. Kosygin's trip to Cairo indicated that the Kremlin viewed the termination of fighting as a question of some importance. However, this Soviet view, as witnessed by Shelepin's October 16 speech, apparently was not endorsed with equal conviction by all Politburo members. Some members of the ruling body may have felt that Israel and the "imperialists" in general deserved a more decisive "rebuff" than they had yet received.

Chairman Kosygin's long three-day stay in Egypt demonstrated that Moscow, because of its desire not to alienate the Arabs, had not quickly imposed, and did not intend to force, a halt in hostilities on the Egyptians. (It should be recalled that Egypt, because of the need to rely on the Soviet airlift, was completely vulnerable to Soviet pressure). Only after it became obvious that the Egyptian Sinai position seemed in acute danger did Sadat acquiesce to a ceasefire. The Soviets did not at any point appear to compel the Egyptian leader to take this decision.

In spite of their quiescence vis-à-vis the Arabs, the Soviets appeared to see no irony in their insistence that the United States actively involve itself in containing the Israelis when Tel Aviv appeared to violate the U.N. ceasefire undertaking. Resorting to the time-honored Soviet recipe for ending Middle East war, the Politburo threatened to unilaterally intervene to stop the Israelis. While the Soviet threat was signaled ambiguously in order to salvage whatever good feelings remained from détente, it seems likely that the Soviets probably did, in fact, intend to deploy at least a small, politically significant sum of ground troops to the Middle East if the Israelis did not stop their offensive. The pre-ceasefire launching of the *Scuds* and the other ominous signals suggesting possible further firings were particularly convincing signs that the Soviets were serious in their concern to avoid an Egyptian "Stalingrad" in the Sinai.

While the American alert probably surprised the Russians, the action of Washington in pressuring Tel Aviv to accept the ceasefire was probably viewed as a more revealing indication of Washington's mettle. Soviet satisfaction with the American response prompted the Russian leadership to reiterate support for the policy of détente after the war.[212]

Moscow's policy during the Yom Kippur War can, therefore, be seen as a continuation of its efforts to support the Arabs' "progressive" aspirations, even at the risk of setting détente back somewhat. The Soviet leadership seemed prepared to permit the war to be prolonged and expanded as long as the Arab belligerents' interests were not endangered and the Arab leaders wished to continue the fight. On the other hand, while the Soviet Union was prepared to facilitate continuation of the war on the part of the Arabs by providing supplies and adopting the appropriate diplomatic stance (such as not agreeing to Western-sponsored ceasefire proposals while the Arabs were not ready to stop fighting), the Politburo was not prepared to offer Soviet assistance, either direct or indirect, which would guarantee achievement of the Arab goal of recovery of the post-1967 occupied territories. In this regard, it should be recalled that Soviet intervention threats were directed toward causing Israel to desist in certain actions against the Arabs (deep bombing and post-ceasefire advances) rather than toward compelling Israel to bow to Arab war aims.

In the course of the war, the Soviets resorted to several moves which were departures from previous Russian practice—resupplying Arab belligerents during the conflict, urging other Arab states to assist the fighting parties, long postponing the establishment of a ceasefire, and employing physical threats associated with possible application of weapons which were strategic in the Middle East context—all of which were novel and disturbing and which indicated that Russians were less concerned to minimize risks than they had been in the past. On the other hand, as the postwar verbal attack on the Chinese implied, the Soviets had recognized some limits; they had not been completely irresponsible. Their more adventurous actions were tempered by a sense of caution and consideration vis-à-vis the United States. Soviet conduct in relation to the Sixth Fleet was indicative of this restraint. The measured and somewhat ambiguous nature of Russian intervention and threats also reflected this caution, as did the lack of direct effort to help realize the Arabs' goals.

In sum, Soviet actions, though more risk-prone and undesirable than in the past, were still within the realm of potentially manageable behavior.

III As we have seen, the Soviet approach to the October 1973 Yom Kippur War had its origin in Moscow's response to Israel's dramatic victory of 1967. At the end of the Six-Day War, the Soviet Union's Middle East clients were prostrate. The Politburo's wager on Nasser and the other Arab "progressives" appeared to be in vain. After years of Soviet support of the "progressives," not only had the latter failed to remove Western influence from the Middle East, but it seemed that as a result of their abysmal 1967 defeat, Western-aligned forces would again hold decisive power in the Near East.

Considering the disastrous failure of the Arabs, the rulers of a nation less wedded than the Soviet Union to maintaining a permanent Middle Eastern influence might well have elected to forgo further sacrifices of arms and money. The Soviet leadership did not chose this option, however. Instead, immediately after the Arab defeat, President Podgorny and Marshal Zakharov hurried to the Middle East to lay the groundwork for the reconstruction of the devastated Arab armed forces.

The Soviet Union thus demonstrated, in the immediate wake of the Six-Day War, that it would not easily countenance a restoration of the Western dominance which had prevailed in the Middle East before 1955. This reluctance to sanction or permit a reversal of Russian fortunes in the area would be a prime factor in determining Soviet policy in the 1967–73 period. The Soviet Union would seek to avoid any appearance of shrinking from support of the Arabs and would challenge forces both inside and outside the Arab world (such as Israel) whose activities seemed to undercut Soviet-Arab ties.

While the existence of a Soviet desire to maintain the allegiance of the Arabs, particularly the "progressives," is manifest, the reason for this acute concern is not equally clear. One can assert that the Soviets wished to deprive the West of a base to encircle the Soviet Union (as Dulles attempted in the 1950s), to control one of the West's major sources of energy supply, to establish friendly regimes in the environs of the Soviet Union's border, and to satisfy Russia's historical urge to expand its power in a southerly direction. While all these assertions are probably true, they do not seem to explain the unique persistence which the Russians demonstrated in pursuing their goals in the Middle East.

The missing element may be that the Near East represented one of the few areas in which a Western or Western-aligned state (in this case, Israel) possessed both the power and the will to reverse Soviet gains.

The preservation of Russian advances seemed particularly important because, not only had the Arab "progressives" aligned their foreign policy with the Soviet Union, they had also introduced significant domestic political, economic, and social changes offering the possibility of the emergence of societies approximating the Soviet pattern. According to the Russian framework of analysis, such societies gave a promise of permanence to anti-Western foreign policy which otherwise might have been lacking.

While Tel Aviv probably had no inherent ideological resentment of the foreign policy or domestic political alignment of its Arab opponents, its use of military means to compel the "progressive" Arab nations to accede to Israel's wishes (first, by maintaining its hold on the post-1967 occupied territories and, later, by active use of military force) tended to discredit the regimes and policies of the "progressive" Arab states as ineffectual. Moscow clearly wished to avoid this impression both in the Middle East and on a wider scale.

Considering the still extant and deeply held basic Soviet view that international politics consists of a "zero-sum" conflict between the shaken and split, though still integral, "aggressive forces" of "imperialism" and the "socialist" nations and their adherents, it was easy for the Soviets to assume that Israel represented, or at least served the interests of, the Soviet Union's enemies. At stake, therefore, in Moscow's view was not simply the Soviet Union's Middle Eastern clients but, rather, the integrity of the entire "socialist"-"progressive" security structure. If Israel was permitted to exercise its military supremacy over the "progressive" Arabs, what would cause other "aggressive imperialist" forces to shrink from moving strongly against other Soviet client states and movements? In Moscow's eyes, Israel (like North Vietnam in American President Johnson's view) seemed to be an instrument striking at the very foundations of international equilibrium.

Because of the perceived importance of the Middle East issue, Moscow concluded that it was essential to reestablish an Arab counterweight to Israeli military power. The rearming of the Arabs, it was probably thought, would not only deprive Tel Aviv of its "free hand" in the Middle East but would also raise Moscow's stock in the Arab world. Indeed, Israel's decision to maintain a hold on the territories seized during the Six-Day War, to an even greater degree than in the past, highlighted the importance of Soviet arms supplies in the eyes of the Arabs. The post-1967 Middle Eastern occupied territories, like their European precursor Alsace-Lorraine, became a focus of revanchist sentiment. The Soviet leadership, ideologically predisposed to aiding "victims of aggression," quickly sensed the advantages to be gained by backing Arab aspirations for recovery of the conquered territories.

Paradoxically, though, the same aroused sentiments which made the occupied-territories issue a matter on which the Soviet Union could capitalize also tended to work against the Russians. The longer the Arabs were denied the occupied territories, the more they would blame Moscow for not providing adequate support. This resentment of Soviet niggardliness was particularly easy to arouse in the case of weapons supplies as the Arabs became increasingly aware that the Soviets were not prepared to deliver the best and most useful arms at their disposal.

CHAPTER SIX † THE SOVIET UNION AND
THREE WARS IN THE MIDDLE EAST

In the span of less than two decades after the initial Politburo decision to supply arms to Egypt, three major wars wracked the Middle East. Though each war began differently, they all ended in the same fashion. At or near the conclusion of every conflict the Soviet Union threatened military intervention. As a result of these threats, in every instance, a superpower confrontation of some sort erupted.

These same end results appeared when there was a vast disequilibrium of military power between the United States and the Soviet Union, and when parity existed. They appeared when the United States and the Soviet Union shared similar goals in relation to the war under way, and when their goals differed. They appeared when relatively warm relations prevailed between the superpowers, and when the United States and the Soviet Union were in bitterest conflict.

If forecasts were called for, one would be compelled to predict, on the basis of historical experience, that if another war were to take place in the Middle East, relations between the United States and the Soviet Union would again reach a state of acute crisis. While superpower confrontations thus far have been largely symbolic, in a situation of ever more equal military power, not only on the strategic level but also in the Eastern Mediterranean, one cannot exclude the possibility that another Middle East confrontation could provide the occasion for the eruption of military conflict between the superpowers.

In view of the extremely grave hazards posed by the Middle East situation, it behooves us to understand both the latitude and restraints manifested in Soviet behavior before and during the three wars of the last two decades.

II Turning back to the period prior to the 1956 Suez War, the Egyptian-Soviet ("Czech") arms deal of 1955 seemed to have been motivated by the desire of the Soviet Union to establish and cement friendly relations with the nationalist "progressive" regime of President Nasser. The 1955 weapons transaction was part of the post-Stalin leadership's campaign to develop ties with non-Communist nationalist regimes that had adopted an "anti-imperialist" foreign policy. As such, the Soviet initiative was an effort to procure political gains at the expense of the West in the Third World and to rupture the security cordon that had been erected around the Soviet Union.

The new Soviet policy orientation toward the postcolonial regimes represented a sharp departure from the dominant attitude of Stalin's final years—an attitude that had held that the emerging bourgeois nationalist regimes differed little from their colonial predecessors. Stalin's views had probably been influenced, at least partially, by the sense that the post-World War II phase of communist expansion had crested (with the failure of the Communists to acquire power in France and Italy) and by the feeling that the Communist movement itself was increasingly subject to deviationist, centrifugal tendencies (for example, note the break with Yugoslavia and the Eastern European purges that followed). Stalin, witnessing these events, was probably drawn toward engineering reconsolidation of the Communist movement. Therefore, he steered overseas Communists less toward coalition with left-wing and nationalist non-Communist groups and more toward lone-handed policies. The Communist North Korean action in attacking the South Korean nationalist, colonial-succession regime was an extreme manifestation of the sectarian approach that Stalin seemed to favor in this period.

The post-Stalin leadership, though rent with internal disagreements, soon began to view Stalin's approach as dangerously counterproductive. Rather than strengthening the Communist movement, the sectarian approach, as manifested in the Korean War, had only spurred a reaction in the West that increased the power of anti-Soviet politicians and accelerated the Western effort to construct a chain of anti-Soviet alliances around the periphery of the Soviet Union. To counter this resurgence of "imperialist" unity, the new leadership began tentatively to resurrect the "collective security" and "popular front" tactics of the late 1930s, which had aimed at isolating and limiting the potential of assertive Fascism. As in the collective security/popular front period, Soviet and Communist cooperation would be based on "least common denominator" mutuality of interests with foreign regimes and groups. The least common denominator required on the part of foreign states would be a generally anti-Western or neutralist foreign policy orientation.

This decision to abandon the late-Stalinist sectarian approach was manifested in the on-again, off-again reconciliation with Yugoslavia and the development of Soviet ties with India and then in the mid-1950s with Egypt. The development of friendly relations with Egypt was particularly striking because the regime was dominated by nationalist military officers, some of whom had expressed sympathy for the Axis in

World War II, and who were actively engaged in suppressing the local Communist movement. Moreover, despite promising rhetoric, the Egyptian regime in its early years was not seriously involved in restructuring society along the socialist lines favored by Moscow. The principal explanation, therefore, for the Soviet move toward Cairo must have been Egypt's foreign policy stance, specifically the aggressive, anti-British stand taken by the revolutionary regime. This stance culminated not only with British military departure from the Middle East, but also the eventual emasculation of the Baghdad Pact (partially as a result of Egyptian-inspired opposition). The Baghdad Pact, of course, had been the political-military instrument designed to preserve British and Western dominance in the postcolonial Middle East.

The new Soviet approach toward Egypt was first embodied in the 1955 arms deal. In view of the military domination of Egypt, the Kremlin undoubtedly viewed provision of arms as an appropriate measure both to appeal to the professional interests of Cairo's leadership and to strengthen Egypt's ability to withstand Western and Israeli military pressure or threats.

Concurrently with Moscow's moves to construct a broader anti-imperialist front on a world scale and in the Middle East, the Russians were also seeking to moderate tensions with the Western powers. The fruits of this first post-Stalin détente were evidenced in the signature of the Austrian State Treaty and the invocation of the so-called "Spirit of Geneva" of 1955. The drive for reconciliation with the West, like the dropping of the sectarian approach to collaboration with non-Communist, neutralist forces, was a response to the excesses of the Stalin period. The dominant element of the Soviet Presidium felt that a "breathing space" with the West was needed to slow or halt the Western push to encircle the Soviet Union militarily and politically, as well as to permit long-needed economic transformations to take place inside the Soviet Union. The development of Soviet strategic missiles, coupled with both a moderation of dialogue with the West and the acquisition of adherents and political dynamism in the Third World, gave the Presidium sufficient confidence to demobilize some three million men (some 50% of the Soviet armed forces) between 1955 and 1960—a highly significant injection of manpower into the labor-short Soviet economy.

While Soviet pursuit of moderated relations with the West and support of anti-Western elements in the Third World were meant to serve the same goal—the easing of Western pressure against the Soviet Union —the two tactics stood in sharp contrast. On the one hand, the West was being soothed. On the other hand, the West's position in the Third World was being undermined. As it turned out, the seeming disjunction of pre-1956 Soviet policy would be the first of repeated instances in which Russian campaigns to moderate East-West tension would be accompanied by assertiveness against Western interests in the Third World.

Some observers were inclined in 1955, and in later years, to treat the evidence of apparently contradictory Soviet behavior as a manifestation of Russian hypocrisy. Other analysts have gone as far as to assert that the Soviet leadership has consciously used détente to mask aggressive actions directed against the West. These criticisms, however, posit a unitary consistent Soviet policy stance that, in fact, may not exist.

FIGURE 1. SOVIET-WESTERN DÉTENTE AND QUALITATIVE CHANGES IN
RUSSIAN MILITARY INVOLVEMENT IN THE MIDDLE EAST

Periods of Détente		*Qualitative Changes*
	1953	
	1954	
Spirit of Geneva	1955 ⟵	Soviet-Egyptian Arms Deal. Provision of Second-Line Soviet Equipment and Small Strategic Bombing Capability.
	1956	
	1957	
	1958	
	1959	
Spirit of Camp David	1960	
	1961	
	1962	
Post-Cuban Missile Crisis/Test Ban	1963 ⟵	Provision of First-Line Soviet Military Equipment and Enlarged Strategic Bombing Capability
	1964	
	1965	
	1966	
	1967	
	1968	
	1969	
	1970 ⟵	Commitment of Soviet Air-Defense Personnel
	1971	
Post-XXIV Party Congress	1972	
	1973 ⟵	Provision of Assured-Penetration Strategic Weapons and Resupply During War
	1974	

In accordance with Moscow's ideological framework, Soviet foreign policy in relation to the capitalist world and its overseas interests has always reflected an amalgam of coexistence and revolution—the contradictory desires both to benefit from friendly relations with the rich and powerful Western nations and to undermine the sources of their strength. The shifting of Soviet foreign policy to favor either of these poles has never been complete. Always a minimum stress on the opposite policy pole, a "reinsurance," has been maintained to permit Moscow to reap rewards from the opposite policy emphasis and to facilitate change in Soviet policy orientation should this be required. Thus, even in the "ultra-revolutionary" period of the Civil War and foreign intervention, Lenin was not blind to the benefits of possible future foreign economic concessions in Russia. On the opposite extreme, even when Soviet relations with the Western allies were closest during World War II, in spite of other conciliatory changes, Stalin did not seek to abolish the Western Communist parties.

The realization of the value of a two-emphasis foreign policy has thus been a constant aspect of Soviet conduct. Because of this two-emphasis tradition, views of individual Politburo members are likely to reflect, not single, consistent foreign-policy lines (such as coexistence at the expense of revolution, and vice versa), but, rather, various weightings of two simultaneously operative factors—coexistence and revolution, or in the more modern and subdued Soviet terminology, détente and support of the "progressive" movement. In the event of political conflict within the Politburo, the various weightings assigned to the two key factors by individual members are likely to differ more greatly and to become more polarized.

Regardless of the degree of leadership conflict, however, a domestic consensus on Soviet policy undoubtedly can more easily be maintained to the extent that *both* key foreign-policy factors—détente and support of the "progressive" movement—are promoted simultaneously. A Soviet leader (*primus inter pares*) who wishes to turn Soviet foreign policy toward a new orientation or emphasis may invite domestic political difficulties for himself unless he "reinsures" himself by compensating a move in one direction with a gesture toward the other policy pole. The need to maintain domestic foreign-policy consensus through compensation and "reinsurance" may well be the root cause of the repeated coincidences between détente and Soviet assertiveness in the Third World. (Conversely, it also may suggest that a Soviet turn in a "hawkish" direction need not breed excessive pessimism in the West.)

Attempts to balance policy, of course, cannot be allowed to excessively discredit or subvert the principal Soviet political emphasis of the moment. For this reason, possible Soviet efforts to "reinsure" policy for the most part have appeared carefully moderated. This moderation has accompanied, and perhaps fortified, the generally cautious Soviet policy orientation of the postwar period—an approach aimed at securing the benefits of détente and avoiding a nuclear confrontation with the West.

As we have seen, in the pre-1956 period, Egyptian leader Nasser had expressed concern with reported French arms shipments to Israel, as well as with a rising threat from the Western powers. The Soviet leadership, probably at least partially as an effort to compensate for its policy moves toward reduction of tension with the capitalist nations, elected to accede to Nasser's request for weapons to protect "progressive" Egypt from an anticipated attack or military pressure. The Soviet decision to dispatch arms, while disruptive of the Western political-military monopoly in the Middle East, was probably not intended to spur war in the region. An outbreak of war provoked by Soviet arms shipments would prejudice the more basic goals of then current Soviet policy—reduction of tensions with the major capitalist powers. Therefore, arms shipped to Nasser were probably intended only to deter a perceived Israeli/Western threat rather than to overwhelm such a challenge or to allow the Egyptians to initiate offensive action. The "reinsurance" move on behalf of Egypt was thus moderated by concern for dominant Soviet goals.

Though the pre-1956 arms shipments to Egypt raised the total of Egyptian tanks by more than 50 percent and the number of jet aircraft by more than 100 percent, Israeli weapons, by virtue of French shipments, also markedly increased. Because of the secrecy with which French deliveries to Israel were handled, it was quite easy for the Russians and the Egyptians to overestimate what Tel Aviv was, in reality, receiving. What appeared on the surface to be a Russian drive to give Egypt military superiority in the Middle East may in fact have reflected far more minimal Soviet designs.

The argument in favor of Russian restraint is further strengthened by the fact that Moscow initially supplied Nasser only with obsolescent and second-line military equipment. Though one could argue that better equipment was simply not available, the provision of improved aircraft (MIG-17's) immediately after the Suez War suggests that the initial Soviet restraint was calculated rather than forced.

The most salient apparent exceptions to the hypothesis of conscious Soviet weapons restraint in the pre-1956 period were (a) the delivery of heavy and medium tanks to Egypt, while Israel was only receiving light tanks and (b) the shipment of thirty-plus IL-28 bombers capable of reaching Israel. Tel Aviv, on the other hand, had virtually no strategic bombing capability.

As was pointed out, however, Soviet provision of heavy and medium tanks was probably due to the fact that light tanks were simply not put into production in the Soviet Union until 1955. As for the IL-28's, while their delivery could be attributed to a desire to give Egypt a limited offensive capacity, it is equally possible to interpret their shipment in a defensive context. The creation of a strategic threat to Israel would force Tel Aviv to allot more of its limited supply of interceptors to strategic air defense and thereby would make Israeli tactical air control and offensive action more difficult.

Therefore, while one cannot be absolutely certain, there are a number of good reasons to believe that pre-1956 Soviet weapons deliveries to Egypt were structured more as a deterrent than as an offensive warfighting instrument. This impression is confirmed by the fact that, in spite of the large relative increase in Egyptian weapons stocks, the Soviets only augmented the Egyptian forces by a very small amount in absolute terms. Egyptian armored forces, for example, the principal offensive ground striking element, were reinforced by only some one hundred tanks—a minute portion of Russian stocks, far removed from later deliveries, which would boost Arab tank inventories into the thousands.

After the 1956 war, the Soviet Union rebuilt the Egyptian armed forces and began to supply weapons to Syria and Iraq (after 1958). The Soviet decision to continue and expand involvement in the Middle East probably stemmed from satisfaction with the outcome of the Suez contest. The Soviet Union, after all, had received a positive response from "progressive" nationalists for its (largely verbal) support of Egypt against the Anglo-French-Israeli attack. Moreover, the nuclear power of Washington now appeared less intimidating, given the United States' failure to back its allies at Suez and the Soviet development of a symbolic ICBM deterrent capacity. Most importantly, of course, the Soviet Union was riding on a crest of optimism produced by Khrushchev's triumph over the Presidium opposition, the Soviet launching of the first Sputnik, the suppression of deviation in Hungary, and the ongoing collapse of the European colonial empires. In this heady atmosphere, it was easy both to attract and support new clients, as well as to be more demanding of them.

In the late 1950s, Nasser launched a vigorous anti-Communist campaign in Egypt. This campaign aroused the Kremlin's ire as did the Egyptian move against the Syrian Communists, undertaken at the behest of Syrian instigators of the Egyptian-Syrian United Arab Republic union. In response to this campaign, Khrushchev rebuked Nasser and a chill set in on Soviet-Egyptian relations.

The downturn in Moscow's relations with Cairo took place against the background of the 1959–60 Soviet-Western détente (popularly known under the rubric "The Spirit of Camp David"). During this period, Soviet and American high-level visits were exchanged, culminated by the visit to the United States of Soviet Communist Party First Secretary Khrushchev and the projected, though ultimately aborted, trip of President Eisenhower to the Soviet Union. The Soviets, buoyed by the belief that the flow of world events was in their favor, seemed eager to return to the moderated relations with the West that prevailed before Suez and the Hungarian uprising. In the Soviet judgment, a pacified West would be less likely to interfere with the "progressive" changes that were taking place at an ever more rapid pace.

The 1959–60 Soviet-American détente was unusual because, unlike the 1954–55 "Spirit of Geneva" interlude and every other period of East-West relaxation of tension in the post-Stalin years, it did not produce any qualitative change in Soviet military involvement in the Middle East. An explanation for this exception was easy enough to find—the Egyptian-Soviet quarrel spurred by Nasser's actions against the Egyptian and Syrian Communists. Such an exception indicates, however, that while increases in Soviet military involvement in the Middle East have generally accompanied periods of East-West détente, this by no means constitutes an "iron law." It also suggests that at times when Moscow's confidence is very high, particularly with regard to the success of the "progressive" movement, it is felt that there is less need to compensate for détente with the West. In this period, the Soviets were acquiring new, seemingly steadfast, clients in Africa, Asia, and Latin America (Cuba). Even in the Middle East, Kassem's Iraq, in its early days, seemed more ready to cooperate with the Communists than to follow Nasser's more independent, nationalist lead. Moscow's powerful and ascendant position in the "progressive" movement seemed to generate no need to balance détente with the capitalist nations.

The U-2 affair and the coming to power of the assertive Kennedy administration in the United States put a chill back into Soviet-American relations. Soviet and American ambitions clashed in Cuba, Berlin, the Congo, and Laos. In this atmosphere of sharpened Cold War, the Kremlin began to sense that the easy successes of the immediately preceding years could not be repeated. The West was stiffening its resistance and major fissures in the Communist camp generated by China's dissidence began to appear. To once again seize the initiative and to counterbalance the growing American ability to destroy the Soviet homeland without risking retaliation, Khrushchev deployed medium-range missiles and light bombers to Cuba. The American administration, in response to this move, confronted the Soviet Union, caused a withdrawal of the Russian missiles and aircraft, and inflicted a diplomatic humiliation on the Soviet Union.

The dangers of confrontation evident in the Cuban Missile Crisis sobered both the American and Soviet leaderships. In the aftermath of the crisis, Soviet pressure on Berlin ceased, the Nuclear Test Ban Treaty was signed, and the "hot line" linking Moscow and Washington was installed. Reflecting a hopefulness with regard to détente on the part of the United States in this period, President Kennedy made his famous American University speech calling for new measures of co-operation between the superpowers.

While the Soviet leadership now worked to conciliate the United States on bilateral issues, its moves *vis-à-vis* the "progressive" movement in the Middle East showed no lack of assertiveness. The Soviet Union and Egypt moved back into closer relations following a cooling of rhetoric on both sides, and Moscow demonstratively strengthened the Egyptians, particularly for their confrontation against traditional, pro-Western forces (backed by Saudi Arabia) in Yemen. These weapons also, of course, strengthened Egypt's hand against neighboring Israel. The perceived need to "reinsure" Soviet ties with the "progressive" states was probably heightened by the increase of anti-Khrushchev factionalism in the Politburo, the growing rambunctiousness of the Chinese, and, most importantly, the sense of defensiveness created by the Soviet humiliation in Cuba and the subsequent feeling of the need to improve bilateral ties with the United States. The Khrushchev leadership had to demonstrate that moves toward the West did not imply a sacrifice of the "progressives."

It should be recalled that from the beginning of the Soviet-Egyptian military-supply relationship in 1955, Moscow had supplied the Arabs with only obsolescent and second-line Soviet military equipment, weapons and equipment that either were no longer used or were not the best available in the Soviet armed forces. Beginning in 1962–63, this policy changed. Commencing slightly before and after the Soviet-Egyptian arms-delivery agreement of 1963, first-line Soviet weapons such as the MIG-21 interceptor and the T-54/55 tank began to be shipped to the "progressive" Arabs. In addition, in a most important move, the TU-16 bomber, a currently deployed Soviet aircraft with a capacity to deliver twenty thousand pounds of bombs on enemy targets, was also provided to the Egyptians for the first time.

The 1963 Egyptian-Soviet pact therefore marked the second basic qualitative change in Soviet military involvement in the Middle East. The 1955 arms deal had established the Soviet Union as a factor in the Middle East political-military equation, and now Moscow was raising the level of its involvement. Henceforth, various first-line Soviet weapons would be supplied to the "progressive" Arabs, and Moscow would endeavor to maintain an upgraded limited Arab strategic-bombing capability. In addition, reflecting at least partially the augmented number of Arab clients of the Soviet Union, the quantitative sum of arms delivered to the Arabs would begin to exceed vastly, rather than to approximate, Israeli weapons holdings.

The Soviets, however, as in the past, did not forsake moderation in seeking to balance their détente policies. Nor, for that matter, was moderation sacrificed when Soviet-American relations deteriorated as the result of the Vietnam crisis.

Soviet weapons deliveries in the pre-Six-Day War period, though massive, seemed structured primarily to provide the "progressive" Arabs with a defensive capability. Though large numbers of tanks and interceptor aircraft were provided, the Soviets were quite restrained in the supply of ground-attack aircraft and tactical rockets. Deficiencies in these weapons categories weakened the Arab capacity to deliver deep and shifting combat fire support and to accomplish battlefield interdiction. Hence, Israel or other opponents would enjoy a greater relative advantage on the line of combat confrontation and could more easily reinforce threatened points than would have been the case if a greater quantity of contemporary ground-attack aircraft and tactical rockets had been provided. Consequently, as the result of Soviet supply decisions, the possibilities for Arab rapid offensive movement were reduced.

Moreover, while the Arabs had received bombers that could tie down Israeli interceptors in strategic air-defensive duties, the Russians had not sufficiently compensated for the subsequent Israeli acquisition of surface-to-air missiles to allow Egyptian strategic bombers to continue to play a decisive role in keeping Tel Aviv's interceptors out of the tactical arena. Hence, Israel's chances to maintain some degree of tactical air control were enhanced, and Egyptian possibilities for offensive action were reduced.

Again, while one cannot be absolutely certain, the apparent gaps in Soviet weapons supplies to the Arabs suggest that the Russians had no desire to give their clients the means to launch an overwhelming, decisive offensive action. Instead, the "progressive" Arabs had been given the means to defend themselves and to engage in, at most, gradual, limited offensive activity. Presumably, the Russians were so restrained in the 1963 period to avoid jeopardizing Soviet-Western détente, and later, to prevent the Arabs from unleashing a catalytic war.

After Israel's 1967 victory, the Soviets again rebuilt the client Arab armed forces in much the same pattern that was employed before the Six-Day War. When the Israelis demonstrated the superiority and effectiveness of their interceptor and ground-attack aircraft during the 1969–70 "war of attrition," however, the Russians added a new dimension to the Egyptian force posture. Antiaircraft missiles (SA-3), which had not yet been provided to the Warsaw Pact nations or to embattled North Vietnam, were sent to Egypt. In addition, some twenty thousand Soviet personnel, including some twelve to fifteen thousand air-defense missile crew members and two hundred interceptor pilots, were provided to augment Cairo's forces. This occasion marked the first time that Soviet combat personnel had ever been deployed to a non-Communist country.

The 1970 dispatch of hitherto unexported weapons and the commitment of Soviet combat personnel constituted the third major qualitative change in the Soviet Middle East military involvement. This important change also marked a partial exception to the general tendency toward coincidence between East-West détente and assertive Soviet moves in the Middle East. Though there were increasing signs of a Soviet move toward closer relations with the Western powers in an effort to assuage the nervousness created by the Czech intervention of 1968, the new, full-blown Soviet détente program would not be officially proclaimed until the XXIV Party Congress in March 1971.

The 1970 qualitative change was not introduced, of course, as a completely free act of Russian volition. Israeli persistence in seeking to force Egypt to the negotiating table by means of application of military power (spurred by Nasser's desire to force the Israelis out of Sinai by inflicting high casualties) compelled the Soviet leadership either to undertake unique measures in support of Cairo or to watch its client be humiliated. While Moscow might well have stood aside if the United States had fully backed Israel, Washington's publicly displayed misgivings about Tel Aviv's course probably signaled that risks associated with even a qualitative change in Soviet military involvement were small.

After the end of the "war of attrition" and the elimination of Israel's "military advantages" along the Suez Canal, Moscow's concerns turned toward wooing the West in accordance with the "Program of Peace" enunciated by General Secretary Brezhnev at the XXIV Party Congress. The Soviet leadership embarked on détente after more than five years of tense relations with the United States dominated by the war in Vietnam. Not only were Moscow's relations with Washington at low ebb during the Southeast Asian crisis, but the Soviets also had aroused the deep apprehensions of Western Europe as a result of their intervention in Czechoslovakia. Western concerns had also been raised by the dramatic Soviet movement from strategic inferiority to parity in the span of only a few years. At the end of the 1960s, Soviet relations with the West, if not totally reminiscent of the days of deepest Cold War, also bore little resemblance to previous interludes of reduced East-West tension.

At the same time, however, it was becoming apparent to the Politburo that the United States would not achieve an easy triumph in Vietnam and, in fact, the American cause was probably doomed to failure.

In May 1969, President Nixon had announced his "Vietnamization" policy and, in spite of temporary aberrations such as the American incursion into Cambodia, United States involvement in the war was clearly shrinking. Moreover, the American president had stated, in his Nixon Doctrine of 1969, that the United States would play a much less central role in future local conflict situations. These events, suggesting a decline in both American fortunes and assertiveness, permitted Moscow to contemplate alteration of its own political position vis-à-vis the West.

The impetus for such a move was provided by the Soviet desire to tranquilize the West in order to: (a) face the growing Chinese military menace more confidently; (b) promote the loosening of Western defense ties and reduction of Western defense consciousness, and (c) gain access to Western technology and credits for Soviet economic development.

By the onset of the 1970s, China had become an important factor in Soviet calculations. The political warfare that had raged between Moscow and Peking during the previous decade had escalated to military clashes and confrontation along the Sino-Soviet border. These clashes undoubtedly caused serious concern in Moscow. China, after all, possessed nuclear weapons and was acquiring a missile delivery capacity. The Peking regime had just passed through a "cultural revolution" that had accentuated the disorder and fanaticism still present in China. Peking's seeming irrationality, coupled with Chinese possession of nuclear weapons, made the prospect of Sino-Soviet war seem real. In the event of the threat or reality of such a war, the Soviets wished to ensure that they would have no distraction on their European flank. Moreover, they also wished to preclude or minimize the political or military significance of any possible Chinese-Western reconciliation.

Promotion of Soviet security interests vis-à-vis China could be realized in the first instance by reducing the anxiety of the Western powers over Soviet intentions. In a situation of high tension, these capitalist states might otherwise make common cause with Peking. In addition to its benefits vis-à-vis China, however, a more conciliatory policy toward the West would have important security benefits in its own right. By reducing the perception of threat from the East, the new Soviet emphasis would tend to discredit "hard-line" Western politicians, who advocated increased military expenditures. A softer Soviet posture would also raise doubts about the necessity of strengthening or maintaining Western defense unity. More generally, a détente orientation would undermine Western foreign policies aimed at isolating and "containing" the Soviet Union. In this manner, Western incentives and means to confront the Soviet Union would gradually be eroded. This would serve to enhance Soviet flank security, lessen the Western urge to support

China, and promote domestic and international evolution in the West in a manner favoring Soviet interests.

The basic security motives for a new Soviet orientation were given added weight by Soviet domestic economic needs. By the beginning of the 1970s, the massive infusions of capital and labor that had fueled previous Soviet economic expansions were now less readily available. New labor inputs into industry, formerly drawn from the agricultural sector, were no longer as easily obtainable as in the past. Capital investment for industrial growth was also restricted because of the need to distribute funds extensively over an enlarged, more complex, and sophisticated economy. Economic growth would increasingly have to be generated by qualitative upgrading rather than quantitative augmentation of the factors of production. Improved use of resources—heightened efficiency of production—would have to replace capital and labor increments as the motor for economic expansion. Increased efficiency could be derived through introduction of more effective systems and equipment employing improved technology. These more effective systems and equipment were often available only in the West and not in the Soviet Union. While improved technology could, of course, be developed in the Soviet Union over time, purchase in the West could provide speedier installation and would reduce developmental costs. Moreover, in many cases, Western firms and banking consortiums, with governmental assistance and encouragement, could provide credits for purchase of this advanced equipment. Thus, Soviet economic expansion could be financed out of future increased output rather than current resources. In order to gain access to Western technology and credits, the Soviets were strongly drawn toward mending their relations with the West and projecting an image of reliability and responsibility.

These various factors combined to produce a major turn in Soviet relations with the West. The German situation was normalized, a strategic arms control agreement was signed, and Soviet summit meetings with the leaders of the United States, France, and West Germany became commonplace. In the wake of these meetings, Soviet-Western agreements, exchanges, and commercial transactions proliferated. The Soviet Union seemed clearly set on making détente with the West a major, long-term object of policy.

Because of the apparently basic importance attributed to the new détente orientation after 1971, the Soviet leadership was quite reluctant to supply Egypt and its other Arab associates with the "offensive weapons" that President Sadat requested ever more strongly to assist in the "liberation" of the occupied territories. Apparently, these "offensive weapons," in the Egyptian view, were arms that could either execute or facilitate strategic bombing or deep interdiction strikes on the Israeli homeland. The Egyptians felt this capability was particularly necessary after the Israelis received high payload Phantom fighter-bombers from the United States. Presumably, possession of "offensive weapons" would allow the Egyptians to deter the Israelis from bombarding the highly populated areas of central Egypt as in the "war of attrition," and thereby make Egyptian offensive action less fraught with danger.

Regardless of Moscow's reluctance to supply the means for a war that might jeopardize détente with the West, Sadat's expulsion of Soviet military personnel from Egypt probably prompted the Russian leadership once again to consider compensating for its warming relations with the capitalist powers. The perception among certain elements of the Politburo of a need for "reinsurance" was probably firmed by the crescendo of criticism and suspicion directed at détente policies by Third World radicals and Peking.

The move toward détente, of course, was not intended to result in abandonment of the "progressive" movement. The Soviet attachment to the "progressives" was real and enduring. Détente, in the Soviet view, was intended not only as a vehicle for solving immediate Soviet problems, but also as a means to heighten the acceptability of "progressive" change in the West and the Third World. In the short run, however, the Soviet effort to seduce the capitalist powers created a feeling among the "progressive" states that Moscow's commitment to anti-Western change was flagging. The persistence of such a belief could create complications for Moscow's pursuit of close relations with the West. Not only would loss of the loyalty of the "progressives" be intolerable (since the Soviets viewed their eventual triumph on a world scale as inevitable), but also no Soviet leadership could afford to open itself up to domestic criticism that it had "sold out" Moscow's "true" friends. "Progressive" criticism would have to be headed off or pursuit of détente would be untenable.

Faced by the need for "reinsurance," therefore, the Soviet leadership decided to satisfy Sadat's request for "offensive weapons" at least partially. Consequently, approximately thirty Scud missiles of 150-mile range were supplied to Egypt to provide an assured means of strategic penetration to the Israeli heartland. In addition, though this is not certain, the Soviets may have committed themselves to providing support to Egypt in the event of an Arab resort to war.

The Soviet provision of means of assured strategic penetration, like the other qualitative changes in Soviet military involvement in the Middle East, was not characterized by a lack of restraint. Though a means of assured penetration was provided, the sum total of incremental destructive power placed in Cairo's hands was not of decisive significance. The thirty-odd 2,000 pound Scud high-explosive warheads could inflict severe damage and casualties in Israeli populated areas but could by no means be said to represent a capability of annihilation. The *Scuds*, therefore, were an important addition to the Egyptian capacity to deter Israeli strategic strikes and possibly were a crucial component influencing Sadat's decision to resort to war. The Soviets, however, did not provide sufficient missiles to guarantee or possibly even to affect the outcome of a future war in Egypt's favor. The Soviet provision of *Scuds* to Sadat can, therefore, be seen as a possible attempt to balance the unfavorable effects of détente on Moscow's ties with the "progressive" movement. At the same time, this balancing move was limited and restrained so that it hopefully would not undermine the basic Soviet goal of improved relations with the major capitalist powers.

As has been seen, four qualitative changes in Soviet military involvement in the Middle East took place between 1955 and 1973. Three of these changes coincided with periods of Soviet-Western détente. While these qualitative military changes were probably not caused by détente, one can hypothesize with some good reason that Moscow's moves toward warmer relations with the capitalist powers generated domestic- and foreign-policy pressures to balance Soviet policy by providing renewed support for the "progressive" movement. While the Soviet leadership was not compelled to respond to these pressures, the historical record seems to indicate that Moscow was particularly prone to raise its military involvement in the Middle East in times of warmer relations with the West.

At the same time, however, the changes in Soviet Near East military involvement have been carefully moderated and measured in order to avoid subverting the dominant goals of Soviet foreign policy and to prevent the "progressive" Arabs, by virtue of an overwhelming victory over Israel, from generating a catalytic war between the United States and the Soviet Union.

III   Soviet actions with regard to the prevention or encouragement of the initiation of war in the Middle East and the limitation of its duration has probably varied in accordance with (a) the degree of support that the Politburo wished to give the Arab "progressives," (b) the extent of success that Soviet clients were enjoying, and (c) the degree to which the Western powers were thought to represent a military danger to the Soviet Union.

The initiation of the 1956 Suez War, of course, was purely an Anglo-French-Israeli-designed operation that the Soviet Union did nothing to immediately encourage or discourage. After the outbreak of the war, probably due to the Egyptian lack of success, the Soviet Union spoke in favor of a rapid end to hostilities. However, presumably because of the fear of provoking Western military countermeasures while the Soviet army was heavily engaged in Hungary, the Russians made no concrete moves or threats aimed at seeking an early end to the fighting. Moscow also did not act to provide supplies or combat personnel to the beleaguered Egyptians.

After some seven days of combat in the Middle East and the termination of major resistance in Hungary, the Soviet leadership made its first concrete political-military move of the war—an implicit threat of missile attack on France and England and a call for deployment of a joint American-Soviet military force to the Middle East. While the missile threat was generally dismissed as incredible in the West, the Soviet proposition calling for establishment of a Russian-American joint force raised concerns in Washington which, when relayed to London and Paris, were instrumental, along with British foreign-exchange difficulties, in bringing hostilities to a close.

Not until three days after England, France, and Israel ended combat, however, did the Soviets make their only direct threat of unilateral military intervention—the assertion that Russian "volunteers" were ready to depart for the Middle East if the invading powers did not evacuate their forces from Egyptian soil. This threat, probably not coincidentally, was issued on the day that military operations in Hungary definitively ended.

One can, therefore, reasonably presume that, in 1956, during the militarily active phases of the Hungarian revolt, the Soviet leadership placed greater importance on avoiding military confrontation with the West than on providing support for Nasser's flagging "progressive" cause. Once the Hungarian distraction was eliminated, the Soviets introduced the highly conditioned threats of a rocket attack on France and England (cast in terms of a hypothetical possibility and not a direct threat) and the dispatch of a joint Russian-American force (which by definition could not be deployed without the concurrence of the United States).

A direct Soviet threat did not emerge, however, until the United States had clearly shown that it shared Soviet views on terminating the tripartite operation and until Washington had succeeded in imposing an end to fighting on England and France. The Soviet leadership, under these circumstances, probably viewed the risk associated with its direct-intervention threat as minimal, while the public-relations advantages vis-à-vis the "progressive" movement were probably felt to be high.

Turning to the period preceding the Six-Day War, the Soviet Union, wishing to fortify the "progressive" Arabs against the heightened threat allegedly posed by Israel and local Western-backed "reactionaries," encouraged the Egyptians to make a show of unity and force on behalf of Syria after the latter country had suffered a military humiliation at the hands of Israel. The Egyptian demonstration of force, however, was rapidly converted into a real threat of war by virtue of Nasser's decision both to expel the U.N. Emergency Force from the Sinai Desert and to blockade Israeli shipping through the Straits of Tiran.

Faced by the possibility of Arab-Israeli hostilities, with the concomitant danger of a Soviet-American confrontation, the Russian leadership shifted its position and repeatedly tried to stem the Egyptian-Israeli move toward war. The Soviet sense of urgency in seeking to forestall conflict was probably heightened by President Johnson's expression of concern regarding the Middle East situation, coupled with the generally threatening nature of Washington's behavior in the early and mid-1960s. Soviet efforts to avert war, however, were to no avail, and on 5 June 1967 the Israeli air force successfully attacked Egypt.

With Cairo's capacity for defense drastically reduced as a consequence of Israel's attack, Moscow, as evidenced by hot line messages to President Johnson, was strongly drawn toward seeking a quick ceasefire. This Soviet expression of restraint was warmly received in Washington. When the Egyptians initially balked at accepting a halt in hostilities, however, the Soviets acceded to Cairo's wishes. The Soviets were apparently willing to tolerate the risks of confrontation as long as the Arabs were prepared to fight. Moscow's desire to fortify the "progressive" movement, as evidenced by the encouragement of an "anti-imperialist" show of force before the war, demanded at least a passive support of Arab wishes during the conflict.

On the other hand, the Soviet leadership, apparently anticipating the inevitability of an early Arab defeat, declined to offer any large-scale concrete assistance to the Arab belligerents during the course of the war. When the Egyptians and then the Syrians announced their readiness to accept a ceasefire, Moscow brooked no delay in pushing an appropriate resolution through the United Nations. The United States, consistently favoring a quick end to hostilities, supported the ceasefire resolution.

When the ceasefire did not take effect on the Syrian front and Israel continued its gains at Syrian expense, Moscow again, near what appeared from the American perspective to be the end of hostilities, threatened military intervention in the Middle East. Moscow's direct threat, again, only came after the United States had indicated on multiple occasions that it shared the by then current Soviet desire for a quick end to hostilities. The conciliatory trend of American policy during the war probably lessened the Russian perception of risk associated with the intervention threat. The Soviet leadership probably assumed that the

United States, as in the 1956 approaches to England and France, would intercede to halt Israeli advances and that no serious reaction would be forthcoming. Such an outcome would be highly desirable from the Russian point of view, since it would gain needed credit for Moscow after Moscow's half-hearted support of the Arab war effort yet would not endanger Soviet national security or Russian Middle Eastern clients. Furthermore, the Russian intervention threat was sufficiently qualified so as not to oblige the Soviets to act even if the Americans did not comply with Soviet wishes. As it turned out, the United States did suggest that the Israelis halt operations, and the only American reaction to the intervention threat—the change in deployment of the Sixth Fleet —was not prejudicial to the Soviet Union's interests.

Moscow's policy in 1967 can therefore be seen as an effort to support and encourage the "progressive" movement, but not at the risk of provoking a confrontation with the United States. After war broke out against Russian desires, the Soviet leadership undertook no moves outside the realm of verbal support which would prolong the Arabs' capacity for resistance. As soon as the Arabs were ready to stop fighting, the Soviet Union instantly acted to implement this wish. On the other hand, the Russians, by not pressing for an immediate ceasefire against Arab wishes, indicated that they were prepared to accept certain low-level risks of confrontation in order to maintain the support of the "progressive" movement.

Again, as in 1956, the only threat of direct Russian intervention came at the conclusion of the crisis and only after a concurrence of views had been achieved with the United States with regard to the conditions of ending the war. Due to the absence of political disagreement with the United States, the Politburo probably considered its intervention gambit as a desirable, low-risk move.

By 1973, Soviet policy was less intent on strengthening the "progressive" movement than on simply maintaining the movement's alliance with the Soviet Union. Anti-Soviet feelings spurred by failure to achieve a return of the 1967 occupied territories and a belief that Moscow was sacrificing Arab interests in order to promote détente were becoming prevalent in even the "progressive" Arab states. After Soviet military advisers were expelled from Egypt in 1972, Russian fears of losing all the hard-earned gains achieved by long support of the Arab "progressive" movement undoubtedly came to a head. In order to prevent further deterioration of the Russian position in the Middle East, the Soviet leadership must have decided when friendly relations were reestablished between Egypt and the Soviet Union in late 1972 and early 1973 that if at all possible, it would not again stand in the way of Arab aspirations.

Hence, when Egyptian President Sadat's emissary Hafez Ismail informed Moscow of the bellicose direction of Egyptian policy in July

1973, the Soviets apparently expressed only cautions and made no public effort to argue against an Arab resort to war. Though private efforts reportedly were undertaken to convince the Arabs to delay war for two to three years, these urgings were apparently not presented as ultimata or, for that matter, even very strong demands. The Soviets, wishing to safeguard their Middle Eastern position, went no further than to signal their reservations.

While the Russians did not wish to lose more ground in the Middle East, they also did not want to jeopardize détente with the major Western powers. During summer 1973, the Soviets therefore reportedly passed vague intimations of an impending Arab attack to the West. The final step of these very veiled warnings was the Soviet decision to evacuate dependents from Cairo and Damascus. While these Soviet actions provided evidence of a measure of tacit cooperation between Moscow and the West, they were far removed from the energetic American and Soviet cooperative efforts of 1967 to forestall the outbreak of war. In fact, even after the evacuation of Russian dependents, when Moscow was certainly fully aware of the imminent attack, there was a notable lack of any Russian efforts to halt the movement toward war.

The difference between 1967 and 1973 may have been accounted for by the more acute Soviet fear of offending the Arabs; Moscow's heightened confidence in its own military capabilities; and the sense that the United States, because of the Vietnam experience, domestic political difficulties, and the desire to preserve East-West détente, was less likely to confront the Soviet Union or its Arab clients. All these factors, combined with the probable belief that the Arabs at worst would suffer a quick limited defeat, prompted the Soviets to adopt a less cautious course than had been the case six years before.

After Cairo and Damascus launched the war on October 6, the Soviet leadership in contacts with Washington and Cairo seemed to indicate that it was in favor of an early halt in hostilities. President Sadat, however, rejected Soviet ceasefire approaches and, concurrently, the Arab attacks achieved limited successes instead of the failures probably expected by Moscow. Relying on the same policy calculus that had prompted the Soviet Union not to openly oppose the Arab resort to war, the Russian leadership, taking account of the Arab successes, shifted from calling for a quick ceasefire to endorsement of Arab war aims and the beginning of air and sea resupply of the Egyptian and Syrian armed forces.

Moscow's unprecedented decision to allow the war to continue, and indeed to encourage its prolongation, probably was founded on two basic considerations—the Soviets' desire to strongly demonstrate support for the "progressive" movement and the perceived belief that the United States, because of differences of view with Israel and other foreign and domestic factors, would not decisively act against the Soviet Union, Egypt, and Syria. When the United States began to resupply Israel, however, and the fortunes of Egypt and Syria began to seriously falter, Chairman Kosygin flew to Cairo and thereby indicated that Soviet policy had again shifted toward serious advocacy of a halt in hostilities. The final fruits of this last Soviet policy shift would be the agreement of Cairo and Damascus to a halt in hostilities and the October 22 joint Soviet-American ceasefire resolution adopted by the U.N. Security council.

The Soviet leadership, therefore, more conscious of the need to seriously back the Arabs due to the rise of anti-Sovietism, was willing to run higher risks than at any time in the past to express solidarity with the "progressive" movement. This more adventurous policy was both prompted and eased by the success of the Arab armies vis-à-vis Israel and the perceived weakness of American backing for Tel Aviv.

The only Soviet direct-intervention threat during the Yom Kippur War came, like its precedents in the Suez War and the Six-Day War, at the end of the crisis. Because of the breakdown of the American-Soviet ceasefire resolution and the nearness to collapse of Egyptian forces, the Soviet Union again resorted to the tried and tested method of goading Washington to apply pressure on its friends and allies. As on previous occasions, the initiation of the intervention threat was delayed until the United States was definitively committed to supporting the same goal as the Soviets—an immediate ceasefire. The haste with which the American Secretary of State departed for Moscow when the Soviets indicated that a ceasefire was possible probably tended to confirm the Soviet impression that the United States would not create serious difficulties for the Soviet Union because of the Soviet threat. Though the extent of American posturing as represented by the October 25 alert probably surprised the Russians, in Moscow's eyes the Middle East intervention threat probably again justified itself as a highly successful tool of war termination.

The 1973 Soviet intervention threat was distinguished from its predecessors by the fact that it was taken more seriously by Washington, given Moscow's greater ability than any time in the past to rapidly transport troops and supplies to the Middle East. Notwithstanding the theatrical nature of Washington's response to the intervention threat, that pressure was put on Israel to terminate operations and Soviet interests were not immediately harmed probably confirmed Moscow's prior view that the political-military risks posed by engaging in threatening behavior against the United States and its friends were small.

In addition to the different degrees of Arab success in the Yom Kippur War, the Suez War, and the Six-Day War, the less cautious nature of Soviet responses in the 1973 conflict (as witnessed by the decisions not to oppose Arab resort to war and to delay implementation of a ceasefire) was probably motivated by a paradoxical evolution of the Soviet power position.

In previous Middle Eastern wars the Soviet Union had enjoyed the important advantage of being regarded as the only reliable and true backer of the "progressive" Arabs. By 1973 the Soviet reputation had seriously deteriorated (principally because of Arab dissatisfaction and impatience rather than any change in the character of Soviet support), and Moscow was at pains to prove its backing of its clients' cause.

On the other hand, in previous wars the Soviet Union stood juxtaposed against Western powers that enjoyed great military advantages over the Soviet Union, not only on the strategic level but also in the local Middle Eastern area. By 1973 the Soviet Union had gone far toward reducing these military deficiencies. Most importantly, the political confidence of the United States had seriously been eroded by the long, frustrating war in Vietnam, the weakness of domestic support of a scandal-ridden presidency, and the endorsement of a foreign-policy stance premised on avoiding conflict with the Soviet Union.

The Soviet Union in 1973, in contrast to 1956 and 1967, therefore found itself in a weak and deteriorating position vis-à-vis its Arab clients but in a strong and ascendant position in relation to the United States. This formula probably caused and permitted the Soviet leadership to take greater risks than at any time in the past in backing the Arab position in the Yom Kippur War.

IV The preceding survey of Soviet conduct before and during the last three Middle East wars has indicated that, while Russian behavior has evolved in a less cautious direction, particularly in the period of the Yom Kippur War, there has been no overall absence of restraint on the part of Moscow. Soviet supplies of potentially decisive arms, such as regionally strategic weapons and weapons permitting overwhelming offensive results on the ground, have often been highly restricted. Furthermore, during the prelude and course of the various Middle East wars, no attempts have been made to directly confront the United States. Soviet intervention threats have appeared only when American and Russian policy positions have coincided.

At the same time, the persistence and effort exerted by the Soviet Union in seeking to maintain its close ties with the Arab "progressives" must be noted. Upwards of 80 percent of total Soviet economic and military aid has been expended on the countries lying between North Africa and the Indian subcontinent. Egypt, Syria, and Iraq received more than 50 percent of global Soviet military assistance from 1954 to

1970.[1] In addition, Egypt alone received from 3 to 16 percent of total Soviet inventories of various ground and air weapons.[2]

Soviet interest in maintaining a position of substantial influence in the Middle East is clearly high. In spite of the defeats which Soviet clients have suffered and the various rebuffs which these clients have given the Soviet Union, in the post-Stalin era the Soviets have never openly turned against the Arab "progressives" as a whole.

Presumably, the Soviet leadership believes that "progressive" nationalist leaders hold the key to eventual exclusion of Western power from the Middle East, an area which contains much of the energy resources of the capitalist world, provides a location along the Soviet Union's borders from which an additional threat to Soviet security could be projected, and encompasses a number of countries which for a long period of time have aligned their foreign and domestic policies in an anti-Western direction.

Therefore, in order to preserve the Soviet stake in this vital area and to symbolically express support for radical movements in other areas, Moscow has sought, to the extent possible, to harmonize its interests with those of the various Arab "progressive" leaders.

Soviet efforts to curry the favor of the "progressive" Arabs have been accompanied by the apparent belief that a long-range coincidence of interest exists between the Soviet Union and the radical Arab regimes. In Moscow's view, not only do the "progressive" regimes serve the interests of the Soviet Union, but the Soviet Union also meets the needs of the "progressive" regimes.

The Soviet perception of a confluence of Arab and Russian interests is apparently founded on the expectation that the domestic- and foreign-policy courses of current and future "progressive" regimes will inevitably clash with Western economic and petroleum interests in the Middle East and the American inclination to support and protect Israel. Such Arab-Western confrontations will not only redound to Soviet benefit but will also cause the "progressive" Arabs to turn to the Soviet Union for necessary military and political support.

Soviet calculations on Western-Arab conflict, of course, could be seriously confounded if the "progressive" Arab regimes remain tolerant of Western economic interests as well as of the security of the state of Israel. Nonetheless, the nagging nature of Middle Eastern problems suggests that Moscow's estimate of future Arab-Western tension might indeed constitute a highly possible development of events in the Near East.

Whatever direction historical evolution takes, however, given the probable Soviet expectation and desire of a continuing role in the Middle East, coupled with the demonstrated evidence of the high priority of the region in Russian eyes, there is little reason to believe that Soviet influence will be permanently excluded from the area. Because of the seeming insolubility of many of the problems of the Near East, it is prudent to assume that Moscow will continue to play an important political-military role in the region.

APPENDIXES

The methodology employed in this paper to evaluate Soviet arms deliveries is based on the following premises. The military contest in war is a political process, not only in the terms employed by Clausewitz (as a means to achieve a political end) but also in the allocative sense. While the ordinary political process allocates positive values (goods, power, and so forth), the military contest of war allocates negative values (death, destruction, etc.). Hence, the definition of politics as the process of deciding "who gets what, when, and how" can usefully be applied to war. The military contest of war can thus be said to decide whether A *or* B (who) gets physically destroyed *or* disorganized, that is, becomes unable to operate purposefully (what), rapidly as a result of a quick annihilation or blitzkrieg attack *or* slowly through attrition (when), by means of fire *or* movement (how).

Fire is projected and movement is executed in order to accomplish four basic offensive tasks: (a) fire support on the line of combat confrontation, (b) interdiction of the movement of enemy forces seeking to

FIGURE 2. WAR

A. *The Military Contest*

B. *Fire/Movement*
Fire is projected and movement is executed in order to accomplish:

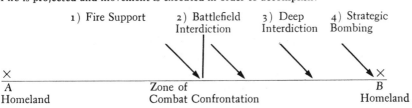

reinforce threatened points and to concentrate for attack on the battle-field, (c) deep interdiction of the movement of enemy supplies and reinforcements from rear areas to the zone of combat confrontation, and (d) strategic bombardment of the enemy's source of supplies and population in his homeland. All these tasks have the common goal of creating a local or general imbalance in favor of one's forces over those of the enemy.

In order to accomplish these various offensive tasks and to defend against the enemy's exercise of the same tasks against one's own forces, some seven basic combat functions can be performed by a military establishment: (a) strategic air defense, (b) tactical air cover and air defense, (c) strategic bomber escort (if strategic bombers are employed, (d) combat-zone fire support, (e) battlefield interdiction, (f) deep interdiction, and (g) strategic bombardment.

Three basic categories of weapons can perform these seven combat functions: (a) interceptor aircraft and various antiaircraft weapons, (b) ground-attack aircraft, tanks, artillery, tactical surface-to-surface missiles, infantry weapons, plus means of transport of men and material, and (c) long-distance bomber aircraft and medium- and longer-range surface-to-surface missiles.

As indicated in figure 3, each of the individual categories of weapons can perform two or more of the seven listed combat functions. Because of the necessity for performing multiple combat functions, a problem of allocation of finite resources arises. Interceptor aircraft that are used to escort strategic bombers cannot be used in strategic air defense, and so forth.

Furthermore, force holdings of the enemy can influence one's own use of forces. For example, should the enemy possess a great strategic bomber threat, one would have to strengthen one's strategic air defense by diverting antiaircraft weapons and interceptor aircraft away from the zone of combat confrontation (thereby diminishing the quality of tactical air cover for one's own ground-attack aircraft and reducing the protection of one's own ground forces against enemy air attack).

Hence, by surveying the distribution of weapons deliveries between and within the three basic weapons categories, one can generally assess the type of forces that the delivering party wished or felt compelled to create for its client. The provision or lack of provision of certain types of weapons will clearly have an important impact on both what the client's forces can accomplish and what the client's enemy can do.

For example, by limiting provision of strategic bombers, the supplying state reduces the strategic offensive capability of the client. This decision also, however, permits the client's enemy to devote more of his

FIGURE 3. WEAPONS AND THEIR MILITARY USES

$(A \rightarrow B)$

1. *Interceptor Aircraft, Antiaircraft Weapons Including SAM's*

A) Strategic Air Defense   B) Tactical Air Cover and and Air Defense   C) Strategic Bomber Escort (Interceptor A/C Only)

A   Zone of   B
Homeland   Combat Confrontation   Homeland

2. *Ground-Attack Aircraft, Tanks, Artillery, Tactical Missiles, Infantry Weapons, and Means of Transport of Men and Material*

D) Fire Support   E) Battlefield Interdiction

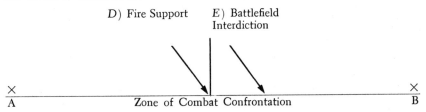

A   Zone of Combat Confrontation   B

3. *Long-Distance Bomber Aircraft* and Surface-to-Surface Missiles (MRBM and Longer Range)*

(Could Be Used for "D" and "E" if Required)   F) Deep Interdiction   G) Strategic Bombardment

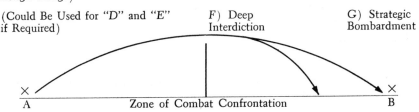

A   Zone of Combat Confrontation   B

* Some current multipurpose fighter-bombers have performance characteristics sufficiently high to be used as interceptors (F-4 Phantom [U.S.] for example).

finite air-defense means to the zone of tactical combat confrontation and thereby reduces the client's tactical offensive capability. By limiting the supply of ground-attack aircraft, the supplying state weakens the client's tactical offensive capability. It also, however, permits the client's enemy to devote less air-defense resources to the tactical zone. This means that the enemy's strategic air defense can be improved and that more enemy interceptors might be spared for escort of strategic bombers to the client's homeland and other targets.

Because of these various trade-offs, the appearance of notable imbalances within a client's armed forces probably represents a limiting decision of considerable import on the part of a supplying state. In addition, failure of a supplier to respond to a weapons procurement on the part of a client's enemy which creates additional imbalances or eliminates force advantages previously enjoyed by a client also represents an important limiting action on the part of a supplying state.

2. MAXIMUM PERFORMANCE DATA OF SELECTED ARAB AND ISRAELI AIRCRAFT

A. ARAB

1. Interceptors (Type/First Flight)

	MIG-17 (1952)	MIG-19 (1953)	MIG-21 (1955)	MIG-25 (1964)
Speed	711 mph	902 mph	1,385 mph	2,115 mph
Ceiling	55,000 ft.	59,000 ft.	59,000 ft.	73,000 ft.
Bombload	1,100 lb.	1,100 lb.	———	———
Radius	435 mi.	425 mi.	350 mi.	700 mi.

2. Ground-Attack Aircraft   3. Bombers

	SU-7 (1956)		IL-28 (1948)	TU-16 (1954)	TU-22 (1961)*
Speed	1,055 mph	Speed	559 mph	587 mph	920 mph
Ceiling	50,000 ft.	Ceiling	41,000 ft.	42,000 ft.	60,000 ft.
Bombload	5,500 lb.	Bombload	4,500 lb.	20,000 lb.	?
Radius	200–300 mi.	Radius	700 mi.	2,000 mi.	700 mi.

B. ISRAELI

1. Interceptors/Fighter-Bombers   *2. Ground-Attack Aircraft*

	Mirage III (1956)	F-4 Phantom (1958)		A-4 Skyhawk (1954)
Speed	1,460 mph	1,454 mph.	Speed	645 mph
Ceiling	55,000 ft.	58,000 ft.	Ceiling	49,000 ft.
Bombload	2,000 lb.	14,000–16,000 lb.	Bombload	7,750 lb.
Radius	745 mi.	920 mi.	Radius	500 mi.

*Controlled as of 1973 only by Soviet personnel.

3. EXCERPTS FROM SADAT INTERVIEW WITH AS-SIYASAH (KUWAIT), SEPTEMBER 9, 1975

a. *Aly Sabry Ouster and the Soviet-Egyptian Treaty (1970)*

"When the struggle reached its peak I summoned the Russian Ambassador . . . and said . . . there was a domestic subject that might affect our relations. I want you to convey it to Moscow. . . . I have decided to eliminate Aly Sabry from the command. . . . The Soviet Ambassador answered me that this did not concern him at all. I told him: 'You are right, but I want you to inform Moscow so that [when] the West and the Western press . . . say that Moscow's man in Egypt has been liquidated . . . there will be no misunderstanding between us. . . .' Aly Sabry was liquidated and all the West said that Moscow's man had finally been eliminated. . . . The month Aly Sabry was liquidated, Podgorny suddenly arrived in Cairo and asked us to sign the treaty that Nasser and I had been urging the Soviet Union for three years to conclude. I told Podgorny: 'Your spectacle before the Egyptian people will be unacceptable if you ask for this agreement to be signed immediately after the liquidation [of the Sabry group]. . . . This means that Aly Sabry was Moscow's man in Egypt.' Podgorny replied that he did not mean this, and that the treaty was an attempt to answer the West. I told him: 'Postpone . . . this treaty. . . .' But he insisted pleadingly that the Politburo in Moscow had adopted a decision and wanted this treaty. I then summoned Foreign Minister Mahmud Riad and said to him: 'The Russians want a treaty. Draft a treaty for them.' We signed the treaty."

b. *Weapons Supply Before the October War* (1973)

"After the withdrawal of the Russian experts from Egypt [1972], enormous quantities of technologically advanced Russian arms arrived in Syria. I did not receive arms except in the summer of 1973. . . ."

c. *Russian Ceasefire Initiatives During the October War* (1973)

"The Russians asked Egypt to cease fire first on 6 October, the day of the war, and on 7 and 8 October. They then sent Kosygin to Cairo [October 16]. . . ."

d. *Dealing with the Russians*

". . . when you send them an urgent message which may be one of destiny, they do not answer you and say that the Soviet leaders are in the Crimea where the Soviet leaders spend four months from May to October. Of course, you have to wait for their return to Moscow, and, of course, they need a month and a half to rest a bit in Moscow. They will then answer you if they ever do."

NOTES

CHAPTER ONE

1. *Washington Post*, 28 November 1973.
2. *The New York Times*, 26 October 1973.
3. Soviet-supplied arms were also used in combat by Egypt in its 1962–67 intervention in the Yemen civil war and by Syria in its 1970 incursion into Jordan.

CHAPTER TWO

1. For British invasion motives, see Anthony Eden, *Full Circle* (Boston: Houghton Mifflin Company, 1960), pp. 467–92; for a more critical view, see Anthony Nutting, *No End of a Lesson* (New York: Clarkson N. Potter, 1967). For French motives, see the remarks of Christian Pineau in Peter Calvocoressi, ed., *Suez: Ten Years After* (New York: Pantheon Books, 1967), pp. 62–64. Regarding Israeli intentions, see Moshe Dayan, *Diary of the Sinai Campaign* (New York: Harper and Row, 1966), pp. 1–19.
2. Mohammed Hassanein Heikal, *The Cairo Documents* (Garden City, N.Y.: Doubleday and Company, 1973), p. 51.
3. Harold Macmillan, *Riding the Storm: 1956–1959* (London: Macmillan Company, 1971), p. 90.
4. Dwight D. Eisenhower, *Waging Peace: 1956–61* (Garden City, N.Y.: Doubleday and Company, 1965), pp. 25–26.
5. Heikal, *The Cairo Documents*, p. 46.
6. Kennett Love, *Suez: The Twice Fought War* (New York: McGraw-Hill Book Company, 1969), p. 101.
7. Ibid., pp. 75 and 707.
8. Ibid., p. 95. Love states that the reports were leaked by British sources who were concerned with Israel's threat to Britain's clients Jordan and Iraq. Another source indicates, however, that the French decision to supply Mystere IV's came after the "Czech" arms deal. See Calvocoressi, *Suez*, p. 67.
9. David Ben-Gurion, quoted in Calvocoressi, *Suez*, p. 67.
10. A. S. Protopopov, *Sovetskii soyuz i suetskii krizis 1956 goda* (Moscow: Izdatel'stvo Nauka, 1969), pp. 63 and 66. It is worth nothing that Protopopov refers to Western charges that the Soviet Union was disrupting the Middle Eastern arms balance but does not directly contradict these accusations. He simply states that the West feared losing its weapons-supply monopoly, which had long been used for "criminal ends" (see ibid., pp. 67–68).
11. Secretary of State Dulles's argument also added the qualification that Israel because of limited population and resources, could not compete in an arms race with the Arab states. Therefore, in his view, means other than arms would have to be used to guarantee Israeli security. See J. C. Hurewitz, *Middle East Politics: The Military Dimension* (New York: Frederick A. Praeger Company, 1969), p. 465.
12. Eisenhower, *Waging Peace*, p. 25.
13. Love, *Suez*, p. 117. The MIG-17's were not yet delivered by the beginning of the 1956 war.
14. Dayan, *Diary of the Sinai Campaign*, pp. 4–5.
15. Ibid.

16. Robert Stephens, *Nasser: A Political Biography* (New York: Simon and Schuster, 1971), p. 161.

17. Humphrey Trevelyan, *The Middle East in Revolution* (London: Macmillan Company, 1970), p. 33, quoted in Stephens, *Nasser*, p. 161.

18. John Erickson, quoted in Calvocoressi, *Suez*, pp. 48–49.

19. Dayan, *Diary of the Sinai Campaign*, p. 5.

20. Ibid., pp. 81 and 221.

21. Love, *Suez*, p. 118. American intelligence, presumably based on U-2 aerial photographs, credited Israel with sixty Mysteres in October 1956 (see Eisenhower, *Waging Peace*, p. 677). The discrepancy between Dayan's figures on Israeli Mystere holdings and the aerial-intelligence photographs may be accounted for by the fact that the additional Mysteres may have belonged to French air force squadrons that had been transferred to Israel to provide air cover during the forthcoming invasion (see Hugh Thomas, *The Suez Affair* [London: Penguin Books, 1970], p. 134).

22. Dayan, *Diary of the Sinai Campaign*, pp. 220–21. Dayan (p. 30) states that Israel requested and received approval for the shipment of 100 Super Sherman World War II–vintage medium tanks from France one month before the scheduled invasion.

23. By way of reservation, it should be recalled that Mystere deliveries to Israel reportedly did not commence until April 1956. The initial "Czech"-Egyptian arms pact that provided the MIG-15's was signed in September 1955 (ibid., p. 81).

24. John Milsom, *Russian Tanks, 1900–1970* (London: Arms and Armour Press, 1970), p. 95.

25. Ibid., pp. 104–12 and 125.

26. Dayan, *Diary of the Sinai Campaign*, p. 80, and Andre Fontaine, quoted in Calvocoressi, *Suez*, p. 68.

27. Calvocoressi, *Suez*, p. 65. Strategic air defense during the war was provided by French air force units transferred to Israel (see Thomas, *The Suez Affair*, p. 134).

28. *Izvestiya*, 1 November 1956.

29. Heikal, *The Cairo Documents*, p. 112.

30. Nikita Khrushchev, "For New Victories of the World Communist Movement" (Speech delivered 6 January 1961), in his *Kommunizm—mir i schast'ye narodov* (Moscow: Gospolitizdat, 1962), vol. 1, p. 35.

31. *Izvestiya*, 6 November 1956.

32. Ibid.

33. John Erickson, quoted in Calvocoressi, *Suez*, p. 23.

34. Eden, *Full Circle*, p. 621.

35. Macmillan, *Riding the Storm*, p. 165.

36. Eisenhower, *Waging Peace*, p. 91.

37. Quoted in U.S. Department of State, *United States Policy in the Middle East: September 1956–June 1957* (Washington, D.C.: U.S. Government Printing Office, 1957), p. 184.

38. While the Russian rocket threat had little impact in the West, it reportedly inspired the Egyptians to make a stand against the English and French in Port Said rather than surrender the city. According to British commander Sir Charles Keightley, loudspeaker trucks toured Port Said inspiring the citizens with the announcement that World War III had begun and that London and Paris were being bombarded by missiles. The Soviet consul general in Port Said at this point assisted in distributing Russian weapons to the citizens of the city (see Thomas, *The Suez Affair*, p. 158, and A. J. Barker, *Suez: The Seven Day War* [London: Faber and Faber, 1964], p. 140).

39. Eisenhower, *Waging Peace*, p. 89, and Protopopov, *Sovetskii soyuz i suetskii krizis 1956 goda*, p. 204. The full text of the letter appears in U.S. Department of State, *United States Policy in the Middle East*, pp. 180–81, and *Department of State Bulletin*, 19 November 1956, pp. 180–81.

40. *Izvestiya*, 6 November 1956.

41. Ibid.

42. U.S. Department of State, *United States Policy in the Middle East*, p. 182.

43. Eisenhower, *Waging Peace*, p. 91.

44. Ibid., p. 90.

45. Ibid., pp. 91–92.

46. Macmillan, *Riding the Storm*, pp. 164–67.

47. Protopopov, *Sovetskii soyuz i suetskii krizis 1956 goda*, p. 206.

48. U.S. Department of State, *United States Policy in the Middle East*, pp. 215–16.

49. J. M. Mackintosh, *Strategy and Tactics of Soviet Foreign Policy* (New York: Oxford University Press, 1963), p. 175.

50. Love, *Suez*, p. 160.

51. Ibid., p. 117.

52. U.S. Department of State, *United States Policy in the Middle East*, p. 246.

53. Dayan, *Diary of the Sinai Campaign*, p. 109, states that one IL-28 bomber on 30 October and one on 31 October "dropped their bombs on open ground, far from city or village, without discrimination and without causing damage." At least one of these bombings took place in Israel proper near Jerusalem (p. 89). Kennett Love, the *New York Times* correspondent, states that according to the message log at Egyptian air force headquarters in Cairo, IL-28 bombers in pairs carried out six raids against Israeli airfields on 30 October (Love, *Suez*, p. 512).

54. Heikal, *The Cairo Documents*, p. 109.

55. Thomas, *The Suez Affair*, p. 144.

56. John Erickson, quoted in Calvocoressi, *Suez*, p. 49.

57. Love, *Suez*, pp. 528 and 724.

58. John Erickson, quoted in Calvocoressi, *Suez*, p. 49, and Barker, *Suez*, p. 60.

59. Dayan, *Diary of the Sinai Campaign*, p. 218.

60. John Erickson, quoted in Calvocoressi, *Suez*, p. 49.

61. Dayan, *Diary of the Sinai Campaign*, pp. 109 and 177–78. Seven of the ten Israeli planes were shot down on October 30 and 31 before the British and French air attacks began.

62. Barker, *Suez*, pp. 101 and 205.

63. Ibid., p. 103. Mohamed Heikal asserts that for all practical purposes, the Egyptian air force was destroyed during the first day of Anglo-French bombing. (Heikal, *The Cairo Documents*, p. 110).

64. Dayan, *Diary of the Sinai Campaign*, p. 54.

65. Heikal, *The Cairo Documents*, pp. 109–10.

66. For a complete description of the military operations in Port Said and vicinity, see Barker, *Suez*.

CHAPTER THREE

1. Nadav Safran, *The United States and Israel* (Cambridge: Harvard University Press, 1963), p. 248.

2. Heikal, *The Cairo Documents*, pp. 134–35.

3. Ibid., pp. 141–42.

4. Walter Laqueur, *The Struggle for the Middle East: The Soviet Union and the Middle East, 1958–68* (Harmondsworth: Penguin Books, 1972), pp. 84–86.

5. Ibid., pp. 86–87.

6. Information on the dimensions and contents of the 1957–65 Soviet-Egyptian arms agreements is derived from George Lenczowski, *Soviet Advances in the Middle East* (Washington, D.C.: American Enterprise Institute for Public Policy Research, 1972), pp. 146–49.

7. Stephens, *Nasser*, p. 391.

8. Avigdor Dagan, *Moscow and Jerusalem* (New York: Abelard-Schuman, 1970), p. 145. Dagan is a senior Israeli foreign ministry official.

9. *Al Ahram*, 1 July 1962, cited in Wynfred Joshua and Stephen P. Gibert, *Arms*

for the Third World: Soviet Military Aid Diplomacy (Baltimore: Johns Hopkins Press, 1969), p. 23.

10. Michael Howard and Robert Hunter, *Israel and the Arab World: The Crisis of 1967* (London: Institute for Strategic Studies, 1967), pp. 50–51.

11. Abba Eban, in *The New York Times*, 20 June 1967, cited in Nadav Safran, *From War to War: The Arab-Israeli Confrontation, 1948–1967* (New York: Pegasus Books, 1969), p. 436, and in Lincoln Bloomfield and Amelia Reiss, *Controlling Small Wars: A Strategy for the 1970's* (New York: Alfred A. Knopf, 1969), pp. 338–39.

12. Howard and Hunter, *Israel and the Arab World*, p. 50; *The New York Times*, 11 July 1967, cited in Safran, *From War to War*, p. 339.

13. Howard and Hunter, *Israel and the Arab World*, p. 50.

14. Safran, *From War to War*, pp. 439–40.

15. Howard and Hunter, *Israel and the Arab World*, p. 50.

16. Ibid., p. 51; Safran, *From War to War*, p. 440; and *The Statesman's Yearbook, 1968–1969* (New York: St. Martin's Press, 1968), p. 1478.

17. Howard and Hunter, *Israel and the Arab World*, p. 51.

18. Ibid., and *The Statesman's Yearbook, 1968–1969*, p. 1148.

19. Ibid., and *The Statesman's Yearbook, 1967–1968* (New York: St. Martin's Press, 1967), p. 1155.

20. Milsom, *Russian Tanks*, p. 114.

21. Ibid., p. 116.

22. Hurewitz, *Middle East Politics*, pp. 479–80.

23. News conference of 25 February 1965, reprinted in *Department of State Bulletin*, 15 March 1965, p. 367.

24. Howard and Hunter, *Israel and the Arab World*, p. 50.

25. Ibid.

26. Dayan, *Diary of the Sinai Campaign*, pp. 152–53.

27. Approximately 3–4 percent of the estimated total fifteen-year production run of T-54 tanks was shipped to the Middle East before the Six-Day War (see *Jane's Weapons Systems, 1969–1970* [New York: McGraw-Hill Publishing Company, 1970], p. 216).

28. Ibid, pp. 203, 209, and 216.

29. Michael I. Handel, *Israel's Political-Military Doctrine* (Cambridge, Mass.: Harvard University Center for International Affairs, 1973), p. 28.

30. Kenneth Munson, *Fighters in Service: Attack and Training Aircraft since 1960* (London: Blandford Press, 1971), p. 152.

31. Safran, *From War to War*, p. 439.

32. Howard and Hunter, *Israel and the Arab World*, p. 50.

33. Hal Kosut, ed., *Israel and the Arabs: The June 1967 War* (New York: Facts on File, 1968), p. 39.

34. Anthony Nutting, *Nasser* (New York: E. P. Dutton and Company, 1972), p. 409.

35. The A-4 Skyhawks, though ordered in 1966, were not delivered until 1968 (see Hurewitz, *Middle East Politics*, p. 481). The Mirage V's, though ordered and paid for by the Israelis, were embargoed by the French government after the Six-Day War (Munson, *Fighters in Service*, p. 151).

36. Israeli Air Force Brigadier General Mordechai Hod stated at a press conference in June 1967 that, "for 16 years we lived with the plan, we slept with the plan, we ate with the plan. Constantly we perfected it" (quoted in Edgar O'Ballance, *The Third Arab-Israeli War* [London: Faber and Faber, 1972], p. 54).

37. John H. Hoagland, Jr., and John B. Teeple, "Regional Stability and Weapons Transfer: The Middle Eastern Case," *Orbis*, Fall 1965, p. 720. The supply of Hawks was the first exception to the previous U.S. policy of abstention from Middle Eastern arms supply.

38. O'Ballance, *The Third Arab-Israeli War*, p. 54.

39. Safran, *From War to War*, p. 446.

40. *Jane's Weapons Systems, 1969–1970,* p. 88. *The Jerusalem Post,* 2 December 1973, provides a one-ton figure for the warhead of the *Kelt* air-to-surface missile carried by the TU-16 bomber. The *Kennel* warhead figure is postulated by analogy.

41. The Soviets would have had to deliver at least thirty more TU-16's or IL-28's to equal the single attack quantitive load imposed on Israel's air defense by the thirty TU-16's deployed in Egypt in 1967 utilizing their maximum of sixty *Kennels* in a stand-off attack. Bombers supplied in excess of these thirty additional aircraft would impose a greater burden on Israeli air defense than the 1967 deployment, provide an additional qualitative edge by virtue of the bombers' maneuverability, and create a tenfold expansion per attacking vehicle (TU-16 vs. *Kennel*) in deliverable destructive power. Such a move, of course, may have raised Egyptian bomber losses in combat and perhaps prompted the United States to supply more Hawks to Israel. An alternative possibility would have been to provide additional fighter aircraft to escort the Egyptian bombers to strategic targets and protect them from Israeli interceptors. The very short combat range (350–75 miles) of the best Soviet interceptor available before the Six-Day War (the MIG-21), however, made such an escort system impractical (the short range of the MIG-21's would make circuitous approaches to strategic bombing targets, evasion possibilities, and prolonged air combat difficult).

42. Khrushchev's letter of April 1959, quoted in Heikal, *The Cairo Documents,* p. 142.

43. One can also speculate that the Soviets believed that additional deliveries, particularly of bombers, would be offset by U.S. shipments of more Hawk missiles to Israel. Shipment of rockets might also deepen American involvement in the supply of other weapons to the Israelis.

44. See Hoagland and Teeple, "Regional Stability and Weapons Transfer," p. 719, for a discussion of development of these missiles. See *The Military Balance, 1966–67* (London: Institute for Strategic Studies, 1966), p. 41, and following issues, for mention of guidance-system difficulties of the various Egyptian missiles.

45. *Jane's Weapons Systems, 1969–70,* p. 88.

46. Norman Polmar, *Soviet Naval Power: Challenge for the 1970's* (New York: National Strategy Information Center, 1972), pp. 45–46.

47. Hoagland and Teeple, "Regional Stability and Weapons Transfer," p. 720.

48. For some thoughts on the reasons for the Israeli decision, see Handel, *Israel's Political-Military Doctrine,* p. 28.

49. Geoffrey Kemp, "Arms Traffic and Third World Conflicts," *International Conciliation,* March 1970, p. 24.

50. Hoagland and Teeple, "Regional Stability and Weapons Transfer," p. 720.

51. I Belyayev, T. Kolesnichenko, and Y. Primakov, *Golub' spushchen* (Moscow: Izdatel'stvo "Molodaya Gvardiya," 1968), p. 61.

52. Munson, *Fighters in Service,* p. 129.

53. See N. S. Khrushchev, "Razoruzheniye-put' k uprocheniyu mira i obespecheniyu druzhby mezhdu narodami," in *O vneshnei politike Sovetskogo Soyuza 1960 goda* (Moscow: Gospolitizdat, 1961), p. 36.

54. *Jane's Weapons Systems, 1969–70,* p. 29.

55. Heikal, *The Cairo Documents,* pp. 142 and 148.

56. *Jane's Weapons Systems, 1960–70,* p. 30.

57. See Theodore Draper, "From 1967 to 1973: The Arab-Israeli Wars," *Commentary,* December 1973, p. 34, for a summary of pre-Six-Day War Egyptian comments in this regard.

58. This statement presumes an alert Israeli air defense. If the Israeli air defense were taken by surprise, as happened to the Egyptian air defense on 5 June 1967, decisive results from an Arab strategic first strike might well have been possible.

59. Theodore Draper, in "From 1967 to 1973," asserts that the Israeli troop-concentration story served only as a "cover" justifying a previously existent Egyptian idea to reoccupy Sinai and blockade the Straits of Tiran. Whether the Israeli troop-concentration story was a cause or a pretext for Egyptian action, it would still seem to be of major importance.

60. Aide-Memoire of the Soviet ministry of foreign affairs presented to the Israeli ambassador in Moscow, 9 November 1966, reprinted in Dagan, *Moscow and Jerusalem*, p. 191.

61. For a summary of incidents, see Kosut, *Israel and the Arabs*, pp. 38–39.

62. Ibid., pp. 39–40.

63. Oral Statement of the Soviet ministry of foreign affairs, 21 April 1967, quoted in Dagan, *Moscow and Jerusalem*, pp. 202–3.

64. Written statement of the Soviet ministry of foreign affairs, 25 April 1967, reprinted in Dagan, *Moscow and Jerusalem*, pp. 203–4.

65. Jan Dziedzic and Tadeusz Walichnowski, *Background of the Six Day War* (Warsaw: Interpress Publishers, 1969), p. 10.

66. Belyayev, Kolesnichenko, and Primakov, *Golub' spushchen*, pp. 21–22.

67. *Pravda*, 27 April 1967.

68. Heikal, *The Cairo Documents*, p. 240.

69. Speech of President Gamal Abdel Nasser at Cairo University, 23 July 1967, reprinted in Theodore Draper, *Israel and World Politics* (New York: The Viking Press, 1968), p. 238. Safran, *From War to War*, p. 277, suggests that the Russians conveyed to the Egyptians an Israeli General Staff document containing what probably was a contingency plan for an attack on Syria.

70. Lyndon B. Johnson, *The Vantage Point: Perspectives on the Presidency* (New York: Holt, Rinehart, and Winston, 1971), p. 289.

71. Charles W. Yost, "The Arab-Israeli War: How It Began," *Foreign Affairs*, January 1968, p. 309.

72. Ibid.

73. *Pravda*, 20 June 1967.

74. Address of President Gamal Abdel Nasser to the Nation, 9 June 1967, reprinted in Draper, *Israel and World Politics*, p. 235.

75. Dagan, *Moscow and Jerusalem*, pp. 212–13.

76. Arthur Lall, *The U.N. and the Middle East Crisis, 1967* (New York: Columbia University Press, 1968), p. 30.

77. Kosut, *Israel and the Arabs*, p. 43.

78. Johnson, *The Vantage Point*, p. 291.

79. Heikal, *The Cairo Documents*, p. 242.

80. Speech of President Gamal Abdel Nasser to Members of the National Assembly, 29 May 1967, reprinted in Draper, *Israel and World Politics*, p. 234.

81. Heikal, *The Cairo Documents*, p. 242.

82. Ibid., p. 244, and Nutting, *Nasser*, p. 411.

83. *Pravda*, 24 May 1967.

84. Dagan, *Moscow and Jerusalem*, p. 217.

85. Ibid., pp. 223–24.

86. Anthony Nutting, *Nasser*, pp. 410–11, maintains, however, that most of Nasser's troops were held in reserve up to one hundred miles from the frontier in a "strictly defensive posture."

87. Belyayev, Kolesnichenko, and Primakov, *Golub' spushchen*, p. 62.

88. Eric Rouleau et al., *Israel et les Arabes: Le 3e Combat* (Paris: Editions du Seuil, 1967), pp. 102–3, quoted in Draper, *Israel and World Politics*, p. 81.

89. *Le Nouvel Observateur* (Paris), 14–20 June 1967, p. 16, quoted in Draper, *Israel and World Politics*, p. 80.

90. Israel Ministry of Defense, *The Six Day War* (Tel Aviv: Israel Ministry of Defense Publishing House, 1967), p. 32.

91. Ibid., p. 33.

92. Israeli pilots on the first strike were reportedly instructed to disregard all targets except MIG-21 interceptors and TU-16 medium bombers (Safran, *From War to War*, p. 322).

93. Belyayev, Kolesnichenko, and Primakov, *Golub' spushchen*, p. 65.

94. Ibid., pp. 65–66.

95. Randolph S. Churchill and Winston S. Churchill, *The Six Day War* (Boston: Houghton Mifflin Company, 1967), p. 78.

96. O'Ballance, *The Third Arab-Israeli War*, p. 68. Egyptian Chief of Staff Amer, air force commander Sidky, and other senior air force officers were caught aloft flying to Sinai during the Israeli attack and were unable to issue relevant orders for more than an hour and a half.

97. Address of President Gamal Abdel Nasser to the Nation, 9 June 1967, reprinted in Draper, *Israel and World Politics*, p. 237.

98. Churchill and Churchill, *The Six Day War*, p. 82.

99. Ibid., p. 66.

100. Egyptian air force unit orders captured in Sinai contained the following phrases: "All units participating in the action are to be prepared to deliver a second concentrated blow on the target 175 minutes after the first concentrated attack. . . . All air units are to be prepared to execute four concentrated attacks per day" (reprinted in Peter Young, *The Israeli Campaign, 1967* [London: William Kimber Company, 1967], pp. 90–94).

101. Churchill and Churchill, *The Six Day War*, p. 88.

102. Aerial photographs of destroyed Egyptian planes (see, for example, Young, *The Israeli Campaign, 1967*, pp. 112 ff.) typically show intact tail sections with principal damage located in the forward areas of the aircraft. This suggests that the Israelis were using infrared guided rockets or bombs that homed in on the warm aircraft engines. The Israelis claim that eight "flights" of Egyptian planes were destroyed while readying for takeoff (O'Ballance, *The Third Arab-Israeli War*, p. 65).

103. Reportedly some one hundred crated Soviet aircraft were present in Egypt (ibid., p. 79). Even if this is true, it was clear that these aircraft could not be assembled under combat conditions within a few days' time.

104. Churchill and Churchill, *The Six Day War*, p. 80.

105. O'Ballance, *The Third Arab-Israeli War*, p. 82, and Israel Ministry of Defense, *The Six Day War*, p. 40.

106. Quoted in Churchill and Churchill, *The Six Day War*, p. 91.

107. O'Ballance, *The Third Arab-Israeli War*, p. 82.

108. Ibid., p. 83.

109. Churchill and Churchill, *The Six Day War*, p. 84.

110. Safran, *From War to War*, p. 323.

111. Ibid.

112. Hussein, *My War with Israel*, cited in O'Ballance, *The Third Arab-Israeli War*, p. 70.

113. O'Ballance, *The Third Arab-Israeli War*, pp. 71–72.

114. Safran, *From War to War*, p. 329.

115. In Tel Aviv and Jerusalem the Israeli civil-defense organization reportedly had trouble convincing the population to take shelter.

116. Israel Ministry of Defense, *The Six Day War*, p. 33.

117. O'Ballance, *The Third Arab-Israeli War*, p. 168.

118. Churchill and Churchill, *The Six Day War*, p. 114.

119. O'Ballance, *The Third Arab-Israeli War*, pp. 168–69 and 171.

120. Israel Ministry of Defense, *The Six Day War*, pp. 46–47.

121. O'Ballance, *The Third Arab-Israeli War*, p. 200. The Israelis, in a self-imposed limitation, did not bomb any closer to Damascus than twenty-five miles.

122. Ibid., p. 168.

123. Interview data.

124. O'Ballance, *The Third Arab-Israeli War*, p. 248.

125. *Pravda*, 6 June 1967.

126. Message of Chairman Kosygin to Prime Minister Eshkol, 5 June 1967, reprinted in Dagan, *Moscow and Jerusalem*, p. 227.

127. Johnson, *The Vantage Point*, p. 298.

128. Michael Bar-Zohar, *Embassies in Crisis* (Englewood Cliffs: Prentice-Hall, 1970), pp. 217–18.

129. Boghdady's comments are cited in Nutting, *Nasser*, p. 419.

130. Johnson, *The Vantage Point*, p. 298.

131. Ibid., p. 299.

132. Bar-Zohar, *Embassies in Crisis*, p. 228.
133. Lall, *The U.N. and the Middle East Crisis*, 1967, p. 57.
134. *Pravda*, 9 June 1967, and Dagan, *Moscow and Jerusalem*, pp. 229–30.
135. Bar-Zohar, *Embassies in Crisis*, p. 238.
136. Lall, *The U.N. and the Middle East Crisis*, 1967, pp. 56–60.
137. Belyayev, Kolesnichenko, and Primakov, *Golub' spushchen*, pp. 69–71.
138. Johnson, *The Vantage Point*, p. 301.
139. Heikal, *The Cairo Documents*, pp. 247–48.
140. Arthur Lall, *The U.N. and the Middle East Crisis*, 1967, pp. 72–77.
141. Quoted in Dagan, *Moscow and Jerusalem*, pp. 232–33. The Israeli representative reminded Fedorenko, in reply, that the Soviet Union, not Israel, had signed a pact with Nazi Germany. This reminder undoubtedly did not ingratiate the Israelis with Moscow.
142. *Pravda*, 11 June 1967.
143. Lall, *The U.N. and the Middle East Crisis*, 1967, pp. 78–79.
144. Ibid., p. 79.
145. Kosut, *Israel and the Arabs*, pp. 106–7.
146. *Pravda*, 11 June 1967.
147. Johnson, *The Vantage Point*, p. 302.
148. Ibid., p. 301.
149. Ibid., pp. 302–3.
150. Bar-Zohar, *Embassies in Crisis*, p. 260.
151. Reported June 10 remark of General Wheeler to a "friend," quoted in ibid., p. 260.
152. Polmar, *Soviet Naval Power*, p. 46.
153. Johnson, *The Vantage Point*, p. 302.
154. *Pravda*, 20 June 1967.
155. Ibid., 22 June, 1967.
156. Alexander Dallin, "Domestic Factors Influencing Soviet Foreign Policy," in *The U.S.S.R. and the Middle East*, ed. Michael Confino and Shimon Shamir (New York: John Wiley and Sons, 1973), p. 50. Syrian Prime Minister Zuayen stated that during a visit to Moscow, some Soviet military leaders told the Syrians in closed session that while they agreed with Syrian policy vis-à-vis Israel, not all their civilian colleagues shared their views (*Al Muntadel* [Syrian Baath party newsletter], cited in Walter Laqueur, *The Road to Jerusalem* [New York: Macmillan Company, 1968], p. 183).
157. *Pravda*, 22 June 1967.
158. Foy D. Kohler, *Understanding the Russians* (New York: Harper and Row, 1970), p. 406.
159. Belyayev, Kolesnichenko, and Primakov, *Golub' spushchen*, pp. 140–41, assert that Egyptian officers responsible for the Six-Day War defeat were associates of the late Marshal Amer, Egypt's former chief of staff, whom they accuse of "anti-Sovietism."

CHAPTER FOUR

Some information in the ensuing two chapters has been derived from interviews conducted in January–February 1974 with government and academic specialists in Israel and Great Britain. I wish to acknowledge especially the gracious assistance of the Office of the Presidency, the Ministry of Foreign Affairs, and the Ministry of Defense of Israel, as well as the academic staffs of Tel Aviv University and Hebrew University. At the request of interview subjects, I have footnoted information derived from discussions simply as "interview data" or as information from "interview subjects."

1. See remarks of Soviet Deputy Foreign Minister V. V. Kuznetsov cited in Lall, *The U.N. and the Middle East Crisis*, 1967, p. 256.
2. Ibid., p. 266.
3. Churchill and Churchill, *The Six Day War*, p. 206.
4. Lenczowski, *Soviet Advances in the Middle East*, p. 150.

5. Belyayev, Kolesnichenko, and Primakov, *Golub' spushchen*, p. 98.

6. Nutting, *Nasser*, pp. 431–32. One academic "interview subject" maintained, however, that the Soviets insisted on (a) providing weapons instructors and (b) possessing the right to alter the organizational structure of the Egyptian armed forces, as conditions for the resupply of weapons in 1967.

7. Eric Rouleau in *Le Monde*, February 1–7, 1968, cited in Safran, *From War to War*, p. 411.

8. Belyayev, Kolesnichenko, and Primakov, *Golub' spushchen*, p. 66.

9. Quoted in Stephens, *Nasser*, p. 514.

10. Nutting, *Nasser*, pp. 428–29.

11. Edward R. F. Sheehan, "Sadat's War," *The New York Times Magazine*, 18 November 1973, p. 116.

12. Joshua and Gibert, *Arms for the Third World*, p. 26.

13. Neville Brown, "Confrontation Across the Suez Canal," *New Middle East*, October 1970, p. 27.

14. Mohamed Hassanein Heikal in *Al Ahram*, 10 July 1968, quoted in *Middle East Journal*, Autumn 1968, p. 493.

15. Yehosafat Harkabi, *Fedayeen Action and Arab Strategy* (London: Institute for Strategic Studies, 1968), p. 9.

16. Mohamed Hassanein Heikal in *Al Ahram*, 7 March 1969, reprinted in Jebran Chamieh, ed., *Record of the Arab World (March 1969)* (Beirut: The Research and Publishing House, 1969).

17. In addition to the four or five major military airfields within Israel's pre-1967 boundaries, an additional five major airfields were acquired on the captured Sinai Peninsula (see Neville Brown, "The Real Capabilities of Soviet and U.S. Weapons . . . ," *New Middle East*, May 1970, p. 11).

18. The combat radius of the MIG-21, the standard advanced interceptor in the Arab inventory, which would presumably be called upon to provide air cover for Arab bombers, was only 350 miles. In the case that air combat or evasion was required, this range was clearly insufficient for participation in a strategic attack.

19. An Iraqi Christian pilot defected to Israel with his MIG-21 interceptor some time before Heikal's article. The MIG-21 was used by the Israeli air force in combat training of its pilots.

20. Statement of Israeli Chief of Staff General Chaim Bar-Lev, 7 September 1969, quoted in *Middle East Journal*, Winter 1970, p. 48.

21. *The New York Times*, 11 November 1969.

22. From June 1967 through the end of 1969, the Israeli air force flew 2,700 combat missions in the Canal Zone alone. Sixty-two Arab aircraft were shot down on all fronts with only eight Israeli losses (Robert Jackson, *The Israeli Air Force Story: The Struggle for Middle East Aircraft Supremacy Since 1948* [London: Tom Stacey, 1970], p. 225). The Israeli military spokesman reported that on one day alone (24 July 1969) the Israeli air force destroyed thirteen Egyptian aircraft that challenged Israeli planes over the canal zone. On 11 September 1969 another eleven Egyptian aircraft were shot down (cited in *Middle East Journal*, Autumn 1969, p. 506, and Winter 1970, p. 48).

23. V. Rumyantsev, "OAR: Bor'ba prodolzhayetsya," *Pravda*, 6 June 1969. (Rumyantsev may be V. P. Rumyantsev, a Central Committee staff member who has dealt with Middle Eastern affairs.)

24. *Strategic Survey 1969* (London: Institute for Strategic Studies, 1970), p. 47.

25. Speech of Gamal Abdel Nasser, 6 November 1969, cited in *Middle East Journal*, Winter 1970, p. 53.

26. I. Belyayev, "OAR: Na vnutrennom fronte," *Pravda*, 27 August 1969. Belyayev, who is now deputy director of the African Institute of the Academy of Sciences, has been identified by Soviet colleagues traveling overseas as an extreme partisan of the Egyptian cause.

27. *Pravda*, 20 September 1969.

28. Obozrevatel', "Zastavit' Izrail' vypolnit resheniya OON," *ibid.*, 2 October 1969.

29. *Pravda*, 7 October 1969. Detailed political-military analysis of the type contained in this article is rarely printed in the Soviet press.

30. Ibid., 10 December 1969.

31. Ibid., 11 December 1969.

32. Quoted in *Middle East Journal*, Spring 1970, p. 183.

33. Lawrence L. Whetten, "June 1967 to June 1971: Four Years of Canal War Reconsidered," *New Middle East*, June 1971, p. 17.

34. Interview of Anwar Sadat by Arnaud de Borchgrave, *Newsweek*, 13 December 1971. One "interview subject" stated that Egypt may have received a commitment in 1968 from the Soviet Union to defend Egypt in certain contingencies. According to the "interview subject," Nasser's trip to Moscow may have been intended to request fulfillment of the Russian commitment.

35. In an interview with James Reston in February 1970, Nasser stated that he expressed an interest in the MIG-23 "two months ago"—perhaps during Sadat's visit to Moscow (*The New York Times*, 15 February 1970). This and other subsequent references to the MIG-23 are believed to refer to the high-performance interceptor aircraft known in NATO terminology as *Foxbat*. It was generally believed in the West that MIG-23 was the Soviet designation of *Foxbat*. It now appears, however, that the *Foxbat* is designated MIG-25. Some analysts maintain, however, that the Egyptians were referring to what is now known to be the MIG-23—the swing-winged *Flogger*—a dual-purpose interceptor/ground-attack aircraft. The latter aircraft was delivered to Syria after the Yom Kippur War in 1973–74 and to Egypt in 1975. Subsequent references to MIG-23 will be marked as follows: MIG-23(25).

36. SAM-3's were probably dispatched to Egypt beginning in mid-February 1970. (see Whetten, "June 1967 to June 1971," p. 18). A U.S. Congressional report indicated that all SAM-3 installations at least initially were entirely in the hands of Soviet personnel (*The Middle East and American Security Policy*, Report of Senator Henry M. Jackson, U.S. Senate Committee on Armed Services, December 1970 [Washington, D.C.: U.S. Government Printing Office, 1970], p. 3).

37. While Soviet combat personnel had served outside the Warsaw Pact area before (air-defense personnel in North Vietnam and strategic missile troops in Cuba), never before had they been deployed in a non-Communist country.

38. *Washington Post*, 4 February 1970, cited in Whetten, "June 1967 to June 1971," p. 18.

39. J. C. Hurewitz, "Superpower Rivalry and the Arab-Israeli Dispute: Involvement or Commitment?" in *The U.S.S.R. and the Middle East*, ed. Michael Confino and Shimon Shamir (New York: John Wiley and Sons, 1973), p. 160.

40. See Yigal Allon(then Israeli deputy prime minister), "The Soviet Involvement in the Arab-Israel Conflict," in *The U.S.S.R. and the Middle East*, ed. Michael Confino and Shimon Shamir (New York: John Wiley and Sons, 1973), p. 152.

41. Ye. Maksimov, "Put' k spravedlivomu miru," *Pravda*, 27 January 1970.

42. Jackson, *The Israeli Air Force Story*, p. 231.

43. From an interview with Gamal Abdel Nasser by James Reston, *The New York Times*, 15 February 1970. Nasser justified his belief that the Abu Zaabal strike was intentional by the fact that there were no military targets nearby (apparently a false assertion) and that the attack occurred during a shift change, that is, at a time when minimum casualties would be inflicted.

44. For an analysis of the anti-Zionist campaign and its links to the Abu Zaabal and other bombing incidents, see Jonathan Frankel, "The Anti-Zionist Press Campaigns in the U.S.S.R., 1969–1971: An Internal Dialogue," Research Paper Number 2, Soviet and Eastern European Research Center, Hebrew University (Jerusalem).

45. *Pravda*, 3 March 1970.

46. Yu. Glukhov, "Nastanet den'," ibid., 4 March 1970.

47. *The New York Times*, 14 May 1970, reported that in the "last few weeks" about one hundred Soviet pilots were sent to Egypt to man three or four interceptor squadrons. The reports of the American dispatch of combatants were initially generated in the Soviet press by a Western press story to the effect that the United States

would no longer automatically deprive American citizens serving in the Israeli armed forces of their citizenship. This U.S. position was not really new since it was the consequence of a 1964 court decision (the *Afroyim* case). The Soviets, of course, made much of the Western story to justify their own dispatch of combatants to Egypt. See, for example, the Soviet foreign ministry press conference reported in *Pravda*, 1 November 1969.

48. Hurewitz, "Superpower Rivalry and the Arab-Israeli Dispute," pp. 160–61.

49. Statement of President Nixon, 18 February 1970, quoted in *Middle East Journal*, Summer 1970, p. 353.

50. Notification of the American decision appeared in *Pravda*, 25 March 1970. It is probably more than coincidental that the intensive Soviet press campaign against Israeli bombings ended in the last week of March. There was another flare-up of propaganda activity in the second week of April after an Israeli bombing attack killed thirty children at a reported school at Bahr al-Baqar, Egypt.

51. The Soviets, in an unusual move, had printed in the Soviet press the following exchange from an anti-Zionist press conference held for foreign correspondents: "Question: Will the Soviet Union deliver the MIG-23(25) (most advanced Soviet interceptor) to Egypt? Answer: Nasser, in an interview with Reston, said the U.A.R. (Egypt) had not asked for such aircraft. There is no necessity to add more" (ibid., 6 March 1970). Nasser, of course, in his interview with Reston, had in fact stated that he had requested MIG-23(25)'s. As the Soviet press typically does not mention specific models and types of military equipment, this question was presumably special and was reprinted with the intention to communicate something to foreigners. The purpose of the message probably was to indicate that the Soviet Union was not yet supplying MIG-23(25)'s but that the United States and Israel should be aware of the Soviet option.

52. The Dayan and Peled statements are cited in *Middle East Journal*, Summer 1970, p. 355. On 14 April 1970 the Israeli army weekly, *Bamachane*, published a statement by Dayan stating that he hoped the Soviets "will establish themselves in places where we shall not be compelled to attack them" and will "leave us enough depth to defend the ceasefire line and carry out other essential operations" (cited in ibid., p. 356).

53. Cited in ibid.

54. Ibid., p. 357.

55. See Whetten, "June 1967 to June 1971," p. 19.

56. *Pravda*, 15 April 1970.

57. I. Belyayev, "Sily soprotivleniya agressoru rastut," *Mirovaya ekonomika i mezhdunarodnye otnosheniya*, May 1970, p. 73.

58. Brown, "Confrontation Across the Suez Canal," p. 27.

59. Ibid.

60. Whetten, "June 1967 to June 1971," p. 20.

61. *The New York Times*, 12 August 1970. Whetten, "June 1967 to June 1971," p. 23, cites "highly reliable NATO officials" as indicating that the Israelis baited the Soviets.

62. Israeli intelligence, based on aerial photographs of burial mounds along the Canal, estimated that two thousand Egyptians were killed during the period from summer 1969 until summer 1970. An additional ten thousand were believed wounded (*Le Monde*, 8 July 1970). From spring 1969 until spring 1970 the Israelis lost 150 killed and about 750 wounded along the Canal. During June 1970, because of increasing Egyptian activity, losses increased to thirty-four killed and one hundred wounded. In July 1970 Israeli losses declined to five killed and twenty-five wounded (see Brown, "Confrontation Along the Suez Canal," p. 28).

63. *Pravda*, 30 May 1970.

64. Ibid., 18 July 1970.

65. Soviet Communist Party General Secretary Brezhnev, on a later occasion, described Nasser's talks in Moscow as "very frank, friendly, and useful" (see Brezhnev's speech at Alma Ata, ibid., 29 August 1970). Description of talks as "frank" gen-

erally signifies that disagreements were present. Brezhnev, in the cited speech, praised Nasser's "constructive attitude," probably indicating that the Egyptian leader, after expressing reservations regarding a ceasefire, then acquiesced to the halting of hostilities.

66. I. Belyayev, "Iz-za chuzhoy spiny," ibid., 21 July 1970.

67. *Pravda*, 30 July 1970.

68. U.S. Congress, House of Representatives, Committee on Foreign Affairs, *The Continuing Near East Crisis* (Washington, D.C.: U.S. Government Printing Office, 1971), p. 8.

69. Ibid., p. 9.

70. Whetten, "June 1967 to June 1971," p. 21.

71. *Strategic Survey 1970* (London: The Institute for Strategic Studies, 1971), p. 48. SAM-2 sites normally contain six launchers each. SAM-3 sites include four launchers.

72. Speech of L. I. Brezhnev at Alma Ata, *Pravda*, 29 August 1970.

73. Leon Romaniecki, "The Arab Terrorists in the Middle East and the Soviet Union," Research Paper Number 4, The Soviet and the Eastern European Research Center, Hebrew University (Jerusalem), p. 3.

74. Henry Brandon, *The Retreat of American Power* (New York: Delta Books, 1974), pp. 135–37.

75. Ibid.

76. Speech of L. I. Brezhnev at Baku, *Pravda*, 3 October 1970.

77. Brandon, *The Retreat of American Power*, pp. 137–38.

78. Speech of L. I. Brezhnev at Baku, *Pravda*, 3 October 1970.

79. Ibid.

80. Statement of Anwar Sadat, 12 November 1971, cited in *Middle East Journal*, Winter 1971, p. 78.

81. According to Golda Meir, Egypt in December 1970 began receiving *Frog* tactical missiles (*Middle East Journal*, Spring 1971, p. 132). *The New York Times*, 10 April 1971, reports that Egypt received some 150 MIG aircraft in previous weeks.

82. See table 1.

83. *The Middle East Journal*, Winter 1971, pp. 59, 62, and 63.

84. "Zayavleniya verkhovnogo soveta SSSR," *Pravda*, 16 July 1970.

85. Sabry was frequently used by Nasser for negotiations with the Soviet Union. His ideological leanings were such that he participated in the Moscow celebrations in honor of the one-hundredth anniversary of Lenin's birthday.

86. *Strategic Survey 1971* (London: International Institute of Strategic Studies, 1972), p. 35.

87. Ibid., pp. 35–36.

88. Sadat speech to the ASU Congress, Radio Cairo Domestic Service, 24 July 1972.

89. Reconstruction of Sadat speech to Egyptian publishers, July 1972, *Newsweek*, 7 August 1972. After the expulsion of Russian advisers from Egypt in July 1972, Sadat explained his decision to leading Egyptian newspaper publishers. *Newsweek* senior editor Arnaud de Borchgrave received information on the contents of the speech from participants. The cited *Newsweek* article is de Borchgrave's reconstruction of the Sadat speech.

90. *The New York Times*, 10 April 1971, reports the delivery of 150 MIG-21 interceptors in recent weeks. The article, apparently erroneously, also reports that a small number of MIG 23(25)'s were shipped to Egypt. This information may have been based on the apparent Egyptian belief after the March 1971 meeting that MIG-23's would soon be arriving.

91. Sadat interview with Arnaud de Borchgrave, *Newsweek*, 13 December 1971. According to Sadat, the training period required to master the SAM-3 missile was eight months. Egyptian air-defense crews that began training in January 1970, when the Soviets decided to ship SAM-3's, were thus finishing their instruction in fall 1970. When Sadat asked for the Russians to stay on temporarily to help operate the

doubled air-defense system, the Soviets, according to Sadat, demanded that the services of the Soviet military personnel be paid for in hard currency, not Egyptian money.

92. Sadat interview with Arnaud de Borchgrave, *Newsweek*, 22 February 1971, and U.S. Department of State statement, 15 March 1971, cited in *Strategic Survey 1971*, p. 92.

93. Speech of N. V. Podgorny at Aswan, *Pravda*, 16 January 1971.

94. Statement of the Soviet government, *Pravda*, 28 February 1971.

95. *Al-Raya* (Beirut), 26 June 1972, reprinted in *Journal of Palestine Studies*, Autumn 1972.

96. *Middle East Journal*, Autumn 1971, p. 507. In July 1972 it was announced that Sabry and his colleagues would be tried for high treason.

97. Reconstruction of Sadat speech to Egyptian Publishers.

98. Ibid.

99. *Pravda*, 29 May 1971.

100. Similar treaties of friendship and cooperation were signed with Iraq and India in the next two years.

101. *Pravda*, 28 May 1971.

102. W. W. Kulski, *The Soviet Union in World Affairs: A Documented Analysis, 1964–1972* (Syracuse: Syracuse University Press, 1973), pp. 454–55.

103. *Pravda*, 24 July 1971.

104. Obozrevatel', "Krovaviy proizvol v Sudane," ibid., 30 July 1971.

105. *Pravda*, 31 July 1971.

106. Ibid.

107. *The New York Times*, 4 November 1971, cites "American intelligence sources" to the effect that Soviet arms shipments to Egypt had been greatly curtailed in recent months and that little of importance was delivered after the Sudan countercoup. On the other hand, the number of Soviet-piloted aircraft was reportedly increased sometime in summer 1971. According to *The New York Times*, 31 August 1971, in addition to the four Soviet MIG-21 squadrons sent in 1971, two Soviet-piloted MIG-21 and two Soviet-piloted SU-11 interceptor squadrons were added "recently" and two more SU-11 squadrons were expected soon. The addition of Soviet-piloted aircraft might have been a by-product of the May Soviet-Egyptian treaty, and the decision for the additional deployment may have preceded the Sudan events.

108. Sadat speech to ASU Congress, Radio Cairo Domestic Service, 24 July 1972.

109. Ibid.

110. A few (perhaps four) Soviet-operated MIG-23(25)'s were in Egypt by early December 1971 (see Sadat interview with Arnaud de Borchgrave, *Newsweek*, 13 December 1971, and reconstructed Sadat speech to Egyptian publishers).

111. Sadat speech to ASU Congress, Radio Cairo Domestic Service, 24 July 1972.

112. For a summary of Soviet naval actions on behalf of India, see James M. McConnell and Anne M. Kelly, "Super-Power Naval Diplomacy: Lessons of the Indo-Pakistani Crisis 1971," *Survival*, November–December 1973.

113. Reconstruction of Sadat speech to Egyptian publishers.

114. Sadat declared on 13 January 1972 that he had given the orders in October for a military assault in December. He said he retracted the order because of the Soviet commitment to India in the Indo-Pakistani war (*Middle East Journal*, Spring 1972, p. 164).

115. On 31 December 1971 the State Department announced that sales of F-4 Phantoms would be renewed. Later, "Administration sources" indicated that forty-two Phantoms and ninety Skyhawks would be supplied in the next two to three years (*The New York Times*, 5 February 1972).

116. Sadat speech at Aswan, 31 January 1972, cited in *Middle East Journal*, Spring 1972, p. 164.

117. Sadat speech to ASU Congress, Radio Cairo Domestic Service, 24 July 1972.

118. *The New York Times*, 20 March 1972.

119. Sadat speech to ASU Congress, Radio Cairo Domestic Service, 24 July 1972.

120. Sadat later stated, in a March 1975 interview with *Al-Hawadith* (Beirut), that the seven points referred to outstanding Egyptian requests for military equipment needed "to complete the strengthening of the Egyptian Army so that we would be ready in November (1972), either for a peaceful solution or for war" (Cairo *MENA*, 19 March 1975.

121. Sadat statement in Cairo, 1 May 1972, cited in *Middle East Journal*, Summer 1972, p. 292.

122. *Al-Akhbar* (Cairo), 16 May 1972, cited in Jebran Chamieh, ed., *Record of the Arab World*, 1972 (Beirut: The Research and Publishing House, 1973), p. 502.

123. Cited in *Middle East Journal*, Autumn 1972, p. 434.

124. The Soviet officer reportedly said to Egyptian Lt. Gen. Sa'ad al Din al Shadhili and other Egyptian officers that "you are like a man with two wives and do not know which one to choose"—an apparent negative reflection on Egyptian manliness (United Press International wire, 16 February 1972, cited in Chamieh, *Record of the Arab World*, 1972, p. 501).

125. Belgrade TANJUG in English, 19 July 1972.

126. See fn. 120.

127. Reconstruction of Sadat speech to Egyptian publishers.

128. Ibid.

129. Ibid.

130. Ibid.

131. *Al Ahram* (Cairo), 18 July 1972, cited in Chamieh, *Record of the Arab World*, 1972, p. 525.

132. *Al Ahram*, 19 July 1972, cited in ibid.

133. Sadat interview with Arnaud de Borchgrave, *Newsweek*, 7 August 1972. According to Sadat, "the facilities on the Mediterranean will continue to be used by the Russians. . . . Washington has known for a long time that 'strategic presence' and 'advisors' are two different things."

134. *Al Ahram*, 18 July 1972, cited in Chamieh, *Record of the Arab World*, 1972, p. 525.

135. *Aviation Week and Space Technology*, 24 July 1972.

136. *Pravda*, 20 July 1972.

137. *Aviation Week and Space Technology*, 24 July 1972. The remaining ten thousand Soviet personnel were about evenly divided between air-defense crews and shore-based naval personnel, and there were approximately two hundred air-defense pilots.

138. Interview data.

139. *Aviation Week and Space Technology*, 7 August 1972, and interview data.

140. See *Le Figaro* (Paris), 21 August 1972; Associated Press wire, 2 August 1972; and *Daily Express* (London), 13 September 1972, cited in Chamieh, *Record of the Arab World*, 1972, p. 529.

141. In October and November 1972, small military revolts aimed at seeking more vigorous action against Israel were put down by Sadat (BBC, 21 October 1972, and UPI wire, 21 November 1972, cited in Chamieh, *Record of the Arab World*, 1972, p. 543).

142. Reuters wire, 16 October 1972, cited in Chamieh, *Record of the Arab World*, 1972, p. 543.

143. Egyptian air force commander General Hosni Mobarak visited Moscow in late November 1972 and apparently received a Soviet commitment to supply spare parts (*Agence France Press* wire, 28 November 1972, and UPI wire, 10 December 1972, cited in Chamieh, *Record of the Arab World*, 1972, p. 548; also see *The New York Times*, 21 October 1972). According to *The New York Times*, 1 November 1972, a Lebanese newspaper reported that the Soviet Union had agreed to return some SAM-6 missiles to Egypt.

144. Vinogradov returned October 3, presumably to arrange the Sidky visit to Moscow (*Middle East Journal*, Winter 1973, p. 61).

145. *Jerusalem Post*, 15 September 1972.

146. See ibid., 4 October and 5 November 1972; Associated Press wire, 24 September 1972; and Reuters wire, 19 November 1972, cited in Chamieh, *Record of the Arab World, 1972*, pp. 409–18.

147. Interview data.

148. *The New York Times*, 13 September 1972.

149. Interview data.

150. *L'Orient-Le Jour* (Beirut), November 1972 (exact date not given), cited in Chamieh, *Record of the Arab World, 1972*, p. 426. Israeli sources indicated that Egyptian aircraft had been present in Syria for more than a year before November 1972 but had not previously gone into action.

151. *Jerusalem Post*, 21 November 1972.

152. See *Al Thawra* (Damascus), the official Syrian Baathist newspaper, and Radio Cairo citations in Chamieh, *Record of the Arab World, 1972*, p. 426.

153. Sadat interview with Arnaud de Borchgrave, *Newsweek*, 7 August 1972.

154. Ibid., 9 April, 1973.

155. See Ye. Dmitryev, "Twenty Years of the Egyptian Revolution," *International Affairs* (Moscow), August 1972, and L. Stepanov, "Tekushchiye problemy mirovoy politiki," *Mirovaya ekonomika i mezhdunarodnye otnosheniya*, October 1972.

156. Sadat speech, 3 April 1974, cited in Foy D. Kohler et al., *The Soviet Union and the October 1973 Middle East War* (Miami, Fla.: Center for Advanced International Studies, 1974), p. 35.

157. *Middle East Journal*, Spring 1973, p. 192.

158. Sadat interview with Arnaud de Borchgrave, *Newsweek*, 9 April 1973.

159. *Pravda*, 9 February 1973.

160. Ibid., 14 February 1973.

161. Ibid., 28 February 1973.

162. Sadat interview with Arnaud de Borchgrave, *Newsweek*, 9 April 1973. The editor of the Egyptian newspaper *Akhbar el-Yom* declared on 24 March 1973 that "in importing arms from the Soviet Union these days Egypt is no longer concerned with the question of the types of weapons [it would obtain from the Soviet Union] after having solved the question of continuity of arms supply" cited in Kohler et al., *The Soviet Union and the October 1973 Middle East War*, p. 36.

163. On 5 April 1973, in Stockholm, Chairman Kosygin acknowledged that the Soviet Union had resumed weapons deliveries to Egypt. Kosygin declared: "We believe Egypt has a right to possess a powerful army now in order to defend itself against the aggressor and to liberate its own lands" (*Novoye vremya*, no. 5, April 1973, cited in Kohler et al., *The Soviet Union and the October 1973 Middle East War*, p. 36).

164. Sadat speech, 3 April 1974, cited in Kohler et al., *The Soviet Union and the October 1973 Middle East War*, p. 37, indicates that the Egyptian leader definitively decided to resume war in April 1973. The exact date of the attack was established later.

165. *Pravda*, 14 July 1973.

166. Ibid., 18 July 1973.

167. Sadat statement, 16 July 1973, cited in *Middle East Journal*, Autumn 1973, p. 489.

168. *Izvestiya*, 30 June 1973.

169. Ibid., 12 July 1973.

170. See Brezhnev's speech in honor of the 70th Anniversary of the Russian Social Democratic Workers' Party (RSDRP), *Izvestiya*, 14 July 1973; speech in Kiev, ibid., 27 July 1973; speech in Alma Ata, ibid., 16 August 1973; speech in Sofia, Bulgaria, ibid., 20 September 1973; and speech in Tashkent, ibid., 25 September 1973. The only direct reference to the Middle East in any of these speeches is one line in the Sofia speech expressing solidarity with liberation struggles such as "the struggle of the Arab people for the liberation of lands seized by the aggressor." For a contrast with the post-Ismail treatment of the Middle East, note Brezhnev's references to the Near East in his Lenin Peace Prize speech, ibid., 12 July 1973; his speech on

American television, ibid., 26 June 1973; and his speech on West German television, ibid., 23 May 1973.

171. *Peking Review,* 12 January 1973.

172. *Izvestiya,* 1 August 1973.

173. Ibid., 28 July 1973.

174. Ibid., 5 August 1973.

175. Interview data.

176. Sheehan, "Sadat's War," p. 115. The writer, who is friendly to the Arab cause, states that Western diplomats in Cairo claim that Sadat originally decided to go to war at the end of April 1973. In April 1974 this was confirmed by Sadat himself (Sadat speech, 3 April 1974). Sheehan asserts (p. 114) that "from May onwards Sadat eliminated 'war' from his public vocabulary, and embarked upon the smoke screen phase of his elaborate preparations." Sadat's elimination of references to 'war,' of course, closely paralleled similar Soviet reticence in the period after Hafez Ismail's July visit to Moscow.

177. *The Military Balance, 1967–68* (London: Institute of Strategic Studies, 1967) and ensuing editions, plus interview data. Figures given, of course, are, at best, educated estimates.

178. Kenneth Munson, *Bombers in Service* (London: Blandford Press, 1972), pp. 75 and 137.

179. *Jane's Weapons Systems,* 1969–1970, p. 30.

180. Ibid., p. 29.

181. Statement of U.S. Assistant Secretary of State Joseph Sisco, 12 July 1970, cited in *Middle East Journal,* Autumn 1970, p. 497.

182. Interview data.

183. James Reston interview with Nasser, *The New York Times,* 15 February 1970.

184. Ibid.

185. Reconstruction of Sadat speech to Egyptian publishers.

186. Sadat interview with Arnaud de Borchgrave, *Newsweek,* 13 December 1971.

187. John W. R. Taylor, *Jane's Pocket Book of Major Combat Aircraft* (New York: Collier Books, 1974), p. 165.

188. Reconstruction of Sadat speech to Egyptian publishers.

189. Interview data. Some observers feel that the MIG-25 is of limited usefulness because of its alleged poor ability to "look and shoot down," that is, to detect and destroy targets, from its most effective zone of operations in the extreme high altitudes. If these observations are true (and they may not be), it is possible to speculate that the Soviets were anxious not to provide the MIG-25 to the Egyptians in order not expose its combat shortcomings to the West.

190. Taylor, *Jane's Pocket Book of Major Combat Aircraft,* p. 235.

191. *Aviation Week and Space Technology,* 24 July 1972.

192. According to interview data, the Soviets in summer 1973 did, however, station a Soviet-piloted TU-22 unit in Iraq.

193. *The Military Balance, 1973–74* (London: International Institute of Strategic Studies, 1973), p. 31 n.

194. Interview data.

195. *Jane's Weapons Systems,* 1969–1970, p. 88.

196. Interview data.

197. *Al Ahram,* 26 November 1971, cited in *Middle East Journal,* Spring 1972, p. 162.

198. Interview data. Required maintenance of the missiles may have been much more simple than Western observers originally hypothesized. The one hundred-odd Soviet personnel remaining Egypt after the expulsion might well have been able to maintain a larger number of SAM's than originally thought.

199. Interview data.

200. Ibid. Some captured Egyptian soldiers declared that they began intensive, day-after-day training on use of the *Sagger* in fall 1972.

201. Belgrade TANJUG in English, 19 July 1972.

202. "The Arab People Hold the Key to Victory," *Peking Review*, 12 January 1973.

203. Interview data. It should also be noted, perhaps significantly, that the provision of ballistic missiles, unlike bomber aircraft, did not cause the Israelis to divert greater numbers of these aircraft into strategic air defense.

204. *The Military Balance, 1973–1974*, pp. 32 and 36.

205. Interview data. In spite of some Western statements, including that of Admiral Thomas Moorer, Chairman of the American Joint Chiefs of Staff (*Washington Star-News*, 10 December 1973), that Syria had received the *Scud*, there are reportedly some grounds for doubting this assertion.

206. Interview data.

207. Ibid.

208. "The True Face of a False Friend," *Peking Review*, 14 September 1973.

209. See, *inter alia*, replies to Arab attacks on: (a) economic agreements with the Soviet Union, Radio Moscow in Arabic, 3 September 1973; (b) Arab allegations that the Soviet Union was helping the United States to beat the energy crisis, Radio Moscow in Arabic, 12 September 1973; (c) Arab allegations that the Soviet Union was obstructing Arab unity, Radio Moscow in Arabic, 18 September 1973; and (d) Arab attacks on the quality of Soviet military equipment, Moscow TASS in English, 21 September 1973.

210. *Izvestiya*, 14 September 1973.

211. Radio Moscow in Arabic, 21 September 1973, attacked various Egyptian journalists who had questioned the sincerity of Soviet support of the Allende regime. In another Radio Moscow commentary in Arabic on September 21, Middle East expert Igor Belyayev, referring to the Arab world, stated: "In the light of recent events in Chile it is clear that every attempt to assert socialism creates sleepless nights for the enemies of the world's progressive forces."

212. Brezhnev Speech at Tashkent, *Krasnaya zvezda*, 25 September 1973. "True, sometimes one can hear statements that the concluded agreements are unsatisfactory as they do not solve real problems (e.g., general and complete disarmament, prohibition of nuclear weapons, and the dismantling of military blocs) . . . once and for all. . . . (They) say that what has been done are half-measures. One can only be amazed at the naivete of such an approach. . . . (Must) one really do nothing and wait for manna from heaven to fall into your hands? No, the principle of all or nothing in no way is suitable in international politics."

213. Egyptian Foreign Minister Zayyat had visited Peking in March, and Egyptian Vice-President Hussein el Shafei visited the Chinese capital September 21–23. The individuals were the highest Egyptian officials ever to have visited China. Shafei stated during his visit that "Egypt is earnestly endeavoring to strengthen Egyptian-Chinese relations . . ." (*Peking Review*, 28 September 1973).

214. Radio Moscow in Arabic, 19 September 1973.

215. Ibid., 11 September 1973.

216. The Sunday *Times, Insight on the Middle East War* (London: Andre Deutsch, 1974), pp. 43–44.

217. Ibid., p. 43.

218. Interview data. Moscow, in its own self-interest, some weeks later denied these reports of Soviet-Syrian tension (Moscow TASS in English, 3 October 1973).

219. The Sunday *Times, Insight on the Middle East War*, p. 46.

220. Radio Moscow in Arabic, 17 September 1973.

221. For example, Radio Moscow in Arabic, 15 September 1973; and Moscow TASS in English, 16 September and 21 September 1973.

222. *Krasnaya zvezda*, 23 September 1973.

223. Statement of Congressman Wolff (N.Y.) in *Congressional Record*, 11 December 1973, p. H11083.

224. Interview data.

225. Ibid.

226. *Le Monde*, 22 September 1973. Al Qadir was reportedly vacationing on the Black Sea.

227. Radio Sofia Domestic Service, 20 September 1973. If Brezhnev in fact met Sadat on September 20, his talks were certainly not lengthy or complicated for he reportedly departed Sofia at 10:00 A.M. on September 21 (*Izvestiya*, 22 September 1973). Brezhnev flew to Tashkent, apparently directly because the local newspaper there shows him arriving in daylight on September 21. In addition to travel time, there is a substantial time difference between Sofia and Tashkent. See *Pravda vostoka*, 22 September 1973, for a daylight photo of Brezhnev's arrival in Tashkent. In one interesting note, all of Brezhnev's traveling companions returned directly to Moscow with the exception of foreign policy aide A. Aleksandrov, who accompanied the general secretary to Tashkent.

228. Walter Laqueur, *Confrontation: The Middle East and World Politics* (New York: Bantam Books, 1974), p. 83.

229. *Krasnaya zvezda*, 25 September 1973.

230. Interview data.

231. *Krasnaya zvezda*, 27 September 1973.

232. It is interesting to note that in the last two to three years, Jews residing in the Trans-Carpathian Oblast of the Soviet Union (an area in which until a few years ago the populations of many towns were more than 40–50 percent Jewish) have achieved unparalleled success in receiving permission to emigrate overseas. Residents of the area predict that within the next few years, the Jewish population in the oblast will be virtually nonexistent. While one can only speculate on the reasons why Jews in this one location have been so successful in their emigration efforts, one reason might be that the oblast represents the only area of the Soviet Union directly touching the borders of Czechoslovakia and Hungary. This fact makes the oblast of some geo-strategic importance, particularly because neighboring Romania does not ordinarily permit Soviet troops to cross its territory.

233. *The New York Times*, 21 December 1973.

234. *Pravda*, 26 September 1973.

235. Ibid., 2 October 1973.

236. The Sunday *Times, Insights on the Middle East War*, pp. 53–54.

237. Interview data. Among these overt acts, *inter alia*, were calls by low-ranking Soviet diplomats at certain Western chanceries on October 3 inquiring whether the respective countries had any information concerning Egyptian and Israeli force build-up.

238. The Sunday *Times, Insights on the Middle East War*, p. 50, asserts in this connection that the Egyptian message to the Syrians warning that the attack was imminent was transmitted only on September 30. The Egyptians' reluctance to provide earlier information of the attack date to the Russians may have been occasioned by security considerations or fear that the Soviets, as in 1967, would intervene and try to stop the Arabs. The Soviets may only have received information on the exact date of the Arab attack shortly before October 3.

239. Chairman Kosygin, perhaps not coincidentally, had raised the subject of the U.S.-Soviet Agreement on the Prevention of Nuclear War a few days previously in a Belgrade speech. As Kosygin reiterated, "the obligation of the parties is precisely expressed to act so as to exclude the arising of nuclear war between them and also between each of the sides and other countries" (*Pravda*, 26 September 1973).

CHAPTER FIVE

Note: Footnotes in this chapter designated as "interview data" were derived from interviews conducted in Israel and Great Britain in January–February, 1974.

1. According to Egyptian President Sadat, October 6 had been chosen, not because it was Yom Kippur, but because it was a moonlit night, there was a favorable current in the Suez Canal, and the Israelis would not expect an attack in the Moslem holiday period of Ramadan. Sadat Interview with Mohamed Heikal, *Al Ahram*, reported in *Jerusalem Post*, 19 November 1973.

2. Interview data.

3. *Washington Star-News*, 4 December 1973, indicates that American intelligence organs received copies of these basic Egyptian and Syrian battle plans in April and September 1973, respectively. The plans were originally drafted with Soviet assistance in 1970–71 (interview data).

4. The Sunday *Times, Insight on the Middle East War*, pp. 68–69 and 86. It is important to note that, because the Soviets had not supplied the Egyptians and Syrians with the means to obtain deep air superiority, the respective Arab air forces were unable to interdict the flow of mobilized Israeli reservists, the overwhelming bulk of Tel Aviv's armed forces, to the front. Therefore, the Arab advantage derived from surprise attack only obtained for the first few days of the contest, until the Israeli reservists arrived. In the Six-Day War, on the other hand, the Israeli surprise attack gained advantages significant for the entire course of the war.

5. Interview data.

6. Ibid. The Egyptians and Syrians typically put their best and newest tanks, the T-62s, into infantry divisions, maintaining their older T-54/55's in their armored divisions.

7. The concrete hangarettes, designed to protect Egyptian aircraft from repetition of the 1967 annihilating Israeli aerial first strike, were installed by the Soviets in Egypt in 1970. See *Aviation Week and Space Technology*, 3 December 1973. Some one hundred Egyptian aircraft reportedly struck, however, at forward Israeli airfields in the Sinai in the opening hours of the Arab attack, causing some damage to runways. See statement of Egyptian Minister of War Ismail. The Sunday *Times, Insight on the Middle East War*, p. 84.

8. Interview data and *Aviation Week and Space Technology*, 3 December 1973. Some *Kelts* may have been targeted at Tel Aviv. See *Jerusalem Post*, 2 December 1973, for an account by an Israeli pilot of an interception of a *Kelt* headed for Tel Aviv in the beginning of the war. This article highlights the slow subsonic speed of the *Kelt* cruise missile which rendered it extremely vulnerable to Israeli air defense.

9. *Aviation Week and Space Technology*, 3 December 1973, asserts that all but five of twenty-five-odd *Kelts* launched were shot down. The five that reached targets, according to the magazine, destroyed two Israeli radar sites and one supply depot.

10. Interview data.

11. Arnold Sherman, *When God Judged and Men Died* (New York: Bantam Books, 1973), p. 37.

12. *Aviation Week and Space Technology*, 3 December 1973.

13. Winston Churchill, "The Yom Kippur War," *The Observer* (London), 16 December 1973.

14. Interview data and *Aviation Week and Space Technology*, 29 October and 5 November 1973. The SAM-6 missile presented two fundamental difficulties: (a) the radar tracking and command links of the missile system apparently "hop" from frequency to frequency, making it difficult to jam a single channel electronically, and (b) the missile uses infrared guidance during the final stages of its interception that apparently is filtered to minimize distraction by aircraft-launched flares or other such deception techniques.

15. Interview data and statement by Congressman Lehman, *Congressional Record—House*, 11 December 1973, p. H11079.

16. The Sunday *Times, Insight on the Middle East War*, p. 94.

17. Interview data.

18. Lehman, in *Congressional Record—House*, 11 December 1973.

19. Statement of Egyptian Chief of Staff Shazli, cited in The Sunday *Times, Insight on the Middle East War*, p. 99. The Egyptians were reportedly very unskilled and slow in setting up the bridges. According to one report, they took four hours to put in place a PMP portable bridge which can be laid down by Soviet troops in under a half-hour (interview data).

21. Interview data.

22. Ibid.

23. *Aviation Week and Space Technology*, 17 December 1973.

24. Though Egyptian officers cited in ibid. claim that the 190th Armored Brigade enjoyed air support, it should be noted that during the early stages of the war the bulk of the Israeli air force was committed to the Golan Front, and Egyptian air defenses along the Canal were still quite effective. Therefore, if Israeli air support was provided, it probably was of a limited nature.

25. Interview data and transcript of Moshe Dayan meeting with Israeli newspaper editors (9 October 1973), *Jerusalem Post Weekly*, 19 February 1974.

26. Interview data. Syrian tank losses were at first believed to be eight hundred to nine hundred tanks. These numbers were later revised to under five hundred. In spite of fierce Syrian resistance in some places, as noted in this paragraph, there were several occasions when Syrians abandoned tanks and other equipment and fled. This phenomenon reportedly did not occur among the Egyptian forces.

27. Interview data. The sea journey from Soviet Black Sea ports to Syria or Egypt takes three to four days.

28. Interview data.

29. Ibid.

30. Ibid.

31. Ibid.

32. *Washington Star-News*, 6 November 1973.

33. United Press International wire, 14 November 1973, and *Washington Post*, 15 November 1973.

34. Interview data.

35. *Baltimore Sun*, 24 November 1973.

36. Interview data.

37. Ibid. and Transcript of Moshe Dayan meeting with Israeli newspaper editors (9 October 1973).

38. Transcript of Moshe Dayan Meeting with Israeli newspaper editors (9 October 1973).

39. Interview data. Israeli Northern Front commander General Hofi had allegedly been taking the more cautious approach, and Defense Minister Moshe Dayan reportedly insisted on the breakthrough. It was hoped that, in the rout that would hopefully follow a breakthrough, significant quantities of Syrian equipment would be destroyed and abandoned as in 1967 in Sinai.

40. Interview data. The strategic bombing of Egypt and Syria could not be carried on simultaneously, in any event, because of a shortage of Israeli aircraft that were much in demand for tactical ground support. It should be noted that, according to some observers, Egyptian possession of the *Scud* had no impact, at least in the first week of the war, on the Israeli decision not to bomb Egypt strategically. According to these observers, Israel did not have confirmation of operational deployment of the *Scud* until October 12. According to others, however, the reported Egyptian possession of the *Scud* did play a significant role in the decision not to bomb Egypt strategically.

41. Transcript of Moshe Dayan Meeting with Israeli newspaper editors (9 October 1973) reports the significant damage incurred at Kibbutz Gvat and several other populated points.

42. Ibid.

43. Interview data.

44. The Sunday *Times, Insight on the Middle East War*, p. 105. In addition to economic targets, military installations and airfields were also bombed, and a number of Syrian aircraft were destroyed on the ground.

45. Interview data.

46. Transcript of Moshe Dayan Meeting with Israeli newspaper editors (9 October 1973).

47. Interview data.

48. Ibid.

49. Ibid.

50. *Aviation Week and Space Technology*, 10 December 1973.

51. Interview data.

52. Ibid. In addition to "people and tanks," the Syrian air force was committed in large numbers to halt the Israeli advance. In the course of these air efforts, the Syrians suffered severe losses at the hands of the Israeli air force.

53. Interview data.

54. Ibid.

55. Ibid. No Russian bodies were recovered, nor were any Soviets captured. Cuban military units were present in Syria but did not appear on the battlefield. As one Israeli remarked, "No cigar smoke was detected near the front lines." Rumors circulated during the war that North Vietnamese air-defense crews were present in Syria. These rumors are believed to be false, however. On the other hand, a few Pakistani pilots were indeed present in Syria.

56. Interview data.

57. Ibid.

58. Ibid.

59. Ibid. Israeli General Ariel Sharon claims that the Egyptians lost 280 tanks in the attack, 149 of which were from the 21st Armored Division, which had been brought over the Canal for the attack (*Maariv* [Tel Aviv], 25 January 1974).

60. Israeli General Ariel Sharon had advocated a trans-Canal operation in the first days of the war. He was opposed by his immediate superiors Generals Gonen and Bar-Lev, who felt that the Israelis must wait until the Egyptians came out of their Canal-side bridgehead so that a decisive defeat could be inflicted upon them. The alternative of Gonen and Bar-Lev won out, presumably because of the primary Israeli emphasis on Syria and the need to concentrate air power and military equipment on that front. On the Egyptian side, an interesting parallel dispute took place between Chief of Staff Shazly, who, in the early stages of the war, advocated rapid Egyptian advances and increased forward commando strikes, and Minister of War Ismail, who wished to consolidate completely the Egyptian bridgehead before moving forward.

61. See The Sunday *Times, Insight on the Middle East War*, pp. 159–76, for a discussion of the Sharon crossing operation.

62. Ibid., p. 171.

63. Interview data. The North Koreans claimed that they were on training exercises, not flying passive air defense. Another group of twenty–thirty North Koreans arrived in Syria after the war. In addition to the North Koreans, a few MIG-25 interceptors, under Soviet operation and control, arrived in Egypt in the final days of the conflict. These interceptors, which presumably represented at least a passive increment to the potential of Cairo's strategic air defense, were used exclusively for reconnaissance over Sinai (though not over Israel proper, as had been the case during the pre-1972 Russian military sojourn in Egypt).

64. *Aviation Week and Space Technology*, 3 December 1973.

65. Interview data.

66. The Syrians are rumored to have requested that the Soviet Union dispatch large numbers of Russian air-defense crews to Syria during the war. If this request was in fact made, it was evidently not satisfied because Soviet air-defense crews operated in Syria only in the Latakia and Damascus sites previously mentioned (ibid.).

67. Quoted in *The Times* (London), 17 October 1973.

68. Interview data.

69. Ibid. Generally, when Russian personnel were attached to Syrian or Egyptian units as advisers or technical assistants, their usual practice was to obey the orders of their Arab superiors and to confine their advice to purely technical matters.

70. *The Times* (London), 20 November 1973.

71. Interview data.

72. Cited in *Jerusalem Post*, 4 November 1973.

73. *The New York Times*, 29 December 1973.

74. Revised estimates of American intelligence agencies, cited in *Baltimore Sun*, 7 December 1973.

75. *The New York Times*, 10 December 1973.

76. The Sunday *Times, Insight on the Middle East War*, p. 218.

77. In a forthcoming article entitled "Soviet Military Doctrine in the October War," Professor Amnon Sella of Hebrew University, Jerusalem, points out the inconsistency between Soviet tactical and operational doctrine and Arab practice during the Yom Kippur War.

78. *Izvestiya*, 5 October 1973.

79. *Pravda*, 6 October 1973. The Moscow TASS wire service (in English) carried reports from Arab newspapers of Israeli troop concentrations beginning as early as October 4 and continuing on October 6. (As mentioned earlier, the only troop concentration involved was the Israeli move of one armored brigade into the Golan area on September 28.)

80. *Krasnaya zvezda*, 6 October 1973.

81. *Izvestiya*, 6 October 1973.

82. According to Marvin and Bernard Kalb, "Twenty Days in October," *The New York Times Magazine*, 23 June 1974, U.S. Secretary of State Kissinger informed Soviet Ambassador Dobrynin on October 6 that an Arab attack was imminent and that Israel had agreed not to strike first.

83. *Pravda*, 7 October 1973.

84. Vladimir Yermakov (weekly "international review") in *Pravda*, 7 October 1973.

85. Interview data.

86. *Pravda*, 8 October 1973. Kalb and Kalb, "Twenty Days in October," indicates that Secretary of State Kissinger did not immediately appeal for a ceasefire because of "Soviet reservations."

87. Interview data.

88. Ibid. Kalb and Kalb, "Twenty Days in October," indicates that by October 10, the Central Intelligence Agency had reported that three Soviet airborne divisions were alerted in Eastern Europe.

89. *The New York Times*, 9 October 1973. Kalb and Kalb, in "Twenty Days in October," state that Nixon, citing the 1972 and 1973 summit agreements, appealed to Brezhnev for a commitment to contain the fighting and to seek a ceasefire. Brezhnev reportedly agreed to consider a ceasefire at the United Nations and expressed the hope that fighting could be contained.

90. Anthony Astrachan, "The October War at the U.N." *Midstream*, December 1973, pp. 52–53.

91. *The New York Times*, 26 October 1973.

92. Sadat interview with *Al Anwar* (Beirut), cited in *Washington Post*, 30 March 1974, and *The New York Times*, 30 March 1974.

93. A purported statement by Soviet Ambassador Vinogradov in *As Safir* (Beirut) contends that the Syrian desire for an early ceasefire was real. According to the account, Sadat told Vinogradov that Egypt wanted to exploit her military advantage and push into Sinai (see *The New York Times*, 5 May 1974).

94. Brezhnev speech at lunch for Japanese Prime Minister Tanaka (October 8), *Pravda*, 9 October 1973; A. A. Grechko, "Bitva za Kavkaz" (article about thirtieth anniversary of World War II Battle of the Caucasus—two paragraphs regarding the Middle East inserted), *Pravda*, 8 October 1973; Account of Suslov and Central Committee Secretary Ponomarev reception of Syrian Communists (October 8), *Izvestiya*, 10 October 1973; Kosygin speech at Tanaka lunch (October 9), *Izvestiya*, 11 October 1973.

95. *The New York Times*, 26 October 1973. Kissinger, in response to the tougher Soviet position, reminded the Russians on October 8 at the *Pacem in Terris* conference that "We shall resist aggressive foreign policies. . . . Detente cannot survive irresponsibility in any area, including the Middle East" (see *Department of State Bulletin*, 29 October 1973, p. 529).

97. *Aviation Week and Space Technology*, 12 November 1973, indicates that Soviet stocks of tanks in Eastern Europe have increased dramatically in the last three

years. According to the journal, Western military experts believe that Soviets may be moving toward a dual-basing armor concept, by which tanks are kept both in home bases in the Soviet Union and in active field storage in Eastern Europe. This practice of pre-positioning military supplies, probably also applied to other weapons, supplies, and ammunition, increases the Warsaw Pact capabilities for quick combat readiness, a constant preoccupation of Soviet military writings in recent years. The availability of these Warsaw Pact equipment and ammunition reserves also permitted the rapid and convenient supply of Arab belligerents during the Yom Kippur War.

98. Interview data.

99. *Aviation Week and Space Technology*, 22 October 1973. There was some indication that the Turks had been subject to some Soviet pressure.

100. Ibid. *Pravda*, 18 October 1973, reported that the Austrian Communist Party newspaper, *Volkstimme*, had called for a cessation of American overflights.

101. American transport and fighter aircraft were only allowed to land in the Portuguese Azores, though aerial refueling was apparently carried out from bases in Spain and elsewhere. As mentioned previously, American aircraft also departed from West Germany. American fighter aircraft landed on U.S. aircraft carriers in the Mediterranean in transit from the Azores to Israel. Transport aircraft were able to fly directly from the Azores to Israel. In view of the April 1974 coup in Portugal, it is possible that the Azores will no longer be available to serve as a way station for Middle East supplies. In the event of a new war, the United States will likely have to "force" its other Western European allies to serve as hosts for such an airlift.

102. Interview data.

103. Ibid. *The New York Times*, 29 October 1973. *Aviation Week and Space Technology*, 19 November 1973, reports deployments of Soviet airborne and air-transport units during the war in Yugoslavia. These reports are believed to be false (interview data).

104. Interview data and remarks of Kuwaiti M.P., *Jerusalem Post*, 15 November 1973. During the Kissinger-arranged postwar disengagement negotiations, Cairo was warned that if it did not keep Moscow informed of the course of negotiations, the Soviet Union would insist on immediate payment of the arms bill. At one point in the troop-disengagement talks, pressure was also applied on Syria.

105. *The New York Times*, 13 October 1973.

106. As mentioned previously, ammunition and spare parts had already been sent to Israel on Israeli planes in the week before the American resupply announcement. The October 15 announcement was significant in indicating that greater volumes of such consumable items would be transported on American aircraft and that replacement of major weapons, such as tanks and fighter aircraft, would be supplied. The delay in the American decision to ship large amounts of arms earlier was apparently due to Secretary of State Kissinger's hope that the Russians could be induced to halt their aid to the Arabs. Kissinger's point of view was allegedly overruled by President Nixon (see *The New York Times*, 21 April 1974).

107. Interview data.

108. Paris Radio Domestic Service, 9 October 1973.

109. See *Pravda, Izvestiya, Krasnaya zvezda*, and other Soviet newspapers, October 9, 10, 11, 1973.

110. *Pravda*, 11 October 1973. Only one Soviet victim of the Damascus Cultural Center bombing was ever named—Aleksandra Petrovna Kalinycheva, chief of language instruction. As no other Soviet victim was either named or cited, there probably were no others (see *Pravda*, 13 October 1973).

111. Kissinger meeting with Mohamed Heikal (7 November 1973), reported in *Al Anwar* (Beirut), 16 November 1973.

112. Radio Moscow in Arabic, 10 October 1973.

113. Kissinger Meeting with Mohamed Heikal (7 November 1973).

114. *Pravda*, 12 October 1973.

115. Ibid., 13 October 1973. The Soviet propaganda campaign was focused on civilian casualties incurred by Israeli bombing. While the Israelis were only engaged

in a strategic bombing of Syria, the Russians, spotlighting incidents in which civilians were hit in strikes on Port Said and areas outside Cairo, tried to give the impression that Egypt was also being strategically bombed.

116. *Pravda*, 13 October 1973, indicates that no Soviets were killed as the result of the sinking of the *Il'ya Mechnikov*.

117. *Krasnaya zvezda*, 15 October 1973.

118. Radio Moscow Domestic Service, 12 October 1973.

119. *Trud*, 18 October 1973. *Trud* added that because of Israeli pilots' fear to execute their missions in the face of Arab air defense, Tel Aviv's pilots were chained to their planes so that they would not be able to eject. In addition, *Trud* declared that eight Israeli pilots who refused to bomb Syrian cities were executed in front of their colleagues. Even the most gullible Soviet reader might be taken aback by these accusations.

120. *Pravda*, 13 October 1973.

121. Ibid., 14 October 1973.

122. Ibid., 15 October 1973.

123. Moscow TASS in English, 15 October 1973.

124. *London Evening News*, 12 October 1973.

125. Interview data.

126. Captain 1st rank V. Pustov in *Krasnaya zvezda*, 13 October 1973.

127. *Izvestiya*, 17 October 1973.

128. Brezhnev, Kosygin, and Podgorny, the Politburo "Big Three," and Politburo members Grechko and Gromyko, the Ministers of Defense and Foreign Affairs, respectively, represented the Soviet Union in the talks. These five may have been the Politburo's "inner circle" charged with handling the war (see *Pravda*, 16 October 1973).

129. Remarks of Kuwaiti member of parliament, Ahmed al Khatib (*Agence France Presse* dispatch), *Jerusalem Post*, 15 November 1973. Alleged Soviet references to going beyond the 1967 boundaries could have referred to the bombing of Israeli cities, as suggested by the TASS Declaration printed October 13.

130. *Pravda*, 16 October 1973. It should also be noted that the October 14 edition of *Pravda*, after a delay of one day more than usual, printed a straightforward, uncritical reportage of Secretary of State Kissinger's October 12 press conference expressing a wish for the end of hostilities as soon as possible.

131. Ibid., 15 October 1973.

132. It should be recalled that the Soviet push for a ceasefire at the end of the "war of attrition" also came at a point when Moscow felt that Israel had been deprived of its "military advantage."

133. Commentary by Valentin Zakharov, Radio Moscow in German, 16 October 1973.

134. *Pravda*, 16 October 1973.

135. Ibid., 17 October 1973.

136. *The New York Times*, 26 October 1973.

137. Speech of A. N. Shelepin at the VIII World Congress of Trade Unions, Varna, Bulgaria, in *Trud*, 17 October 1973. Shelepin was removed from the Politburo in April 1975.

138. *Pravda*, 17 October 1973.

139. *Izvestiya*, 17 October 1973.

140. *Krasnaya zvezda*, 17 October 1973.

141. *Pravda*, 18 October 1973.

142. TANJUG Domestic Service, 19 October 1973. According to "Egyptian sources" cited by Marvin and Bernard Kalb, "Twenty Days in October," Kosygin told Sadat that the Soviet Union was ready to enforce the ceasefire alone, if necessary.

143. The Sunday *Times, Insight on the Middle East War*, p. 182.

144. *The New York Times*, 26 October 1973. According to Kalb and Kalb, "Twenty Days in October," the Soviet ceasefire proposal called for total Israeli withdrawal from all occupied territory, including the Old City of Jerusalem. Kissinger reportedly rejected the proposal as a "non-starter."

145. It should be noted that Kissinger (in ibid.) claimed that the idea for an American-Soviet joint military force had never been publicly or privately broached to him before October 24. Even if true, this statement may not contradict the Yugoslav account of an "international peace force" including, but not limited to, the United States and the Soviet Union.

146. *The New York Times,* 26 October 1973. Kissinger later told a group of American Jewish intellectuals that he gave the Israelis four extra days of fighting time by delaying the conclusion of the Israeli-Egyptian ceasefire (see *Jerusalem Post,* 10 February 1974). "Informed American officials," however, indicated that, in fact, the secretary of state moved for a ceasefire as soon as Moscow was prepared to support one on the basis that a total Israeli victory would make later negotiations impossible (see *The New York Times,* 21 April 1974). Kalb and Kalb, "Twenty Days in October," implicitly endorse the Kissinger version and report that Brezhnev was prepared to dispatch Foreign Minister Gromyko to Washington if Kissinger would not come to Moscow.

147. *Krasnaya zvezda,* 20 October 1973. Col. Leont'yev pointed out that Iraq, Algeria, Jordan, Morocco, Saudi Arabia, and Kuwait supplied military units to Egypt and Syria.

148. *Izvestiya,* 19 October 1973. A few other isolated anti-Semitic references also appeared in this period. *Krasnaya zvezda,* for example, on October 17 published a cartoon entitled "Form and Content" which showed a stereotyped "Jewish-nosed" aviator flying eagle-shaped planes dropping bomb loads in the shape of the Star of David on Damascus.

149. *Pravda,* 18 October 1973.

150. *Nedelya,* 8–14 October 1973.

151. *Literaturnaya gazeta,* 17 October 1973. Sagatelyan is nominally associated with the *Izvestiya* foreign news department.

152. The Sunday *Times, Insight on the Middle East War,* p. 188.

153. *The New York Times,* 26 October 1973.

154. Ibid.

155. *Pravda,* 23 October 1973.

156. *Pravda* and *Izvestiya,* 24 October 1973.

157. *Pravda,* 24 October 1973.

158. The Soviet press had not mentioned the October 22 rocket firing. Sadat's reference in his October 16 speech to the use of rockets to strike deep into Israel was also omitted from the Soviet press. Sadat's rocket threat, however, was broadcast to the Arabs. Radio Moscow in Arabic on October 16 pointed out that President Sadat had stated that "the Egyptian Army possesses missiles which are capable of hitting targets deep inside Israel. Egypt realizes its responsibility for using such missiles and therefore refrains from using them." These sentences were omitted from the TASS English wire dispatch (October 16) reporting on the Sadat speech.

159. The Sunday *Times, Insight on the Middle East War,* p. 203.

160. *The New York Times,* 25 October 1973.

161. *Pravda,* 26 October 1973.

162. Ibid.

163. Ibid.

164. Interview data.

165. *Izvestiya, Trud,* and *Krasnaya zvezda,* all on 26 October 1973 and Moscow TASS in English, 25 October 1973.

166. *Pravda,* 26 October 1973.

167. *The New York Times,* 21 November 1973. According to Kalb and Kalb, "Twenty Days in October," Secretary Kissinger had repeatedly warned Soviet Ambassador Dobrynin on October 24 that the presence of troops from one of the Great Powers in the Middle East war zone was unacceptable to the United States.

168. *The New York Times,* 10 April 1974. Kalb and Kalb, "Twenty Days in October," state that Dobrynin requested an "immediate" reply to the Brezhnev note. Kissinger reportedly told Dobrynin not to "press" the United States and suggested

that the Soviet Union should not undertake any "rash or unilateral" moves before the United States replied to the Brezhnev note.

169. There are five "defense conditions." American forces are normally at Defense Condition Two. Before the Yom Kippur War, the last time that Defense Condition Three was proclaimed was after the 1963 slaying of President Kennedy. During the Cuban Missile Crisis of 1962, U.S. forces were raised to Defense Condition Four—"readiness for combat."

170. Secretary of Defense Schlesinger declared on October 26 that Soviet airborne troops were placed on alert some five or six days before the American alert (see *The New York Times*, 27 October 1973).

171. *Baltimore Sun*, 29 October 1973. Kalb and Kalb, "Twenty Days in October," report that on October 23, American intelligence agencies reported that a number of Soviet army and logistical units in the Ukraine had been put on alert. On October 24, the agencies purportedly indicated that four more airborne divisions, in addition to the three divisions alerted in the beginning of the war, had been placed in a state of heightened readiness. In addition to the seven alerted divisions (fifty thousand troops), Kalb and Kalb report that an airborne command post was established in southern Russia and that military orders had been intercepted that might suggest that Russian intervention was imminent.

172. Statements by Secretary of Defense Schlesinger, *Washington Post*, 27 October 1973.

173. Colonel Robert D. Heinl, Jr., USMC ret., in *Overseas Weekly*, 12 November 1973. Kalb and Kalb, "Twenty Days in October," state that twelve AN-22 giant transports were observed flying toward Cairo on the morning of October 24.

174. Ibid. The Soviets have always stressed that airborne units cannot operate long in a combat role without support from more heavily armed and mobile conventional units (see I. I. Lisov, *Desantniki* [Moscow: Voyenizdat, 1967], pp. 242–45). Operation of airborne units in a politically symbolic role, of course, is not excluded. Perhaps significantly, the Soviet military journal *Voyenniy vestnik*, October 1973, carried an article on desert airborne operations.

175. *Newsweek*, 3 December 1973. Secretary of Defense Schlesinger listed the Soviet naval build-up as one of the chief causes of concern (see *Washington Post*, 27 October 1973).

176. Interview data.

177. *The New York Times*, 9 November 1973. Some other senior naval officers disagree with this assessment.

178. *D.M.S. Intelligence Newsletter*, 2 November 1973.

179. *U.S. News and World Report*, 24 December 1973.

180. Interview data.

181. *U.S. News and World Report*, 24 December 1973.

182. Ibid.

183. Interview data and *The New York Times*, 21 November 1973.

184. Interview data; *Aviation Week and Space Technology*, 5 November 1973; *Washington Post*, 21 November 1973; and *The New York Times*, 22 November 1973. Kalb and Kalb, "Twenty Days in October," states that the nuclear material reached the Egyptian port of Port Said on the morning of October 25—immediately following the proclamation of the American alert.

185. *The New York Times*, 22 November 1973.

186. *Washington Post*, 22 November 1973. Photographs of the Egyptian missile installations, according to the *Washington Post*, were taken by American SR-71 reconnaissance aircraft over Egyptian airspace. It should be noted that during the first two weeks of the war, in addition to flights of Soviet long-distance aircraft over the Middle East, the Soviets orbited four reconnaissance satellites: *Cosmos* 596 (launched October 3, three days before the war, retrieved October 9, six to eight days earlier than usual), *Cosmos* 597 (launched October 6, returned October 12), *Cosmos* 598 (launched October 10), *Cosmos* 599 (launched October 15). No return data are available on the latter two. During the Indo-Pakistani War of 1971, the Soviets launched four satellites of the following duration: five days, six days, one day, and ten

days. The standard Soviet reconnaissance and survey sequence is twelve days (see *The New York Times*, 18 October 1973).

187. *Washington Star-News*, 22 November 1973.

188. *The New York Times*, 22 November 1973, points out that nuclear warheads emit low levels of radiation. Moreover, they are not substantially different in shape from conventional warheads. For this reason, it is difficult to confirm their presence either with radiation-detection devices or with photographic reconnaissance equipment.

189. *The New York Times*, 26 October, 1973.

190. *Chicago Tribune*, 27 October 1973. While Kissinger and Schlesinger sought to underplay the significance of the American alert, President Nixon described the events surrounding the alert as "a real crisis . . . the most difficult crisis since the nuclear confrontation over Soviet missiles in Cuba in 1962" (*Baltimore Sun*, 27 October 1973).

191. *The New York Times*, 26 October 1973.

192. *Time*, 29 October 1973.

193. Quoted by Winston Churchill, MP, in *Jerusalem Post*, 16 December 1973.

194. *Pravda*, 27 October 1973.

195. Ibid.

196. Ibid., 28 October 1973.

197. Ibid. In a commentary on 4 November 1973, *Pravda* accented the dissatisfaction of the Western European nations with the alert and the American resupply efforts to Israel. Cautioning overly optimistic readers, however, *Pravda* pointed out that some of the criticism of the American dispatch of arms and ammunition to Israel from Western European stocks was generated by the feeling that these shipments "weaken the position of the West in relation to 'Soviet aggression in Central Europe.'"

198. Soviet Central Television and Moscow Domestic Service in Russian, 27 October 1973.

199. Interview data.

200. On the domestic level, the Soviet press also attacked dissidents who protested Soviet action. In response to physicist Andrey Sakharov's call for the Western states to take retaliatory action against the Soviet Union for aiding the Arab belligerents, *Pravda*, citing the Italian Communist newspaper *L'Unita*, declared: "Sakharov is always on the side of the imperialists. Yesterday he spoke in favor of the Chilean rebels and today in favor of Israel. . . . This time it was worse—an open call to foreign states to take measures against his own country. . . . This should open the eyes of those in capitalist countries who think Sakharov is a serious person" (*Pravda*, 16 October 1973).

201. Ibid.

202. In addition to propaganda supporting the Arab cause and denouncing U.S. and Soviet actions, the Chinese had the following exchanges with the Arabs. On September 23, Mao Tse-tung and Chou En-lai met with Egyptian Vice-President Hussein el Shafei in Paking. El Shafei's visit, probably a source of Soviet concern, given his very high rank, was probably made to alert Peking of the imminent war. El Shafei was quoted as saying, "We shall liberate our territories by every means and through actions in all fields." Chairman Mao stated, "We are always in support of you" (see *Peking Review*, 28 September 1973). On October 8, after the outbreak of war, Foreign Minister Chi Peng-fei, meeting with the Egyptian and Syrian ambassadors and the representatives of the Palestine Liberation Organization, "sternly condemned Israel for launching a massive aggression" and expressed "admiration and firm support for your fighting spirit." No material help was offered, however (*Peking Review*, 12 October 1973). Chou En-lai on October 11 met with the Egyptian and Syrian ambassadors and asked that messages of support be forwarded to Sadat and Assad (*Peking Review*, 19 October 1973). On October 18, in a move which certainly must have raised Soviet ire, Sadat sent a message to Chou En-lai which stated in part: "We are deeply appreciative of the friendly Chinese people's firm stand in support of the Arab peoples . . ." (*Peking Review*, 26 October 1973).

203. *Renmin Ribao,* 26 October 1973, reprinted in *Peking Review,* 2 November 1973.

204. B. Koloskov, "Pekin i blizhnevostochniy krizis," *Izvestiya,* 20 November 1973.

205. *Pravda,* 7 November 1973.

206. Col. A. Leont'yev, in *Krasnaya zvezda,* 4 November 1973, emphasized that "Western observers" noted the Egyptian success in seizing some three thousand square kilometers of territory in Sinai and destroying large amounts of Israeli tanks and airplanes. Citing the Western press, Leont'yev maintained that the Arabs scored a "psychological victory" because they (the Egyptians) held on to "a significant part" of the territory captured during the war.

207. Lt. General M. Naumenko (Doctor of Military Science), in *Krasnaya zvezda,* 12 November 1973, stated that Israel's "myth" of air superiority was "dethroned." In a false statement, probably indicating that the Soviets envisaged a far more active use of tactical aircraft than did the Arabs, Naumenko claims that at the beginning of the war, "The military command of the Arab countries . . . brought the majority of its aircraft into the air. Syrian and Egyptian aircraft clashed in air battles with Israel at the far approaches to defensive objectives. Israel could not seize the initiative in the air and protect its Ground Forces from serious damage inflicted by Arab air forces." With regard to air defense, Naumenko spoke highly of the effectiveness of Soviet SAM's in an electronic-countermeasure (ECM) environment. He stated that the success of air defense was a product of "precise organization of the Egyptian and Syrian air defenses, close interaction of the various means of air defense, reliable direction (command and control) of them, survivability of combat units, and camouflage."

208. Col. A. Leont'yev, in *Krasnaya zvezda,* 4 November 1973, states that the Israeli spearhead penetration to the West Bank on a narrow (seven-kilometer) width of front permitted Israel to avoid placing a broad front of Israeli troops within range of Egyptian long-range artillery on the west bank of the Canal, where Egyptian air defense could also deprive Israeli forces of air cover. The spearhead thrust permitted Israel to destroy Egyptian air-defense positions, to cut off ammunition supplies to the Egyptian Second and Third Armies, and to raise the combat spirit of Israeli troops. Interestingly enough, though mentioned in Soviet commentary, the significance of antitank weapons was not highlighted to the same extent as were air-defense weapons. This difference of emphasis may be due to Soviet military doctrine's heavy emphasis on the usefulness of the tank. (It should be pointed out that most Soviet discussions of tank warfare are pitched in the context of a nuclear-war environment, where the threat of infantry-operated antitank weapons might be significantly reduced.) A similar treatment of the antitank issue was included in a retrospective article by Col. N. Nikitin and Col. S. Petrov, "Agressiya Israelya v oktyabre 1973 goda," *Voyenno-istoricheskii zhurnal,* no. 11, 1974. Nikitin and Petrov, quoting Western accounts, state that antitank weapons are highly effective but that tanks are indispensable for offensive activity.

209. Nikitin and Petrov, "Agressiya Israelya v oktyabre 1973 goda," pp. 85–86, stressed that the Arabs possessed a three-to-one tank and artillery advantage over the Israelis and a two-to-one aircraft advantage.

210. Ibid., p. 87.

211. Ibid., p. 88.

212. For a typical reference to the virtues of détente and superpower cooperation during the Yom Kippur War, see P. Demchenko, "Trudniy put' k miru na blizhnem vostoke," *Mirovaya ekonomika i mezhdunarodnye otnosheniya,* December 1973.

CHAPTER SIX

1. U.S. Department of State, Bureau of Intelligence and Research, *Communist States and Developing Countries: Aid and Trade* (Research Study RECS-15) September 1971, pp. 2–4 and 18–19.

2. Ibid.

SELECTED BIBLIOGRAPHY

BOOKS AND PAMPHLETS

Non-Soviet

Barker, A. J. *Suez: The Seven Day War*. London: Faber and Faber, 1964.

Bar-Zohar, Michael. *Embassies in Crisis*. Englewood Cliffs: Prentice Hall, 1970.

Bloomfield, Lincoln, and Reiss, Amelia. *Controlling Small Wars: A Strategy for the 1970's*. New York: Alfred A. Knopf, 1969.

Brandon, Henry. *The Retreat of American Power*. New York: Delta Books, 1974.

Calvocoressi, Peter, ed. *Suez: Ten Years After*. New York: Pantheon Books, 1967.

Churchill, Randolph S., and Churchill, Winston S. *The Six Day War*. Boston: Houghton Mifflin Company, 1967.

Confino, Michael, and Shamir, Shimon, eds. *The U.S.S.R. and the Middle East*. New York: John Wiley and Sons, 1973.

Dagan, Avigdor. *Moscow and Jerusalem*. New York: Abelard-Schuman, 1970.

Dayan, Moshe. *Diary of the Sinai Campaign*. New York: Harper and Row, 1966.

Draper, Theodore. *Israel and World Politics*. New York: The Viking Press, 1968.

Dziedzic, Jan, and Walichnowski, Tadeusz. *Background of the Six Day War*. Warsaw: Interpress Publishers, 1969.

Eden, Anthony. *Full Circle*. Boston: Houghton Mifflin Company, 1960.

Eisenhower, Dwight D. *Waging Peace: 1956–61*. Garden City, N.Y.: Doubleday and Company, 1965.

Finer, Herman. *Dulles Over Suez*. Chicago: Quadrangle Books, 1964.

Hammond, Paul Y., and Alexander, Sidney S., eds. *Political Dynamics in the Middle East*. New York: American Elsevier Publishing Company, 1972.

Handel, Michael I. *Israel's Political-Military Doctrine*. Cambridge, Mass.: Harvard University Center for International Affairs, 1973.

Harkabi, Yehosafat. *Fedayeen Action and Arab Strategy*. London: Institute for Strategic Studies, 1968.

Heikal, Mohamed H. *The Cairo Documents*. Garden City, N.Y.: Doubleday and Company, 1973.

Howard, Michael, and Hunter, Robert. *Israel and the Arab World: The Crisis of 1967*. London: Institute for Strategic Studies, 1967.

Hurewitz, J. C. *Middle East Politics: The Military Dimension.* New York: Frederick A. Praeger Company, 1969.

Israel Ministry of Defense. *The Six Day War.* Tel Aviv: Israel Ministry of Defense Publishing House, 1967.

Jackson, Robert. *The Israel Air Force Story: The Struggle for Middle East Aircraft Supremacy Since 1948.* London: Tom Stacey, 1970.

Johnson, Lyndon B. *The Vantage Point: Perspectives on the Presidency.* New York: Holt, Rinehart, and Winston, 1971.

Joshua, Wynfred, and Gibert, Stephen P. *Arms for the Third World.* Baltimore: The Johns Hopkins Press, 1969.

Kohler, Foy D. *Understanding the Russians.* New York: Harper and Row, 1970.

Kosut, Hal, ed. *Israel and the Arabs: The June 1967 War.* New York: Facts on File, 1968.

Kulski, W. W. *The Soviet Union in World Affairs: A Documented Analysis, 1964–1972.* Syracuse: Syracuse University Press, 1973.

Lall, Arthur. *The U.N. and the Middle East Crisis, 1967.* New York: Columbia University Press, 1968.

Laqueur, Walter. *Confrontation: The Middle East and World Politics.* New York: Bantam Books, 1974.

——. *The Road to Jerusalem.* New York: Macmillan Company, 1968.

——. *The Struggle for the Middle East: The Soviet Union and the Middle East, 1958–68.* Harmondsworth: Penguin Books, 1972.

Lederer, Ivo J., and Vucinich, Wayne S., eds. *The Soviet Union and the Middle East: The Post World War II Era.* Stanford: Hoover Institution Press, 1974.

Lenczowski, George. *Soviet Advances in the Middle East.* Washington, D.C.: American Enterprise Institute for Public Policy Research, 1972.

Love, Kennett. *Suez: The Twice Fought War.* New York: McGraw-Hill Book Company, 1969.

McGuire, Michael; Booth, Ken; and McDonnell, John, eds. *Soviet Naval Policy: Objectives and Constraints.* New York: Praeger Publishers, 1975.

Mackintosh, J. M. *Strategy and Tactics of Soviet Foreign Policy.* New York: Oxford University Press, 1963.

Macmillan, Harold. *Riding the Storm: 1956–1959.* London: Macmillan Company, 1971.

Milsom, John. *Russian Tanks, 1900–1970.* London: Arms and Armour Press, 1970.

Munson, Kenneth. *Bombers in Service.* London: Blandford Press, 1972.

——. *Fighters in Service: Attack and Training Aircraft Since 1960.* London: Blandford Press, 1971.

Nutting, Anthony. *Nasser.* New York: E. P. Dutton and Company, 1972.

——. *No End of a Lesson.* New York: Clarkson N. Potter, 1967.

O'Ballance, Edgar. *The Third Arab-Israeli War.* London: Faber and Faber, 1972.

Pennar, Jaan. *The U.S.S.R. and the Arabs: The Ideological Dimension.* London: C. Hurst and Company, 1973.

Polmar, Norman. *Soviet Naval Power: Challenge for the 1970's*. New York: National Strategy Information Center, 1972.

Romaniecki, Leon. *The Arab Terrorists in the Middle East and the Soviet Union*. Jerusalem: Hebrew University Soviet and Eastern European Research Center, n.d.

Rouleau, Eric, et al. *Israel et les Arabes: Le 3ᵉ Combat*. Paris: Editions du Seuil, 1967.

Safran, Nadav. *From War to War: The Arab-Israeli Confrontation, 1948–1967*. New York: Pegasus Books, 1969.

———. *The United States and Israel*. Cambridge: Harvard University Press, 1963.

Sherman, Arnold. *When God Judged and Men Died*. New York: Bantam Books, 1973.

Smolansky, Oles M. *The Soviet Union and the Arab East under Khrushchev*. Lewisburg, Pa.: Bucknell University Press, 1974.

Stephens, Robert. *Nasser: A Political Biography*. New York: Simon and Schuster, 1971.

The Sunday *Times. Insight on the Middle East War*. London: Andre Deutsch, 1974.

Taylor, John W. R. *Jane's Pocket Book of Major Combat Aircraft*. New York: Collier Books, 1974.

Thomas, Hugh. *The Suez Affair*. London: Penguin Books, 1970.

Trevelyan, Humphrey. *The Middle East in Revolution*. London: Macmillan Company, 1970.

U.S. Congress, House of Representatives, Committee on Foreign Affairs. *The Continuing Near East Crisis*. Washington, D.C.: U.S. Government Printing Office, 1971.

U.S. Congress, Senate, Committee on Armed Services. *The Middle East and American Security Policy*. Washington, D.C.: U.S. Government Printing Office, 1970.

U.S. Department of State. *Communist States and Developing Countries: Aid and Trade*. Washington, D.C.: U.S. Government Printing Office, 1971.

———. *United States Policy in the Middle East: September 1956–June 1957*. Washington, D.C.: U.S. Government Printing Office, 1957.

Yodfat, Aryeh. *Arab Politics in the Soviet Mirror*. New York: Halsted Press, 1973.

Young, Peter. *The Israeli Campaign, 1967*. London: William Kimber Company, 1967.

Soviet

Belyayev, I.; Kolesnichenko, T.; and Primakov, Y. *Golub' spushchen*. Moscow: Izdatel'stvo "Molodaya Gvardiya," 1968.

Gantman, V. I., et al. *Mezhdunarodnye konflikty*. Moscow: Izdatel'stvo "Mezhdunarodnye Otnosheniya," 1972.

Grechko, A. A. *Na strazhe mira i stroitel'stva kommunizma*. Moscow: Voyenizdat, 1971.

Khrushchev, N. S. *Kommunizm—mir i schast'ye narodov*. Moscow: Gospolitizdat, 1962.

———. *O vneshnei politike Sovetskogo Soyuza 1960 goda.* Moscow: Gospolitizdat, 1961.

Kulish, V. M., ed. *Voyennaya sila i mezhdunarodnye otnosheniya.* Moscow: Izdatel'stvo "Mezhdunarodnye Otnosheniya," 1972.

Lisov, I. I. *Desantniki.* Moscow: Voyenizdat, 1967.

Malinovskiy, R. T. *Bditel'no stoyat na strazhe mira.* Moscow: Voyenizdat, 1962.

Protopopov, A. S. *Sovetskii soyuz i suetskii krizis 1956 goda.* Moscow: Izdatel'stvo Nauka, 1969.

Pukhovskii, N. V. *O mire i voine.* Moscow: Izdatel'stvo "Mysl'," 1965.

Sokolovskiy, V. D., ed. *Voyennaya strategiya.* 3d ed. Moscow: Voyenizdat, 1968.

Suslov, M. A. *Izbrannye rechi i stat'i.* Moscow: Izdatel'stvo Politicheskoi Literatury, 1972.

Tsvetkov, V. G., et al. *O voyenno-teoreticheskom nasledii V. I. Lenina.* Moscow: Voyenizdat, 1964.

MAGAZINES AND SERIES

Non-Soviet

Aviation Week and Space Technology
Commentary
Congressional Record
Department of State Bulletin
D.M.S. Intelligence Newsletter
Foreign Affairs
International Conciliation
Jane's Weapons Systems
The Jerusalem Post Magazine
Journal of Palestine Studies
Middle East Journal
Midstream

The Military Balance
New Middle East
Newsweek
The New York Times Magazine
Orbis
Peking Review
Record of the Arab World
The Statesman's Yearbook
Strategic Survey
Survival
Time
U.S. News and World Report

Soviet

International Affairs
Mirovaya ekonomika i mezhdunarodnye otnosheniya

Nedelya
Voyenniy vestnik
Voyenno—istoricheskii zhurnal

NEWSPAPERS

Non-Soviet

Baltimore Sun
Chicago Tribune
Jerusalem Post
Jerusalem Post Weekly (overseas ed.)
Le Monde
London Evening News

The New York Times
The Observer
Overseas Weekly
The Times
Washington Post
Washington Star-News

Soviet
Izvestiya   *Pravda*
Krasnaya zvezda   *Pravda vostoka*
Literaturnaya gazeta   *Trud*

INDEX

Algeria, 146–47, 151
Amphibious landing equipment, 109, 128
Arms deliveries, French: to Israel, 182; post-Suez, 25, 31, 33, 96; during Suez War, 7, 9–10, 11–12. *See also* Mirage
Arms deliveries, Soviet: to Iraq, 115–16, 183; limitations on, 114–15, 197; nuclear materials in, 162–63, 164; payment for, 146; post Sabry/Sudan (1971–72), 91–92, 94, 105, 112; pre-October War (1972–73), 99, 105, 112–15, 120, 122; pre-Six-Day War (1957–67), 24–27, 28–29, 31–33, 35–37, 186; resupply of, during October War, 130–31, 138, 145, 172, 173; after Six-Day War (1967–69), 66, 68, 83, 104, 108, 186–67; and Suez War, 10–12, 14, 177, 179, 182–83; to Syria, 83, 87–88, 89–90, 97, 105, 108–12. *See also* Czech-Egyptian arms agreement; *Frog*; IL-28; *Kelt*; *Kennel*; *Kitchen*; MIG; *Sagger*; SAM; *Sandal*; *Scud*; *Snapper*; Soviet-Egyptian Treaty; SU; Tanks; TU; ZSU
Arms deliveries, U.S.: beginning of, to Israel, 27–28, 31; during October War, 131, 137, 146; after Six-Day War, 72, 76, 77, 83, 93, 190; during Suez War, 27–28, 31. *See also Phantom*
Arms deliveries, West German, 27–28
Artillery, Egyptian, 105, 107, 109, 126

Bangladesh, 92
Bar-Lev Line, 73, 125–26, 150
Brezhnev, Leonid, 79, 82, 83, 93, 98, 99, 100, 119, 121, 143, 144, 154, 187; ceasefire and, 156, 160, 164, 165; internal dissent and, 153
Bulganin, Nikolai, 8, 15

Ceasefires: October War, 137, 144, 145,

147, 148, 151, 153, 172, 195–96; Six-Day War, 52–55, 193; Syrian, 55–56; violations of, 157–58, 159, 160, 172; War of Attrition, 80–81. *See also* Kissinger, Henry; United Nations
Chile, influence on Middle East of, 118, 123
China, 184, 185, 188; criticism of Soviet policies by, 100–101, 114–15, 156, 167–69, 173, 190
Czech-Egyptian arms agreement, 7, 9–10, 14, 177
Czech intervention, 187

Détente, 180, 181, 185, 186, 187, 191; October War and, 144, 147, 150, 166, 168, 172, 173; Soviet view of, 118, 119, 123, 169–70, 188–89, 190; "Spirit of Camp David," 183–84; "Spirit of Geneva," 179, 180, 184
Dobrynin, Anatoliy, 1, 122, 160
Dulles, John Foster, 10, 174

Egypt: in Arab politics, 22, 23–24, 25; expulsion of Soviet advisers from, 94–95, 103; military performance of, 47–49, 128, 140–41; Soviet military advice to, 49–51, 71, 125, 138–39, 171; strategic position of, pre-1967, 31, 34–37. *See also* Arms deliveries, Soviet; Artillery, Egyptian; Nasser, Gamal Abdel; Sadat, Anwar; Soviet Union
Eisenhower, Dwight, 15, 16, 17, 184
England: role of, in Suez War, 7, 14n., 15–16, 17, 96, 192

France: role of, in Suez War, 7, 9–10, 11–12, 14n., 15, 17, 192
Frog-3, -7 (missile), 35, 105, 107, 132

Grechko, Marshal, 94, 99, 122, 144, 153

THE JOHNS HOPKINS UNIVERSITY PRESS

This book was composed in Electra text and display type by The Maryland Linotype Composition Co., Inc., from a design by Susan Bishop. It was printed on 50-lb. Publishers Eggshell Wove and bound in Joanna Arrestox cloth by Universal Lithographers, Inc.

LIBRARY OF CONGRESS CATALOGING IN PUBLICATION DATA

Glassman, Jon D
  Arms for the Arabs.

  Bibliography: pp. 235–39
  Includes index.
  1. Russia—Foreign relations—Near East. 2. Near East—
Foreign relations—Russia. 3. Russia—Foreign relations—Egypt.
4. Egypt—Foreign relations—Russia. 5. Jewish—Arab relations—1956–1973. I. Title.

DS63.2.R9G55 327.47′056 75-29254
ISBN 0-8018-1747-1